The Emotional Challenges of

Strategies and stories of those who stayed

Ellie Baker

First published in 2014 by Smeaton Publishing
PO Box 1
Mangatangi
RD 3 Pokeno
2473

Edited by Sue Copsey (www.suecopsey.com)
Designed by Marie Low (http://mariejlow.wix.com/portfolio)

Cover design and illustration by Marie Low
Circular background cover image from © Ychty /Dreamstime.com
Text Illustrations by James Copsey

www.migrantemotions.com

To David, and those who understood

Contents

Introduction

My father was dying in England, and I was living twelve thousand miles away with my New Zealand husband and our three preschoolers.

'If you are going to come, you have to come now,' my sister said. This time there was no question. I arrived in England three days later, and had ten days with Dad before he died.

Facing the sickness and death of your parents from a distance is one of the more obvious and distressing challenges of being an immigrant. At that time, I had been away for ten years. Fifteen years on, I have now been an immigrant for more than twenty-five years. There have been struggles during that time, but these days I am a more settled immigrant who can appreciate that I have a great life.

Within my great life there is always the hovering question of a trip back to my homeland for comfort, catch-up, celebration or compassion. From talking to other immigrants, it is clear most feel similarly about the question of the next trip back.

Other common experiences shared by immigrants include: feeling an outsider, guilt at leaving loved ones behind, using up a significant proportion of your finances and holiday leave on trips 'home', and dealing with different cultural celebrations.

When I was first confronted with these challenges, I looked for a self-help book to dig into for guidance. There were plenty available to help with the parenting challenges I was facing – toddler taming, positive parenting, raising boys, raising girls, and so on. When I was struggling with parenting, the suggestions, explanations and empathy in these books helped. No equivalent book on immigration seemed to exist, but I did find comfort in talking to other immigrants and hearing how they coped with situations comparable to mine. A book would have helped.

This is the book I was looking for.

A note re terminology

The following terms have been used throughout the text:

Emigrate – to leave one's own country with the intention of settling permanently in another

Immigrate – to come to live permanently in a foreign country

Homeland/country of origin – the country being emigrated from; the country with which a person identifies, where one's family and lifelong friends live. (If a person has lived in more than one country, 'homeland' refers to the country in which their formative years were spent, for example until adulthood.)

Adopted country/host country – the country to which a person has emigrated

Immigrant couples – couples who *both* have a homeland elsewhere, and who immigrated together

Mixed marriages – where one partner comes from the country being emigrated to, and the other partner comes from elsewhere

The interviewees

The Emotional Challenges of Immigration is a collection of the experiences of twenty-five women, all immigrants by choice (i.e. they do not include refugees). Their names have been changed.

Most migrated to New Zealand, but their experiences are universal, and should therefore help any immigrant, no matter where they have chosen to live.

I interviewed women because it was mainly women with whom I had conversations when I was struggling with being away from my homeland, however the stories and strategies will resonate with men, too. The women were aged between twenty-five and seventy-seven at the time of interview, and emigrated from nine different countries: Canada, England, India, Ireland, Germany, The Netherlands, the Philippines, South Africa and the United States of America. All had been an immigrant for at least two years at the time of interview.

They include single, married, and separated women; women without children, with children, and with grandchildren. Some were focused on a paid career; others on the unpaid career of mothering or a combination of both. The common thread that links the interviewees is the issues faced as a result of being an immigrant.

Each chapter of the book concentrates on a particular issue, for example dealing with cultural differences; how to keep in touch; what to do when a family member back home is sick; how to fit in. You will read about the women's experiences and their reactions to these situations. At the end of each chapter there are key points and strategies to help you in a similar situation.

For readers who are not immigrants, this book will provide a valuable insight into the emotional challenges faced by immigrants. If someone you love has immigrated or emigrated, perhaps this will help you understand some of their feelings and behaviours.

For those considering emigrating – and I imagine this will include young couples of mixed nationalities – reading this could give you a peep into the future. Emigration is so much more than paperwork and removal companies.

After reading this book you will be a great deal more informed and prepared than I was – or any of the immigrants I interviewed. The practical information, such as ways to keep in contact and the realities of visits 'home', will enable you to reassure the family and friends you leave behind that you will still be in each other's lives.

The tough times can be overcome. Twenty-four out of the twenty-five interviewees are still in their adopted countries at the time of writing, demonstrating that it is possible to learn to live with all the challenges immigration brings.

Keep this book handy when the 'missing' is hardest. At those times, I hope it will ease your missing and lift your spirits so you can focus on and be thankful for what you have, rather than being sad about what you miss.

Introducing ...

Amber, from England, was in her mid-twenties when she first visited her adopted country. She liked it so much she stayed on, and has now lived there for seven years.

Anita (age forty at the time of interview) migrated with her husband and two preschool children from India. They were keen for a better life. She has been in her adopted country for ten years.

Anne decided at age eighteen to study for her degree overseas. Originally from the USA, she liked the country she studied in so much, she stayed on after finishing her degree. She has been away from her homeland for twelve years and is married to Andrew, a native of her adopted country.

Charlotte migrated from England when she was in her mid-thirties, with Mitchell, her husband-to-be. She has been a migrant for two years. They moved to their adopted country for a better lifestyle.

Christina migrated from South Africa with her husband and two small children, fourteen years ago. They moved for improved career prospects.

Elizabeth and Jim migrated with their two preschoolers when they were in their early twenties, hoping for a better life for their children. They have lived in their adopted country for five years.

Emma, Martin and their two children left Germany and crossed the world in search of a quieter life, more than ten years ago. Emma was in her early thirties at the time. Since then they have had another child.

Hanneke has been an immigrant for thirty years. She and Arie had always talked about living somewhere different. They were in their mid-forties when they left The Netherlands. One of their teenage daughters emigrated with them; the other decided to stay in The Netherlands.

Jasmine, from the Philippines, met Jack when he was working in her country. They married, and when Jasmine was in her early thirties they migrated to Jack's homeland as Jack's mother was sick. They have lived in Jack's homeland for twelve years and now have two children.

Jenny met Colin when he was visiting her homeland, England. She was thirty-one when they decided to migrate to his homeland. Marriage and three children later, Jenny has been an immigrant for nearly fifteen years.

Jessica was ready for an adventure. She and Nick met in her homeland (USA), and after travelling together decided to marry. She was thirty when she migrated to Nick's homeland. That was nearly thirty years ago. They have two adult children.

Katy met her future husband in his homeland while she was in her late twenties and travelling. She has been an immigrant for twenty years, and they have three children.

Lena met her future husband, Ben, in her homeland, Germany, when he was a visitor there. She visited him in his homeland when she was thirty, and later they married and had a child. She has been a migrant for fifteen years.

Madeleine fell in love with Bruce, an American, when he was working in her homeland, England. She was in her late twenties when she migrated to the USA as his wife. They now have two children. She has been an immigrant for twenty years.

Monica met Donald on a trip to his homeland. Her curiosity was sparked enough that she returned to see how the relationship would develop. They married, and Monica migrated. She was in her late twenties. Now, with three children, she has been in her adopted country for more than twenty years.

Nina and Perry migrated from India when their child was two. They wanted to try living in a different country for two years, and would stay if they liked it. They have been there for nine years.

Olivia has been a migrant for four years; she left the USA when she was in her mid-twenties. She and her husband, Stuart, decided they preferred the opportunities offered in Stuart's homeland, so moved there.

Rachel migrated with Peter and their two preschoolers when she was in her mid-thirties. She has lived in Peter's homeland for seven years.

Rebecca and Brent grew up in England. Four years ago, when Rebecca was in her mid-thirties, they took up an opportunity to change their lifestyle and migrated with their preschoolers to a country where some of Brent's family members were living.

Sophie met Michael when they were both working overseas. They spent time in Sophie's homeland, England, but Michael's career opportunities were better in his homeland, so they decided to continue their lives there. Sophie was thirty when they moved twenty years ago. They have two children.

Susan and John had a romance in England when both of them were travelling. Over a few years the relationship was rekindled in different countries, until John invited her to live with him in his homeland. So, more than twenty years ago, Susan left her homeland of South Africa to be with him. Since then they have had three children and are still in John's homeland.

Sylvia and her husband migrated from England to their adopted country nearly forty years ago, when she was in her early twenties. They have two children.

Teresa met her husband when he was in her homeland. They went out for a while, then decided to settle in his homeland on the other side of the world. She was thirty when she migrated eight years ago.

Vanessa, George and their three children migrated to their adopted country three years ago, when Vanessa was in her late forties. They were ready to live in a different country. As they had family in New Zealand and had lived there previously (before they had children), they thought it would be a good place to move to.

Yvonne and her husband Mark migrated from Northern Ireland when they were in their mid-twenties. They decided to try out a different country and settle there if they liked it. Four children and more than twenty years later, they are still enjoying living in their adopted country.

 My story

I don't remember making a conscious decision to live in New Zealand. I came here for six months, and a series of (perhaps) fortunate events led to me staying. I have been here for more than twenty years now.

In 1987 I landed in New Zealand. I was on my 'overseas experience' – that search for adventure sandwiched between the education experience and the settling-down experience. I had travelled through Indonesia and Australia with an English travel partner, but as he needed to return to England, I had become unattached. I was ready for another adventure, in New Zealand, the cooler country of the Antipodes.

Within six months of arriving I had fallen in love with the country; its sharp sun that gives the landscape and sky a luminescence; the clean air and clear waters; the unblemished beaches, and national parks and reserves so extensive you can walk for three days without seeing evidence of another human, other than unpowered tramping huts.

I loved the can-do attitude of the people, their resourcefulness and their pride in their country – something I felt was comparatively lacking in England in the 1980s. I loved the mana (power) of Maori. The vibrations of a kapa haka (Maori cultural dance) would flush through my blood and leave me with moist eyes and a need to re-pace my breath. I loved the outdoor emphasis, the longer summer, and the fact that although the population was slightly more than a twentieth of the UK's, there were buzzing cities with employment opportunities, entertainment and events. Auckland was clean and spacious.

Then there was the man I met around this exciting time. This particular native was keen to impress me with all he and his photogenic country had going for it. He was passionate about his country and his life. Before long I was loving this man David, as well as New Zealand.

In that independent, brave (my mother's term — I would say naive) state of a traveller-at-heart kinda girl, it seemed appealing to stay 'just a little bit longer'. Even when I had to rush home for a series of family events, I was not ready to leave either my new love or this recently loved country, nor was I keen to return home and call an end to the discovery and adventure that comes with travelling. So I stayed on.

In my mid-twenties, it didn't occur to me that if I moved to New Zealand I might miss the people who knew and loved me. I might miss the familiarity of my background, from the calls of 'apples pound a pound' in the market to the density and mix of people in the London Underground rush hour. I was too absorbed with the beauty and youth of the landscapes around me to worry about that. I was enthusiastic about the life I was living. It seemed a good idea to commit to it. Three years later, David and I married.

We had our wedding in England, which made sure David was able to get to know my family and my background. On the day of the wedding, he needed more time to get to the church than I did, so I had the bonus of circling our town twice in a white Daimler with Dad. We passed familiar pubs, schools, shops and bus stops as I prepared for my public announcement of commitment.

Making our entrance, I asked Dad to slow a little as we marched down the long aisle. I had walked and genuflected in this aisle hundreds of times as a child and teenager, but never before with so many familiar people looking at me. I was glad to see the Kiwi [New Zealand] men had kept their morning suit jackets on, in spite of protestations at overdressing and the August heat. I loved watching and listening to my sisters sing harmoniously from the choir stalls — the same choir stalls that my friend and I had used to practise our newly learned sign-language alphabet until the organist scowled at us.

As David and I nestled in the Daimler, I realised my mouth ached from smiling. When family and friends applauded us into the reception at The Ridgeway, our family home since I was four, I beamed a grin again.

We extended our stay in England for a year so my family could be around for the arrival of our firstborn, Christopher. In all we stayed eighteen months, which gave David a clear picture of my background.

David was keen to return to New Zealand. He was ready to surf in the

Pacific again; ready to soak in hot pools. He wanted to put his accounting qualifications to use. And I was keen to make a home for our family. The three of us and nine pieces of luggage made our way back to New Zealand.

Without jobs or accommodation, we defaulted to staying with David's parents, and David picked up temporary work as a builder's labourer. He seemed happy. He was living with and being fed by both his new wife and his mother, working outside by the beach in summer, and had a son who adored him. I had a new role as a stay-at-in-laws'-home mum. I decided to try and think of this as a new adventure in life.

One wet day, above Christopher's wailing, I heard the phone ring. It was my mother. David's parents were out and he was busy in the attic of the single-story home. As Mum talked, Christopher cried. One of my hands pushed the earpiece harder to my ear, the other stroked the cheek of our four-month-old in his baby seat. Being a new mum, I didn't consider putting Christopher somewhere safe and walking out of earshot. Instead, I focused on my mother's voice and hoped she didn't hear the croak building up in mine. Through the strained phone cord there was a connection with family and friends I had been missing. I was desperate to hold on to this link. I didn't want to interrupt the conversation, even to call out to David for help.

'Really, I'm fine Mum. It's such a good life.'

After a while, Christopher's cries became louder, and, as neither Mum nor I could hear the other, we said goodbye. I held Christopher close. His skin smelt of family. His white hair darkened with my tears. As he nestled into my neck he pushed the lump in my throat. When I had soothed him, I put him into his cot. Then, with one foot on the step-ladder, I yelled, 'David!' David came down the ladder to see what was wrong.

It was all wrong. It was wrong that he couldn't hear me or the phone call or Christopher's cries. It was wrong that our son had been crying. It was wrong that a cherished phone call was cut short. Most of all, it was wrong that I was away from my family and friends and that we were immersed in his. It was my first awakening that I was an immigrant, and, as such, there were going to be more challenges than I had ever thought.

Clutching the edge of the kitchen table, I spoke. 'I am feeling isolated and thrown off balance here. I have none of my reference points: my parents, my siblings and friends who are bringing up small children. It is November. I should be in boots, kicking autumn leaves and wrapping Christopher in a blanket, woolly hat and mittens, not keeping him in the shade and smothering him in sun cream. I want my mother to see Christopher more. I want to hear her reassurances that our son is beautiful and his behaviour normal.'

I suggested that if we were to stay in New Zealand, I somehow needed more support. I wasn't sure how to get it, but a good start would be to place more importance – in fact a near reverence – on all phone calls or connections from England.

I am still not particularly proud of my outburst, and I wouldn't recommend this course of action – but I don't regret it. The mix of Mum's phone call and Christopher's cries pushed my anxieties into the open. The quiet that followed gave us both time to sit back and realise what a big step we had taken: new to parenthood, a permanent job and home to find, and then the sudden realisation that, with me being an immigrant, there were issues we had to face. I wasn't scared for us as a couple, but I was scared for me. I was no longer a whimsical traveller, but a wife and a mother and an immigrant far away from family and friends in England.

How naive of me to assume that my proven traveller independence would carry me through every stage of life. Once I became a mother and a wife, I wasn't independent. I had to rethink. Motherhood and marriage as an immigrant had to be my new adventure. In this adventure I needed to learn to cope with missing the support and presence of family and friends.

I coped. Twenty-five years on, David, my New Zealand friends, my children and my family have helped me through the challenges of being an immigrant. A busy life with children to look after has provided plenty to be thankful for, even on the sadder days. I have a great life and now am a far more settled immigrant. I often love life here. I delight at seeing the Southern Cross in a clear night sky. My eyes become teary when it is now my children joining in the kapa haka or their school song with pride.

I still have tough times. I pine for the aura of Europe's history and diversity, but the hardest times are missing family at celebrations and not being able to be with them as often as I would like.

In earlier days, when there were few people to empathise with during distressing times, I threw a Denby china cup to the ground. It made a satisfying smash, scattering chunks of china over the floor. Later I met other immigrants who felt similarly to me – not about smashing Denby china (although, had they tried it, they probably would have found it most satisfactory), but who had been upset at similar situations. Sharing other immigrants' woes lessened the frustration I felt. (It must have helped, because our china has remained intact since I started talking to other immigrants.)

My challenges as an immigrant have been learning opportunities, which is another way of saying I've made the wrong decision sometimes. No doubt I will continue to get some things wrong, but that is okay.

Interviewing twenty-five wonderful immigrant women has reinforced to me that there are challenges specific to immigrants. I have laughed and wept with these women as they told me their stories of visits home, the excitement of visitors, and the distress of feeling an outsider. When I meet new immigrants and hear their experiences – how they stand out because of their appearance, accent, or sense of humour; how they try to build up a support network and learn new systems – I realise how settled I have become. And when I meet immigrants who have been here longer than me, they give me an insight to future challenges and how to overcome these.

Every year, a flock of bar-tailed godwits that spend the southern summer near to where we live fly off on their migration to Alaska. As they go, I am reminded that migration is part of our planet's bigger picture. I have a home and am loved on two opposite sides of that planet. I have a great deal to be thankful for.

David has learnt to suggest ways to make a visit back to England manageable, and is interested in my family and friends in England. He is a loving husband and father, and we have four lovely children. We live on a 'lifestyle block' (the New Zealand term for a small farm or piece of land in the country with room for animals), with a caring community around us. We are able to laugh regularly, enjoy homegrown food and keep entertained.

I still miss my family, my friends, my roots, English history … but I have become more used to the missing. I have learnt that, as an immigrant, you may be physically separated from your family and friends, but there are opportunities to connect, contribute to, and so remain involved in each others' lives. It is good to know I am not the only person dealing with the feelings of missing. Immigrants have emotional challenges, but they can be overcome. You too can overcome these emotional challenges, freeing yourself up to focus on enjoying your life more.

1 The new immigrant

Only those who will risk going too far can possibly find
out how far one can go.

- T.S. Eliot (1888-1965)

The first experiences of being in your adopted country can be thrilling. Fourteen
of the women I interviewed made a conscious decision to emigrate. Houses
were sold, belongings were packed and they launched into life in another
country.

For the remaining interviewees, migration was more of an evolution than
a conscious decision. For example, Anne came to her adopted country as
a student, Amber came here for a visit, and Lena and Susan came to their
boyfriends' country to be with them 'for a while'. All stayed.

Whether a conscious-decision immigrant or an evolved immigrant, you are
likely to have similar experiences, from the time you announce your migration
to the first weeks, months and years of being in your adopted country.

During the initial period of being an immigrant, the differences can be
stimulating, but also overwhelming. You may seek out familiarity. For families
giving immigration a trial run, family members may have different feelings and
opinions about how the trial is going.

 ## Telling your family

The announcement that you are emigrating can create a stir or two. Hanneke,
her husband Arie and their daughter emigrated more than thirty years ago: 'My
parents were distraught. My mother kept asking questions. We couldn't answer
many of them because we didn't know [the answers]. Friends were disappointed
and angry that they hadn't been included in the decision-making; others were
keen, asking to see where we were going on a map. I laugh at how my mother-in-
law reacted. I was so nervous because there were two grandchildren involved.

We went to Arie's mother and she leant forward with big eyes and asked, "How much is a ticket?" We replied that we didn't know because we were funded by the government. "I'm not talking about you, I am talking about me, because I am going to visit you and if I know how much it is I can start saving now." She visited us within a year.'

When Jenny told her mother she was going to emigrate to her fiancé's homeland, 'My mother said she didn't want to talk about it. I felt, *sod you then; you don't care.* Now I realise it was that she *couldn't* talk about it.'

When Elizabeth told her family that she, her husband Jim and their young children were emigrating, she never really believed they would. She let Jim go ahead with the arrangements. When everything was organised, Jim's parents wished them well, but Elizabeth's parents didn't believe Jim and Elizabeth would actually leave. Her mother was so convinced Elizabeth was not going that she booked a holiday to ensure she was not around when they were due to emigrate. 'I had texted Mum to say we were leaving. Mum said we couldn't go. So I had to get on the plane like that.'

In retrospect, my own immigration feels evolutionary – a series of events that kept me in New Zealand. There was never an announcement that I was emigrating. From my parents' perspective, the 'announcement of emigration' was probably when I rang them from New Zealand to tell them I was engaged to David. At the time, I didn't realise the impact this announcement would have. I couldn't see beyond the excitement of finding a man I wanted to spend the rest of my life with.

David and I sat close with the phone on the table between us. I was excited as I pushed the buttons, anticipating schoolgirl-type visions of whoops of delight and congratulations – after all, they had met my intended at a barbecue during their visit the year before. At the time he was introduced as a friend, and I suspected they were happy to hear that he was just a friend, although they probably weren't convinced, especially as he was the only friend at the barbecue.

Once Mum and Dad were on the phone together, I announced, 'I'm engaged!' There was an awkward silence, followed by stumbling congratulations. I'm glad they didn't ask, 'Who to?' but the phone felt heavy and hot, like a fired gun in a murder scene.

Looking back, how could they delight in my engagement to a New Zealander when that meant I would probably be living away from them?

Packing and leaving

Monica met her future husband while on holiday. When she actually emigrated to his country, she felt she was making this big move, and she didn't want to dwell on it in case she changed her mind. 'It was so scary to think of leaving the country, leaving my mother, father, and sister. Leaving all I knew to come out to a new country. I do believe in "you make your bed and you lie on it". My container was coming out with lots and lots of stuff. I brought everything; I thought that would help me to come here. I brought all my memorabilia and thought I could surround myself with stuff to make me feel better. I thought I wouldn't go ahead with it if I thought too long. I bought the ticket, got on the plane, and that was that.'

 # first impressions

You are a new immigrant. Life can be both exciting and scary. You are in a different country and you are a novelty. There may be a honeymoon period; there is also the reality of the big change you have made in your life.

Most immigrants experience mixed emotions during their first six months or year in their adopted country. Christina, who emigrated with her husband and two small children, remembers only spending all night and day breastfeeding her daughter. She said it was probably a blessing that she didn't have time to think.

Anita, who emigrated with her husband and young children when she was thirty, decided to change her mindset. 'When I came here, I cut myself off emotionally. I didn't get depressed. I didn't want to go on missing. You deny yourself the luxury. I think we were an over-emotional family, so we had to do it. You have to turn off the button.'

Culture shock

Culture shock refers to the feeling of disorientation we can feel when experiencing a new culture. It takes a while for our brains to process all the differences – in smells, sights, sounds, temperature and language, as well as the differing norms of human behaviour – so it's understandable that culture shock is also termed 'brain shock'. Sometimes so many differences in a short period can cause a sense of panic, confusion or disorientation.

On Olivia's first night in New Zealand, her mother-in-law encouraged her to join her at the beach to collect pipis (a shellfish which can be dug below the sand at low tide). Olivia, a self-confessed pampered American, thought *Oh no, what have I done? Why do you have to go to the ocean to get food? Don't you have a grocery store?*

She said, 'I remember my mother-in-law with this bag and my husband with his pants rolled up, going towards the ocean. I knew my mother-in-law wasn't poor, so why were we going to the ocean to pick food? I know why now, but at the time it was, *What in the world am I doing?*'

It didn't stop there. 'The next day she suggested I put my washing on "the line". I asked where her dryer was. She told me she didn't have one. When I asked why not, she said, "Why should I?" I couldn't understand; my mother-in-law wasn't broke and yet she didn't have a dryer? At the time, I thought she must be very odd. She must be the only Kiwi with a clothesline. But then I found out that these weren't oddities, but were features of the country we were now living in.'

Vanessa described registering the different colours and shapes of the plants, and the fact that the sunlight was different: 'Everything was new ... [I] couldn't look anywhere and see familiar surroundings. It was all a bit odd. It was exhausting.'

As a new immigrant, you might feel you have prepared yourself for differences in climate, but when faced with the reality of, for example, higher temperatures or humidity, the extent of the differences may surprise you.

Even if the climate is similar to that of your homeland, the design of the houses may be different, reflecting the environment and culture of your new country. For example, they may be built to keep out snow in Sweden or the sun in Spain, or be designed to accommodate a high population density. There may be emphasis on maintaining a traditional or historical style of building, or on making the most of a view rather than protecting from the wind. The buildings may have been built to last for centuries – or only decades.

Olivia noticed the difference. 'I had never known the elements before then. Well, I was noticing them now! We were living in a house which wasn't insulated. When summer was over, Stuart said, "You are going to need to be warm when you go to bed. Start wearing long johns and skivvies [light jumper]. No more sleeping naked and we'll need an electric blanket." It was so cold. I was bawling. I was lonely. It was culture shock.'

The culture shock carried on for Olivia as the differences in food preparation continued to surprise her. 'I was used to pre-packaged food, convenience food. I didn't know how to cook. I do now. My mother-in-law would ask me to make a white sauce, and I thought, *Can't you buy that?* Everything in the grocery store was foreign to me. I thought, *What am I going to eat?* The first couple of weeks I lost weight because everything tasted different.'

So many changes at once can be draining. Don't be surprised if seeing something familiar in a shop or in a book, or hearing a familiar accent, lightens your day. The search for the familiar is a survival mechanism.

Leslie emigrated from New Zealand to England, her husband's home country. During a visit to New Zealand, Leslie told me of her frustration that her daughter, Anna, wanted to read only the books they had brought from England. 'I keep showing her all these new things – even new books – and yet she keeps going back to the same books.'

I suggested that perhaps Anna was holding on to the only familiar item around her, besides her parents and brother. She couldn't embrace all the new things she was seeing. It was too much.

When Vanessa immigrated with her husband George and their growing teenagers, the crowded motel room in which they stayed for their first three months offered respite from the overwhelming exposure to their new surroundings. The plain walls, non-descript furniture, and familiar TV programmes such as *The Simpsons*, provided welcome relief after days learning the systems and geography of their new city and country.

You can do the research and know in theory what is going to happen, but the reality of the experience can still surprise you. Even those you would imagine are well-placed to cope can struggle, as Olivia found out. 'As an anthropologist, I'm supposed to know what it's like to live in another country, in another culture, but I wasn't acclimatising, I wasn't adapting. For the first six months, I cried and cried, and I even had a time or two where I thought I might have to go back. I'm embarrassed now to think that I wanted to go back because I was cold and I didn't have baked beans the way I liked. But everything was different.'

 ## Closing ranks

Vanessa noticed that her family became closer as they were challenged by the differences in their new environment. 'As new immigrants we had to close ranks, as a family we knitted [nestled] together. Our eldest was seventeen and had already done a lot of pulling away [in our homeland]. At that time, he hadn't wanted to spend a lot of time with us, but all that changed when we moved here. He figured, "This is strange, this is different. How am I going to get on with this?" We became close as a family because of immigration … We are more supportive of each other's needs and can share the differences we find. We all knew we were taking a chance. We would have challenges in difficult times, but we could support each other.'

 ## Trial run

Immigrant couples may have an understanding that they are going to live in their new country for a few years before they make a definite decision to stay.

Rebecca and Brent, who immigrated with young children, decided on three years as a trial period. 'I knew I would go up and down … It's been three years and I'm on my second job, so I've got a fair idea of what it is about.'

At the end of the trial period, one person may want to stay more than the other does. Before you consider rushing back, remember that you have made connections; you have probably made friends here and if you go back, you will have to go through the disconnecting and reconnecting process with everybody. You will have a new perspective on your homeland (see chapter 6).

If your family and friends feel you are going for a 'trial run', they may not take your immigration as seriously as you do. Rebecca found friends and family from England would ask, 'So, have you finished your trip? Is it time to come back now?' and, 'When are you going to stop travelling?'

Reminding your family and friends of the extent of your commitment to your adopted country may help them to accept your migration. For example, let them know that you have a permanent job, a car, residency or citizenship, or have bought furniture or a house. In my earlier years in New Zealand, I would say, 'I won't say I'm never coming back. But I am going to be here for a long time.'

Key points

1 Announcing you are emigrating will cause mixed reactions.

2 Your family and friends may not share your excitement at emigrating, as they see the implications of you being away.

3 Beware of denial. Migrating is a huge move, sometimes too big to feel true for you and/or your family and friends.

4 When you first arrive, there may be an overwhelming awareness of differences. This can be tiring and disorientating.

5 Emigrating families and couples are likely to feel closer once they are in a strange environment.

6 Immigration is exhausting.

7 Do not expect friends and familiarity to happen at once. The first two or three years may be difficult.

8 Sometimes the unfamiliarity of new surroundings is overwhelming, so something familiar is a relief. Children will cope, but familiar things will be particularly important for them.

9 If you have a trial run in your new country, make it a realistic trial.

Strategies

- Expect some people to be upset. Some may even advise you not to go. Be ready; be sure of your conviction. Ask them about their feelings, fears and/ or anger. You may be unaware of some issues in their life. They may need more time to accept you are leaving. Rely on those who are supportive of you to carry you through.

- Those who are not supportive may need to see you happily living in your adopted country before they can share their support and happiness with you.

- Allow yourself time to adjust and to get used to all the changes. Explore ways of accepting all the changes. Acknowledge the differences – take photos, draw the plants.

- Keep the differences in perspective. As Nina says: 'In the first few years you should focus on the reason you came rather than what you find different. The differences are out of your hands.'

»

»
- Be gentle on yourself in the first few months. It is a huge effort to move, let alone change countries.
- Don't be concerned if you find yourself enjoying something familiar. The familiar is a holiday for your senses that have been overwhelmed with new features to process.
- Search for helpful websites, for example under *immigrant advice, settling, immigrant integration.*

2 Life as an immigrant

In your adopted country, the air and light are different, the cars have unfamiliar number plates, the supermarkets stock unknown brands and conversations are peppered with strange jargon and colloquialisms.

At some stage the honeymoon-type excitement of being in this new place fades. Around this time you become aware that it's not only the environment that's different – it's the people, too. You may feel like an outsider; you have different reference points and humour to those around you. You feel you stand out as 'an immigrant'.

You need to learn the systems of your new environment. Accept that, as an immigrant, some aspects will excite you, while others will grate. The realities of your new life may not meet your expectations, but over time, and with a healthy support network, you can adjust to and enjoy your adopted country.

feeling like an outsider

No matter how long it is since you immigrated, there will be times when you feel like an outsider. I have met immigrants who have lived in the same place for more than fifty years who still feel the differences:

Nina: 'By my looks I will always be known as an Indian.'

Anne: 'It is down to the people you are around. I have had a deep and profound sense of belonging here, but then someone will say something and it makes you feel like a foreigner.'

Charlotte, of Caribbean heritage, was raised in England, where there is a large Caribbean population. When she immigrated to New Zealand with Mitchell, she was in her mid-thirties. 'Although Auckland is multicultural, there are very few people who are black – Africans, West Indians. I was driving around thinking *Where are they?* So I joined a Trinidadian band.' The bandleader was from Trinidad; the rest of the band was not.

'In England I could go to a West Indian takeaway and eat the same food that my parents cooked. Kiwis don't know who I am. I don't know where I fit ethnically here. It is isolating for me.'

Appearance isn't the only thing that can lead to feelings of isolation. An immigrant has an accent (see Chapter 3). The way you sound stands out, whether you like it or not. Being a novelty can be a plus – people within earshot may be interested in you – but at other times you may become weary of being the odd one in the room.

Charlotte: *'I would actually reduce speaking to a minimum because I didn't want to stand out, which increased my sense of isolation.'*

Well-travelled and open-minded people may see an accent as interesting, while others may misinterpret you and make judgements. As a young university student, Anne didn't want to be judged as American before she was judged as a person, so she spent a long time studying the accent of her adopted country. 'Accent is a funny thing, because it is very changeable, but at the end of university, you couldn't tell that I was from the States on the first meeting.'

However, when people knew her better and found out that she was from the States, she was accused of 'trying to hide something'.

The more your accent stands out, the more you will stand out. People you meet will know you were not born in your adopted country and may make a point of it. This can sometimes be painful. You could do as Anne did, and pick up the accent of your adopted country, or you could adjust your accent so you stand out less.

An immigrant from Malaysia said he felt there was a limit to how much he was willing to adjust. He became tired of people correcting his English pronunciation. 'I have learnt a second language. I speak it well, even though it is very different to my original language. Can't you accept I've made huge moves to get where I am? I am not bothered if sometimes it is a bit incorrect. As long as you can understand me, I do not need to speak in the same accent as you.'

As an immigrant, you stand out because of your appearance, your accent and also your actions. Incidents will happen that, due to innocence, ignorance or naivety, you will end up feeling awkward. Jessica considered herself a good cook, and enjoyed making salads and ethnic food. When she first emigrated from California nearly thirty years ago, she took a plate of Mexican food to a rural community meal. No one ate it. The community was used to 'meat, potato and veg' meals. They considered her contribution foreign food. She said, 'I thought they could at least try it.'

Elizabeth made a blunder as a mother at preschool: potato printing. 'It wasn't until we set it up we were told it was culturally insensitive [to use food for play]. Awkward, embarrassing, isolating.'

These experiences are trying. They are reminders that not only are you different, but also that you have acted wrongly. This is not easy to accept, especially as it is unlikely there will be others around who can empathise with you. It will probably happen a few times, so you may need to toughen up. You can feel bad or rise above the incident. Try to conjure up tolerance, empathy and understanding. If all else fails, try and get others to see your point of view, as Hanneke has.

Hanneke, from The Netherlands, had to speak a second language in her adopted country. She speaks English well, but finds that when she is searching for the right word to use, the delay can be uncomfortable. 'If you mispronounce, people are very willing to laugh. It hurts.' Over the years she has developed ways of getting people to understand that mistakes come easily when you are learning something new. 'If the situation arises where I can ask them to pronounce a word in my language, I do, because then they can appreciate the effort which goes into speaking another language.'

While Hanneke has come up with tactics for dealing with the hurt, Anne points out that in having to adjust yourself, there is 'a whole side of you that you can't express'. Similarly, Jessica found adjusting an effort. 'I had to do all the changes. No one was prepared to listen to how I do things. That was really hard, but I've done it now.'

Sophie had been an immigrant for more than ten years before she realised how much she was restraining herself. 'Now I say what I think and I am not ashamed to. When you first come over you can't; you feel you'd better not. It took me a long time to think, stuff you, if I don't say it I will bottle it up.'

The adjustments you make to fit in are not easy. But if you want to fit in, it is usually worth the effort.

 # Fitting in

Charlotte was a marketing manager, so she was used to identifying where people 'fit' in society. When she moved to New Zealand, she couldn't work it out. A guidebook on Auckland suggested what each area of the city had to offer. She and her husband chose where to live based on the guidebook, however, a querying 'oooh' from friends and associates suggested that area wasn't right for them.

The choice of urban or rural is an important one when considering whether you will fit in – the lifestyles are very different. In a rural environment, you may rely on your immediate community for social engagement and you are likely to see the same people at different events. In an urban environment, your contacts are less likely to overlap. An immigrant moving from a rural environment in their homeland to an urban one in their adopted country, or vice versa, will have significant adjustments to make, on top of those needed for changing country.

Jessica, from San Francisco, found it difficult to fit into Nick's small rural hometown. She tried to make the relationship work with her new in-laws. However, she was told early on by her mother-in-law that 'you won't be a local for fifty years'!

Jessica: 'I didn't know where they were coming from, nor they me. I think we may have got off on the wrong foot. I always felt I didn't live up to what they wanted me to be. It was not a good fit, and as Nick had been overseas for over ten years it [going back to his hometown] probably wasn't a good fit for him either. It wasn't until we moved away that I felt I could settle in and be myself.'

Sylvia and her husband emigrated more than four decades ago, just after they were married. Sylvia's husband quickly made friends at his office and the golf club. Sylvia found making friends less easy. She felt isolated.

Sylvia: 'I found it tricky to go off and play golf, etc. I was teaching in a small school with few people and he was in an office. Our social networks were very different. [In my homeland] I had always been surrounded by people. I found it very hard. I had to start from scratch.'

It was not until they moved, started a business together and had children that she found opportunities to make friends.

You will choose the extent of the adjustments you make. If they feel like hard work or sacrifices, consider the bonuses of your adopted country – the things that make it worthwhile being there. In my experience, the effort put into adjusting or coping with differences lessens over time. You become more accepting of the differences, and, as you become more familiar with your host country, they develop into normality and become less jarring. While they are there, treat them lightly – laugh if you can, even if you are the only one laughing.

 # Misplacing your sense of humour

Humour varies from country to country. A poignant feature of being an immigrant is that you often can't immediately share the humour of the country you are in.

What is culturally sensitive and or politically correct differs, depending on the stage of each country's attitude and language. Your sense of humour may not go down well, as Jenny and others found:

Jenny: 'I'm sick of making a joke and having to apologise for it.'

Rebecca: 'My sense of humour is quite sarcastic. I have had to temper my sense of humour quite a bit, otherwise people think I'm a real bitch.'

Yvonne: 'I have had to pull back from my comments as they may be received wrongly. I seek friends who can handle it or I have to be guarded, which is frustrating.'

Not being able to share a sense of humour means that people may not find you funny, and you may not find them funny.

Rebecca: 'Sometimes at work they all laugh at things I don't find funny.'

Olivia: 'At work I have told jokes that fell so flat, and there are other times where people have told jokes which I have actually been really offended by.'

Susan and John's relationship began when they were in Europe. John had then looked Susan up in her homeland, South Africa. After continued correspondence, she thought it would be worth seeing what it was like to live in his country for a while.

'What he said must have been funny, because everyone's laughing.'

'When I first came, I couldn't understand [their accent]. We went on a fishing trip and everyone was cracking jokes. We came home and John said how much he laughed and laughed at the jokes. I told him, "I didn't understand a word they said." At the time I had laughed with a limp "ha ha". I had to. I was stuck on the boat with them … I'm sick of laughing at jokes where I can't understand what they are saying. I remember quite clearly thinking *This is just not for me if I have to hear another joke.*'

Sometimes an unknown cultural reference could be the reason for missing the joke. Olivia, an American, likes telling an entertaining story and making people laugh. 'I did a duathlon. I was at the finish line and there was a radio announcer there. He was interviewing people and approached me: "So now you've finished the race, you feel great, so what are you going to do next?" I grabbed the mic and said, "I'm going to Disneyworld!" Now in America, that would have been hilarious because there is a famous thing about |saying you are| going to Disneyworld. There were thousands of people there and you could have heard the crickets. I thought that would have been a great reply, but the audience was the wrong nationality. It was so funny, but not a soul got it.' Olivia was still laughing while the interviewer mumbled a tentative 'Okay(?)'.

Some have found differences in sense of humour are not a big deal.

Lena: 'It is not a major issue. Some people laugh at Mr Bean, some don't. If you don't get the joke, you can always smile and pretend you got it.'

Bear in mind that attempts at humour should intend to cause laughter rather than offence. Over time you may come to appreciate the national sense of humour, or find people whose humour is similar to yours. Some parts of this book are intended to be humorous, but some readers probably won't find them funny. Hopefully some parts will at least make you smile.

I do believe humour is a way you can engage with people. Not being able to share humour is a disadvantage, as Charlotte pointed out. 'Not sharing the sense of humour can be isolating because I can't relate to people in a relaxed way. The communication is really transactional.'

When I go to England I really relish the familiar humour there. I am glad to be laughing so much that my stomach cramps, and I am slightly sad that I am not around that humour more. Over time, I have found people in New Zealand who appreciate English humour, and I have come to appreciate some of the New Zealand humour. For me, it's important that I have people around who can laugh with me.

To ensure you can 'have a laugh' as an immigrant, you could seek out people with a similar sense of humour to yours, or you could learn more about the people, culture and humour of your adopted country. Let go a little, and over time, there will be people who will laugh with you.

 ## finding out what works for you

As a new immigrant, you need to make connections with people.

Olivia: 'Do anything that can get you involved in the community and build a social group. You are not in your home country any more. You are here. It is very easy to become isolated as an immigrant. In the first six months I wanted to go back; I wasn't engaging. By going out and engaging with the local community, you feel more belonging ... Join clubs or get involved in voluntary organisations. Whatever floats your boat.'

If you have small children, there are places – parks, preschool groups, coffee clubs, and so on – where parents and children gather and establish friendships easily. In cultures where dogs are pets, walking with your dog in a popular dog-friendly place can be an easy way to start a conversation.

Sports, drama, music, education and cultural clubs provide an opportunity to meet like-minded people. Have a look on your community notice board, at the town hall, library, information centre, and on web pages, for activities or groups in your area.

Madeleine has found involvement rewarding. 'I found that belonging to and participating in organisations and groups certainly helped with my need to feel I belong. I have been told I am respected in the community as being an involved person and having many connections. That makes me feel very good.'

Since immigrating, Nina has moved cities to become more involved with a wide group of people. When she and her husband first immigrated, they 'latched onto' an Indian community. Surrounded by Indian people and customs, they found it difficult to mix with people of their adopted country. They felt they had swapped one India for another. They thought of returning to India, however, a job opportunity in a different city came up for her husband. 'We went there [the different city] with the idea it was going to be a make or break. We decided we wouldn't seek out Indian people, but would integrate with the society there. That was the winning thing, we actually got to know other people. Many of them were immigrants or people who have travelled, and we became more integrated into the society.'

When Nina's mother-in-law came out later to be with them, they felt she needed Indian company to give her more time to integrate, so they then approached Indian groups. 'This way we now have two groups of friends, and it works well.'

Mixing with more than one group in your community gives you a better chance of meeting people with similar interests, and shared interests often lead to friendship. Furthermore, if you mix with more than one group, you are less likely to feel let down if a group you are in breaks up or does not suit you. As Lena suggests: 'Really get involved with everyone. Don't mope around, you may get homesick. Go to the library; find out what is going on. People are number one. Get involved. Find like-minded people.'

As well as joining groups, you could look at what is immediately around you. What will help to make you feel happy or more settled? Elizabeth is delighted with her adopted country as she loves the outdoor life. Sylvia found having pets and a garden made her feel more settled.

What has helped me feel settled? I like to be part of a group, especially one with a purpose, even if the purpose is only to enjoy each other's company. Over the years I have joined woodwork classes, singing groups, writing groups, preschool groups, school groups and book groups. I have been involved in church, children's camps, paid work and voluntary work. David and I have hosted numerous celebrations at our home for family and friends. Wrapped up in winter jackets and woolly hats, we have cheered on our children's sports teams from the sidelines, chatting to other parents and supporters. All of these groups have given me a sense of attachment, belonging and community. I have gained plenty of positive experiences from these communities and I believe I have contributed to them. The more you put in, the more you will get in return.

Part of your personal growth is finding out what works for you. The difference for an immigrant is that their reference points are geographically distant. Consider for a moment the reference points or conditioning that would influence you or your decisions. The distance of these influences is an opportunity rather than a handicap. You have freedom to choose with an open mind.

Jenny realised being a full-time mum was important to her. Her siblings and their partners have chosen different paths, working full time. 'I feel quite isolated from them, but I am happy with what I'm doing. It works well for me to be a stay-at-home mum.'

Anita, a new immigrant, hadn't learned to drive in her native India. In her adopted country, the only way to get around was by car, as there was little public transport where she lived. Not being able to drive prevented her from mixing with others, and she was unable to take her children to places. Not driving was a 'handicap', which she put up with until her mother came to live with them. Anita felt she couldn't restrict her mother to staying in their home; she used the opportunity to make a change, and learned to drive.

What works for you may not work for your husband or partner, but this doesn't need to be a problem. Jessica enjoys going to the opera, but her husband Nick is not keen. The difference in their tastes didn't appear until their children were less dependent. 'Now I will go with someone else. It doesn't matter that he doesn't want to. It takes time to realise what is important to you.'

Creating a new self

When you go to a new country, you have the opportunity to reinvent yourself. In her homeland, Elizabeth was shy, and wouldn't drive: 'I wanted to be happier and now I am. On the plane over, I thought, *You are coming to a new place, the other side of the world. You can do whatever you like.* I have opened up more, become more confident; I'm driving. No one is over my shoulder watching me.'

Lena was thirty when she arrived in her adopted country from Germany. 'I am a completely different person than I was. I have the freedom to try new things. There are no restrictions around me.'

Anita and Madeleine recognised the opportunities in being physically distant from their families:

Anita: 'In my homeland [India] I was staying with my mum. Here, I don't have to struggle so much. You can look after your children without extra help. This means I have more time with the children. In India there were so many people around you all the time that you didn't spend much time with the children.'

Madeleine: 'On the positive side, I was able to escape some of the baggage I had from growing up, and felt I could reinvent myself. I definitely wanted to have a fresh start and build my own life with my husband.'

 # Health and education - adapting to new systems

Assuming that the health and education services in your adopted country will be similar to those in your homeland may cause problems. Before you emigrate, learn as much as you can about these systems, and when you arrive, approach these services with an open mind. The differences may end up being beneficial for you.

If you experience problems, then get help through different avenues: talk to citizens' advice, the people around you; contact your local politician, change doctors or schools. The problem may not be a national one, it could just be the area, school, hospital or clinic, or even a personality clash.

It may be fair to assume that, as a new immigrant, you have only scant knowledge of your adopted country's system. Unfortunately, this lack of knowledge is sometimes confused with lack of intelligence or ability – such an assumption will depend on the attitude and perception of the person you are talking to. It may also depend on how that person ranks their own education and health systems compared to those of your homeland, on a global scale.

When Vanessa immigrated, she was told that her ten-year-old daughter was a below-average student. In her homeland, Vanessa's daughter had been an above-average student. When the parents questioned the difference, they were told, 'The reading standard here is above that of most other countries … the system is different here and you haven't understood the system yet.'

Vanessa later discovered that the teacher had been doing the assessment incorrectly. An independent assessment found her daughter's score to be above the average of their adopted country. As well as doing the assessment incorrectly, the teacher had also assumed that the reading standard of the adopted country was higher. If Vanessa hadn't had her daughter tested independently, she may have remained in a class below her ability for a long time. This incident and others persuaded them to change schools. Their daughter progressed well and enjoyed her time at school.

As an immigrant, especially a new immigrant, you may be reluctant to react or speak out, as you want to feel loyal and uncritical towards your adopted country. Consider the consequences if you say or do nothing. Every system has weaknesses that may be worth addressing.

Great expectations and romance

> It's not what happens to you, but how you react to it that matters.
>
> - Epictetus (AD55-135), Greek philosopher

Disappointments often follow expectations, especially if the expectations are high. However much you research the country you are adopting, you won't really know what it's like to live there until you arrive.

You may be disappointed with some of the differences. How you adjust to those disappointments will affect your life as an immigrant.

Mixed marriages (different nationalities)

Most marriages have a reality check some time after the wedding. Your new stage of life becomes dappled with a few disappointments. Some you deal with, others you learn to live with (even if that takes a lifetime.) As an immigrant, big disappointments may feel harder to cope with because you are away from the support of those in your homeland.

Madeleine (English) met Bruce, an American, when he was in England. They moved to America soon after they married. She was expecting to do all the things they had talked of before they were married, but 'All the ambitions and life he'd shown disappeared overnight.'

Madeleine's expectations had to be abandoned. It turned out they were not going to move out of his small rural community. Her social life had changed from jet-setting in London to going to her in-laws next door to do her laundry. 'I didn't even know what day it was because each was the same.'

Jessica, an American, met Nick in California, and on hearing he was a tour guide joined his tour to Peru. They married, and Jessica felt confident that she was ready to exchange her homeland for his rural town. Before meeting Nick, she had regularly wined and dined in San Francisco. Nick's parochial hometown '… was so different. You couldn't even buy a wine glass. There was only one place to eat. The food was shocking. I didn't have any friends. It was cold. It didn't help that they [my in-laws] were critical. That first year was so hard … I was naive. It was totally different to what I thought I was coming to.'

When Imogen followed her boyfriend Richard to his homeland with the idea of staying, she faced many challenges. She hated it when she first came. She was staying at Richard's mother's home where, on the wall, there were pictures of each of her adult children and their partners, including Richard with his ex-girlfriend. In addition, Richard's mother would call Imogen by his ex-girlfriend's name. Imogen described herself as 'a cot case.' She became so fed up with it that after a while she put a nametag, *IMOGEN*, on herself and on her bed.

When Richard's mother asked why she did that, she said it was so she could get her name right.

In a mixed marriage, the in-laws have a very important part to play. My mother-in-law was a great support. Having started travelling in her retirement, she was always interested in England and my family there. She and my father-in-law rarely made their thoughts on our parenting known, they would look after the small children when asked, always welcomed us into their home, and often turned up at birthdays until neither could drive. My mother-in-law realised the importance for me of having a sense of family in my adopted country. She was willing to do all she could to provide that.

In contrast, in a conversation I had with Desmond, father-in-law of immigrant Bella, he complained that Bella didn't fit into the family because she was different. I remember hiding my clenched fists in folded arms and breathing deeply before I said, as softly as I could, 'Your family is the only family Bella has had near her for the last twenty years. She probably finds your family different too, but as she doesn't have her family near, she probably tries to make the most of yours.' He nodded his head gently and admitted that he had never thought of the situation from her perspective.

As a mixed-marriage couple, you may have an understanding that you will alternate between countries, living for a few months or years at a time in each. This may work well if you have support networks and employment opportunities in both countries, however, as time goes on, you and/or your children may be reluctant to change countries, friends, schools or work often.

Katy met her husband while travelling. She has lived in his homeland for all of their married life. While her children were preschoolers, they would often spend three months a year in her homeland. Spending long periods away became increasingly difficult when the children became involved in sports and school, but the family did spend a year away at one stage, and then again when two of her children had left school.

It can turn out so differently

Hanneke was all set to emigrate with her husband Arie and two teenage daughters, but at the last minute, one daughter decided not to come, and that daughter is still living in The Netherlands. Hanneke is sad that her daughter is not with her, '… but you can't dwell on it or be miserable about it'. She has had '… to be pleased with the few times I can embrace her, talk with her and kiss her'.

Your expectation may be that when your children grow up, your family stays intact in your adopted country. This does not always work, as there is a strong connection with your homeland. All of Hanneke's older (aged over seventy) immigrant friends have some of their children or grandchildren living overseas.

Your children may not adjust to the move as easily as you anticipated, even if they are quite small. When Christina and her family were new immigrants,

Christina had to deal with her son being bullied, and her thirteen-month-old daughter suddenly going from speaking well to not speaking at all. It took her daughter a while to start speaking again.

The migration process is strenuous, even when you have done it before. Vanessa and her husband George immigrated to New Zealand more than twenty years ago. After five years, they returned to England. Three children and seventeen years later, they decided to come back to New Zealand. Vanessa knew this would be a new migration experience. Her memories of New Zealand were nearly two decades old. The country had changed, and, unlike before, she was now a parent – and a parent of teenagers, which comes with its own challenges.

Immigrating a second time, and with the view of it being a new experience, the emotions were still stronger than she anticipated: '... difficult emotions, like pain – you never remember them well. How could you live with that? How could you remember with clarity? Like childbirth, you don't remember it with full clarity; you remember it in black and white rather than Technicolor.'

Key points

1. No matter how long you have been in your adopted country, there may still be times when you feel like an outsider. Sometimes this may be painful. Your accent and your mannerisms make you stand out. You may feel isolated and choose to keep quiet instead of being sure you are heard. Cultural differences can cause mistakes.

2. The fact that you stand out means that you are a novelty. People may see you as interesting and want to hear what you have to say.

3. Sense of humour differs in different countries. Be prepared for people not to laugh when you make a joke. Work and social situations can highlight the differences in sense of humour. It can be upsetting to be unable to share a joke. There may be offence caused or offence taken when humour is misunderstood.

4. Embrace the opportunity to reinvent yourself. Get rid of the 'baggage' you do not want.

5. Be ready for the challenges the 'new you' brings. Changing behaviour takes time.

6. The health and education systems will be different to those of your homeland.

7. Some people are unaware and sometimes unthinking. They may assume that, being an immigrant, you lack intellect and life experience.

8. As a new immigrant, you may feel weak and unable to assert yourself.

9. Mixed marriages have a treasure chest of challenges to process.

10. Immigration does not solve all problems; it may create new ones.

»

11 Your children and grandchildren may repeat the cycle and become immigrants too.

12 There may be emotional challenges you haven't anticipated, however much research you have done.

Strategies

- Accept and embrace the feeling of being from another culture, or a novelty. There may be times when this allows you to do something you would never have done in your homeland. Celebrate your difference. Mix with those who enjoy your differences.

- As an immigrant, be ready to apologise for the joke, or state that what you said was a joke. Be ready to say that often, then laugh, even if only inside. Get to know the sense of humour of the people in your host country, individually and collectively. Relax, enjoy it.

- Be prepared to expand yourself. Look for interests in your adopted country and talk about them to other people. You didn't immigrate to repeat the life you had in your homeland.

- Have a thick skin while you appreciate and try to understand the people in your host country. Get others to pronounce words in your language.

- Find out about the health, education and other systems of your adopted country. You are an immigrant, not ignorant. Find out who to contact to make a difference.

- Allow a settling-in time for your children. If there are issues, wait a while before reacting to a perceived negative situation. If you are convinced action is necessary, then act.

- Don't be afraid to question. Work out what is best for your child and stick with it.

- With mixed marriages, do as much research as you can to make sure you know not only the person you are going to spend the rest of your life with, but the place you are going to live in, too.

- Be prepared for extra adjustments. Consider them character building.

- Acknowledge you made the decision that felt right at the time. Enjoy it.

3 Prejudice, misunderstandings, assumptions

Prejudice is the child of ignorance.

- William Hazlitt (1778-1830), English philosopher

At the heart of racism is the religious assertion that
God made a creative mistake when He
brought some people into being.

- Friedrich Otto Hertz (1878-1964), Austrian sociologist

Immigrants stand out because of the way they look, speak or act. Comments, assumptions, misinterpretations and generalisations are made about them or their homeland. In many cases, these comments are not intended to cause offence, but they may. It can be frustrating for the immigrant, as often the 'assumer' is not open to correction or enlightenment. You may need to grow a thick skin, see the humour, and be patient and tactful. If prejudice or racism gets too much, a course of action may be needed.

Jenny: 'They assume they know what it's like to be English. Suggestions are made that, as they speak the language, they are basically English too. Well, you are not actually.'

Vanessa: 'It can be annoying to hear them assume they know how it is. They may have some ancient relatives from Scotland or England, but they don't know what it is like now. It is annoying.'

Susan: 'Being South African, people are expecting you to be racist. I avoid race issues. I freeze rather than partake in them.'

Anne was at university in her adopted country during George Bush's term as US President, and the Iraq War. Some people avoided her purely because of her nationality. 'It was strange to have that as a personal reason not to interact with you. They don't know what my opinions are.'

 # Accents

Having an accent can cause misunderstandings, as well as entertaining and enlightening moments. Monica's future husband, Donald, was a dairy farmer, and she was ready for him to impress her. They were up in a hot air balloon drifting over a rural area.

Donald said, 'You can tell that area is a dairy farm and that area is a beef farm.'

Monica looked down, but all she could see were green fields. She was amazed he could identify the difference from such a height. She asked, 'How can you tell?'

He replied (or so she thought), 'That area has no cow shit.'

She scanned below her and still only saw green fields and a few buildings. She couldn't pick out whether or not there was cow poo in the fields.

'That's amazing. Does one type of cattle have a different diet, so they don't poo?'

When Donald turned to her dumbfounded, her response was, 'What is it? I'm agreeing with you. I think it's amazing. I'm just wondering if, because they have different diets, all the energies go into making the beef rather than pooing?'

He replied, 'I didn't say cow *shit*, I said cow *shed*.' |A cow shed is a large milking shed.|

In another example, when David and I were in London, recently married, he was describing our New Zealand house to my brother. David described its sunny aspect and, elaborating, continued, 'What I love is a really big deck.'

With David's New Zealand accent, my brother heard 'dick', not 'deck'. My brother thought my future husband a bit of a 'deck'. It took a while for the translation and explanation to sink in and leave my brother with a more favourable impression of his future brother-in-law.

Madeleine (English, and married to an American) found her children spoke with an English accent until they went to school, when their accent became American.

My children's accents changed too. Hearing their New Zealand accents helped me face the reality of life in my adopted country. My children were going to be New Zealanders. They may have an interest in England, but their connection with England is unlikely to feel as strong as mine.

Accepting the reality of your children identifying with a different nationality to yours can be difficult. However, once you have done so, there is an opportunity to feel a connection with your adopted country – I may not feel like *I* am a New Zealander, but I am a mother to four of them.

Grandparents may find the difference in accents a challenge. The accents not only remind them that their grandchildren are different, but that they are distant, too.

Monica's parents struggled with her being away from them: 'My parents say they don't understand the children. It's not that difficult. Perhaps they don't try very hard.'

From Monica's parents' point of view, they may feel it should not be an effort to listen to their grandchildren. The grandparents were not the ones that moved.

Anne's grandmother said to her, 'America is my home, you shouldn't have an accent.' (Anne had worked on picking up the accent of her adopted county – see Chapter 2.)

Time or circumstances may lead you to adjust your accent, as Anne did. Sylvia (from England) found she modified hers: 'In early days, when my accent was broader, people would do a double take and feel they had nothing in common with me, so would excuse themselves. Very quickly I changed, and I felt I became accepted. My friends from those days still call me Pommie. It is a fond name.'

Monica pointed out that sometimes your original accent surfaces. 'Donald says when I get angry, my cockney accent stands out. Also, when I'm talking to my dad, my accent is stronger.'

If you retain your accent, people might treat you as a new immigrant, even though you have been in your adopted country for a long time. Jessica's in-law was surprised she knew where a particular town was: 'Fancy you knowing, you're not even from this country.'

She thought, *Gosh, I've been here twenty-eight years. Why shouldn't I know?* But she chose to keep this thought to herself. I empathise with her holding back, and may have done the same. As an immigrant, you have to become used to being reminded that you are different, thanks to your actions, accent, appearance and what you say. It can be difficult to be reminded you don't share the same history, but how you respond is your choice. Jessica has become tolerant of hearing she is 'not from here' and chooses not to make an issue of such comments.

With her strong German accent, people assume Lena is a recent immigrant. 'They still ask me where I'm from and make a point of it. I've been here fifteen years. I call it home. When will others see it as my home?' Although she finds such comments frustrating, Lena also chooses to say nothing.

Languages, accents and dialects can make it difficult to match the written and spoken word. When my children were learning to read, they would see the written word 'bed' and hear it as both 'bid' and 'bed'. The same with pin and pen, pig and peg. Fortunately they quickly worked out which was which.

Sylvia, being a teacher, found that children would come and ask her to spell things, '... and I didn't always get what they were saying. I would ask them to put it into a sentence so I would get the correct word.'

Those exposed to more than one accent can sometimes forget which accent is which. During a trip back to London, I was in a local pub with my sisters. Standing at the bar, we each ordered a half of lager. The bar attendant remarked how alike we looked. I was delighted to be recognised as their sister, and thought nothing more of the comment, but one of my two sisters turned to me and said, 'You would feel really at home in this pub, wouldn't you?'

I wasn't sure what she meant. I did feel at home alongside my sisters, but I didn't think she was referring to that. Still in a jet lag stupor, I scanned my memories for past times in the pub that would make her suggest me feeling at home. The pub was local, but not 'a local pub'. We had gone there that night because it was near our parents' home and was often nearly empty. When I asked why, she replied, 'The barmaid's accent – she's from where you are.'

It turned out she was from Australia (Australia, New Zealand – not much difference as far as the Northern Hemisphere is concerned, they are both very far away). It was irrelevant that my sisters didn't recognise the difference between a New Zealand and Australian accent, but a revelation to me that I didn't register the difference between an English accent and an Australia/New Zealand one. The three accents had become a jumbled form of normality to me.

Language challenges

I admire those who speak a second language in their adopted country. On Lena's first trip from Germany to the English-speaking country she would later emigrate to, she couldn't understand a word people were saying, even though she had studied English for seven years.

When she first arrived, there was no one to meet her. Her accommodation and transport arrangements fell through. Her schoolbook English did get her from the pay phone at the airport to accommodation.

Later, she married an English-speaking man who encouraged her to practise her English by making phone calls.

'You have to immerse yourself,' she says. Audio books from the library also helped her. She persevered and picked up the language, but struggled with colloquial English. Her husband often swore. Lena didn't realise the offensive nature of his words until she used them in conversation with a group of 'garden ladies'. A chorus of gasps and raised eyebrows let her know she had made a mistake.

Nina's husband Perry is a lecturer. He has helped her avoid such pitfalls – his students correct his colloquial English, and he shares this information with Nina.

 **Experiences**

A little knowledge is a dangerous thing.
- Alexander Pope (1688-1744), English poet

Travel expands the mind
- Anon

Individuals may sometimes make comments about your homeland and its people that you find annoying, or even offensive.

Often it is the less-travelled who make the more hurtful comments. German immigrants have been asked if they are related to Hitler, Americans have been assumed to be responsible for American foreign policy, South Africans are assumed to be racist, and the English apparently live in permanent rain or fog. It's upsetting to hear negative comments about your homeland, but it will happen and you will have to deal with it.

Olivia: 'I was in a community group, and someone made a compliment about Americans. "Americans are confident: they go out and get it." I relished the moment, but then there was a retort: "Yeah, they go out and invade countries." It was very negative. I was about to raise my hand, however, a new guy there said, "As the token American here I would like to express that although we are Americans, we cannot be lumped with government policy. It is not fair." These are prejudices. I just brush them off my shoulder. If I feel the need to address it, I will. But it's often not worth addressing. I just let it lie.'

Nina: 'People have fixed impressions of how Indians are. It is only in the last ten years more professionals have emigrated. Previously it was always the business or the labour class ... Eight years back, there was surprise we could speak English so well, not realising it is such a common language in India.'

New immigrants may have the worst experiences. Christina's family was subjected to racism by a neighbour when they first arrived. 'We had dead birds dropped on our lawn, then nails in our driveway, three to four days in a row. I picked them all up. Then he made a voodoo doll. I thought, *This is enough.* I decided he was not going to chase us out of the neighbourhood, so I reported him to the police. Then it stopped.'

As a new immigrant, Anita was unsure when was the right time to step in. 'We were quite trusting of the school. There were other immigrants there. One of them taught our children. We considered ourselves global citizens. We shouldn't feel inferior.

'I suddenly realised my very intelligent child had no friends. The teacher said it was because she was a high achiever. Others – adults and children –

said she was being picked on by the teacher. I brought it up with the teacher. I asked whether she had a problem with my daughter's behaviour, and she said no she didn't. The teacher apologised for her behaviour and said she would try not to do it again. But the prejudice didn't go away. My daughter missed many privileges. She couldn't understand why she was not included. We didn't want her to feel that. It was so sad.'

Anita had been so glad about the extra tuition hours she was getting from the school for her daughter's special needs that she didn't want to make a fuss. 'I had told my daughter that sometimes you have to put up with a bad boss. Now I realise she had to deal with more than that.'

Lena's daughter made a stand. 'She gets teased at school, "You are the German one." That really upset her. She had to write a report about herself, and she started, "I was born here."'

Jasmine, from the Philippines, often feels uncomfortable at her husband Jack's family gatherings. The couple met when Jack, a New Zealander, was working in the Philippines, and moved to New Zealand when Jack's mother became sick. Jasmine helped care for her, and they have lived there since.

'Sometimes I feel I don't belong here,' says Jasmine. 'When we go to funerals and birthdays, people look at me and make me feel like I shouldn't be there. Sometimes I don't go to funerals because I don't want to go through with that. I feel sad when I can't go. It is sad. It is Jack's loved ones and I can't be there too. It is too painful for me to go.'

Between 1945 and 1972, British subjects were subsidised to immigrate to Australia and New Zealand. Adults were charged ten pounds sterling for their voyage, and children travelled free. These immigrants became known as Ten Pound Poms, Poms being slang for British. When Sylvia immigrated in the early 1970s, people would react to her broad accent – often with laughter. On one occasion, a man heard Sylvia's accent and challenged her. He told her that he had a handicapped brother, and felt that government money would have been better spent looking after his brother than on funding immigrants. Sylvia said the confrontation made her appreciate that there was resentment about the flush of British immigrants, and felt she had to be careful about what she said and when.

Sylvia's experience reminded my husband David of the resentment against the British at the time. In 1972, when All Black Keith Murdoch was sent home from a British Tour, a New Zealand local radio station promoted 'Punch-a-Pom day'. David remembers that the saying quickly developed into a jesting, 'Punch a Pom today'.

Nina suggested that we have to be careful not to be oversensitive. 'Some [immigrants] have [fear of] racism so ingrained in them, they come expecting it and see things which are not there.'

Rebecca and Emma are originally from countries to which many people have migrated. They now realise what it feels like to be an immigrant – making social blunders, and not knowing the systems and behaviour of the country – and recognise that the judgements they had previously made were unfair.

Great Spirit, grant that I may not criticize my neighbour until I have walked a mile in his moccasins.

- American Indian prayer

Key points

1   There will be ignorance about your homeland. Some people will assume that you bring with you all the attitudes and stereotypes (real or imagined) of your homeland.

2   Some people do not wish to be corrected or informed about your homeland.

3   Some people are inclined to remind apparent outsiders that they are different.

4   An assumption will probably be made that if you have an accent, you are a recent immigrant, and therefore know little about the country (see Chapter 2).

5   You can adjust or change your accent.

6   After a time, the accent of your adopted country will feel like normality.

7   When you are in your homeland, your accent is likely to be moderated by your adopted country, and vice versa.

8   Living in a country with a different language is a challenge.

9   People may consider you inferior to them because you are an immigrant.

10 You may feel or suspect incidences of racism or prejudice. You may be more sensitive and responsive if the incidences involve your children.

11 Attacks or prejudice towards races may not occur because you are an immigrant, but rather because of what is going on in the attackers' lives. Unfortunately, you are the scapegoat.

12 You may be oversensitive to racism or prejudice, especially if you are feeling unsure about your adopted country.

13 As an immigrant yourself, you can reflect on judgements you may have previously made on immigrants when you were in your homeland.

Strategies

•   Practise reflective listening, and if people native to your adopted country are receptive, gently tell them how being an immigrant is for you.

•   Suggest that not all people from your homeland are the same. Ignore those who want to pigeonhole you.

•   Be patient.

»

»

- Seek out those who will listen to your point of view and who do not stereotype.

- Don't worry if your accent stands out, unless it really troubles you. If it does, you can adjust your accent (see Chapter 2).

- When confronted with someone who wants to remind you that you are different, it may be because they have reasons to increase their own sense of ownership or belonging by excluding you.

- When you do not understand what is being said or done, ask people who are willing to help.

- Immerse yourself in the language. Borrow audio books to help learn the language of your adopted country.

- Laugh at the mistakes you make and learn from them. Be ready with a few good replies to stereotyping, or brush the comments off.

- If racism is obvious, then act on it. Report it to a higher authority of the organisation, community or group.

- Be aware of your own prejudice and avoid passing this on to children. Your adopted country is their homeland.

- Do not expect local people around you to change. They have probably been here all the time and they did not ask you to come. Don't get upset if they don't understand you straight away. Recall how you felt about immigrants when you were in your homeland.

4 Support network

Whether you realised it or not, you had a support network in your homeland: friends, family, work colleagues, a neighbour, or someone who knew you well enough to help in a time of need.

In your adopted country it is equally important to have a similar support network. You can create this network in a variety of ways, but you do have to get out there and create it. It's not going to come to you. A bonus is that receiving and giving help, and relying on someone in some way, will increase your connection with the country you are living in.

New immigrants Rebecca and Brent's pact to accept every invitation at least once helped them meet people. 'It was very easy to feel shy in this new environment, but we had to say yes to people. If you don't like them, if you feel it's hideous, then you don't have to go back. The rule was you could not say no; you have to get out there.'

Vanessa described making friends as a long process: 'It starts off with a hello and then you talk a little bit more. You can't really fast-forward a friendship even though perhaps you'd like to. You just have to allow it to happen. Don't be afraid that perhaps you're not making all the friends you would initially like to. You're probably quite exhausted as a new immigrant.'

 ## Build it up

My support network built up mainly through a preschool organisation. I spent time with other mothers, joining them in running and maintaining the preschool. There were meetings and working bees (volunteers gathering to fundraise or complete a task). We had a shared interest in the community and parenting. While there I made plenty of blunders, but because they knew me as someone who was willing to contribute, I was able to build up enough of a rapport with them to feel accepted. Through this group I had people around me who knew my children, knew me and my way of parenting. If an emergency happened, or even if I desperately needed time out, such as for a dentist's appointment or a relaxing haircut for my sanity, there were friends I could call on to look after my children. I did the same for them. Giving and receiving help felt homely.

My support network has made a huge impact on me. When my father died, when I had miscarriages and when our three daughters were born, my adopted-country friends would offer to take care of my children and provide me with ready-cooked meals. The support felt like a godsend each time. At their times of need I could reciprocate, which not only had the delightful feeling of being able to give, but also increased my sense of belonging in my community.

Being a mother with babies or small children can be a great time to meet other people at clinics, day care, school or preschool. The network you build up at that time can stay with you as your children grow and together you face the challenges of schools, health, adolescence, leaving home and beyond.

Work is another opportunity to get to know people well. You spend many hours with colleagues. When you have a task to do, consider making time to stay a little longer. Start a conversation, offer a comment or compliment.

You could join a community activity, evening classes, church, sports team, walking group, or start a book club (see Chapter 2). If you can offer a skill, make a contribution or a connection, you are on the right track to having people around you who are willing to be there if you need them. Find what suits you. Go back to the same place so people become familiar with you. Get to know people. When they know you better then they will become part of your support network.

Immigrant clusters

Immigrants often gravitate to people of the same nationality, language and/or culture. This can provide a readymade network of people with empathy for, and experience of, the challenges of immigration. In these cluster groups you can literally speak the same language and discuss issues that trouble you.

At the book club that Rebecca started up, French-speaking members drift seamlessly in and out of French, while she and the other English members share 'jokes about Ronnie Corbett'.

Monica and other preschool mothers from England used to meet once a month, stick a Union Jack flag in the ground and have lunch.

To have a group of friends who come from the same country as you is helpful, and provides a good network, but consider whether you are relying too heavily on them. Having a healthy mix of friends is rewarding (see Chapter 2).

Making friends as an individual

To like and dislike the same things,
that is true friendship.

- Sallust (86-34 BC), Greek philosopher

My mixed marriage meant that I had the foundation of my husband's friends and family, so there were people around me who cared.

Immigrating couples or families will be eager for new friendships, having left most, if not all, of their established social and family networks behind. But in these cases, network building may take longer (see chapter 16).

Sallust (see quote above) said friendship was based on common interests. Finding an individual with matching interests is easier than meeting a couple with matching interests, or even discovering a family where everyone has similar interests. Perhaps it would be wise to find individual friends first and build on those.

Whether single or married, there will be plenty of opportunities to make friends, either individual or shared. As mentioned earlier, a good start would be to go somewhere or join something where your chances of finding someone with similar interests are high, for example community classes, a dancing group, sports club or church. Over time, a person from one of these groups could become your greatest friend.

 # 'I don't need help.' Yes you do

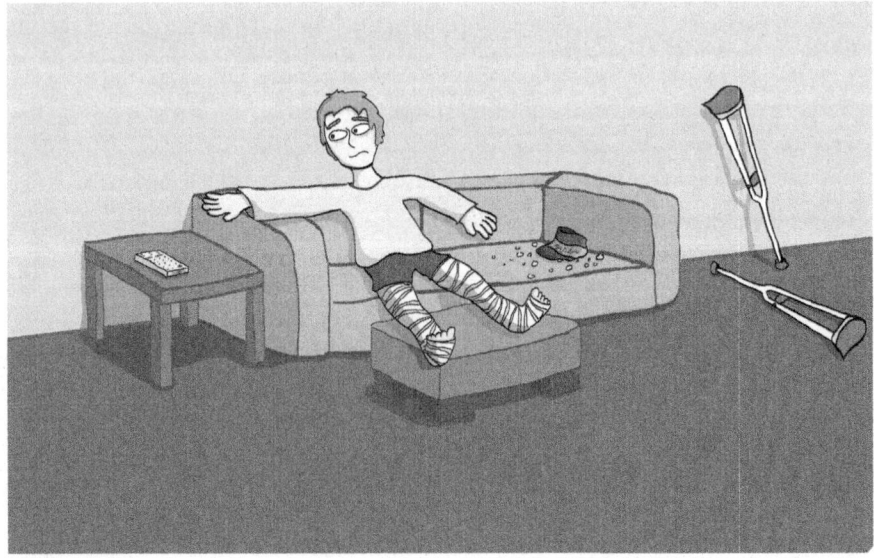

'I'm quite capable of managing by myself.'

If you haven't built up a support network, you need to consider carefully what will happen if you become sick, break a leg or need to go to hospital. Are there people who could help you?

Elizabeth was sick in hospital. The social services recognised that her husband Jim couldn't take any more time off work, but somebody needed to take care of the children while Elizabeth stayed in hospital. As there was no apparent support network, the social services suggested that the children go into care. Jim and Elizabeth were quickly motivated to ask for help from the people they knew. Help was given and their support network was established.

When Charlotte was unwell, her homesickness became stronger. 'I was at home recovering after my operation – no nurses. During the day, I would cry. I don't know why, but I would cry. I think I felt so far away from my family. There was one person to check me each day and I'd think gosh, how would I manage if she didn't do this? I am quite surprised I didn't go home at this stage. It is only because I was so poorly |that| I stayed.'

Charlotte's one person would bring magazines and anything else she needed. It was important to have someone to check on her during the day. This was a limited support network, but it was enough.

Lena missed family support when she had a house fire. 'When I had the fire, I asked my ex-husband to come and help. He didn't. My parents couldn't come and help either.' Fortunately she had neighbours who helped.

A support network is a natural progression of getting to know people in your community, neighbourhood and workplace. If you have engaged enough with at least one or two people, they may be willing to help you in a time of need.

 ## Changing networks and friendships

Building up friendships and support networks takes time. As a new immigrant you may feel you don't need to make many new friends as you already have enough in your homeland, and you may be holding on to a sense of loyalty to those homeland friends. However, you are geographically distant, and, should you need help, your homeland friends can give only emotional support.

Of the people around you now, who could help? If you are putting a great deal of energy into maintaining friendships from your homeland, consider transferring that time and energy to nurturing relationships with new acquaintances in your adopted country (see Chapter 5).

In a mixed marriage, your support network is likely to include your spouse's family – probably the only family you have in your adopted country. If you separate, and loyalties are divided, your spouse's family could become unavailable to help you at this time when you need support (see Chapter 17). It could be worth making sure you have sufficient alternative support.

Key points

1 You need a support network, especially if you have children.

2 You need to engage with people in your adopted country to feel a sense of belonging. It takes effort, but a sound and reciprocal support network increases this sense of belonging.

3 Organisations or groups can also give you a sense of belonging.

4 If you mix only with people of your own nationality, you may feel less engaged in your adopted country.

5 Immigrating couples or families may find it harder than immigrants in mixed marriages to find friends with common interests.

Strategies

- Get out there. Join clubs and walking groups; build up your friends and community. Get to know your neighbours. Attend or volunteer at preschool, school and sports functions. Offering your help or skills is a good way to build up a support network.

- Say yes to invitations. You may love the event.

- Look for communities you fit into best. Look for the goodness in the people you are now mixing with. Allow friends into your life and allow time to develop the friendships.

- Join more than one group or club. Then if a group no longer suits you and you want to leave, you still have people to engage with.

- If you lose some of your support, seek a replacement.

5 Keep in touch, or else!

Charlotte: 'Sometimes he suggests I'm in a funny place. He suggests I phone home. After the phone call I feel connected again.'

Keeping in contact

I once read that a key to happiness is to have contact with somebody every day. Having contact with my family and friends in England gives me a sense of happiness. I don't make contact as often as I could, but it is uplifting when I do.

Email and Skype, and social media sites like Facebook and Twitter, have made contact much easier. A quick email, Facebook message, Tweet or text (or whatever is the latest application on the internet) makes a connection – for a moment, you are in their thoughts and you know you will be in theirs. The connection, however small, is comforting.

Use of the Internet and email properly took off in the mid-nineties, when it became affordable for people to have a home computer. Before then, immigrants' contact with their homeland was by 'snail mail', visits, and, as they became cheaper, phone calls. My uncle, who emigrated from England to Australia in the sixties as a 'Ten Pound Pom', said that in the sixties and early seventies, if he'd wanted to make a trip back to England, he would have had to re-mortgage his house. And at that time, the cost of phone calls was so high that they were made only in exceptional circumstances. He wanted to keep in contact with his siblings, nephews and nieces, so he sent us tapes made on a reel-to-reel tape recorder. The reels were the size of an outstretched hand, and the tape recorders were the size of an airline carry-on bag. We listened to recordings of his children – our cousins – speaking in a funny accent, and in response made recordings along the lines of, 'Hello, my name is Eleanor, I am seven and I like swimming and going to Brownies. Goodbye.'

It all seemed very odd to me as a child, watching the reels go round as they recorded our messages to these stranger-cousins. I'm sure I would rather have been playing, but I don't think I had a choice. I guess my parents were doing as I do now – making sure we had some connection with our cousins and extended family. Our parents' efforts paid off, as decades later, with email, Facebook and easier travel, we have reconnected with our cousins. They are no longer stranger-cousins, even though we were brought up on opposite sides of the world. When I see them, I notice that their faces, expressions and mannerisms mirror those of my siblings, father and grandparents. I realise then that the connection is more than a shared interest in family, it is tribal.

The desire to keep in contact was as strong in the sixties as it is now. However, the expectations are higher today, because connecting is so much easier. New immigrants tend to find they contact many people frequently. When Olivia first arrived in her adopted country, she would spend a whole weekend phoning and emailing friends and family. 'In the beginning my weekend was structured to call this person then that person. I found that I was living inside all weekend; I was living my life in the USA. I wasn't living my life here. I wasn't out making friends, I wasn't out doing anything like seeing the country, joining clubs. I was only going to work and the gym. I found that all my free time was spent catching up with people: "Don't forget me, I'm still here." I would go through this calling list of everyone and then get hold of my family, then other people there too. With my job, I was travelling and meeting people. I may be away for four days and the last thing I wanted to do on a Saturday was to spend the day on the phone. I didn't want my life to be about work and calling people in the States. You get to think, that is not a life.'

Realising she had to decrease the amount of time spent contacting people in the States, Olivia reduced calls to her friends to perhaps once a month, and rang family at set intervals. This has made the amount of contact work well for her. It did mean she had to let go of some of her old friends, or reduce the intensity of the contact, but it gave her room to make friends in her adopted country.

Emma has found that she has decreased contact with her brother. 'When we first moved here, my brother didn't contact me at all. We are still not as close as we were before. He has gone his way and I have to go my way.'

The people you keep in frequent contact with change at different stages of life. This applies whether you are an immigrant or not. For an immigrant, distance often forces the change. Although I don't keep in frequent contact with some of my homeland friends, when I do, the event is delightful.

The Internet has made contact easier, and with so many different ways of connecting there are plenty of opportunities for an increased level of engagement. Through Skype, Sylvia watched her young nephew show her his new room. He took the laptop around his bedroom describing his toys. She loved seeing him in action. That instant visual is fantastic.

Christina told me how, when her brother got married, they prepared for the wedding in one bedroom and Skyped the activity. She was able to see the bridesmaids parading around in their dresses making sure their hair and make-up was just right. Her mother joined in the show too. Christina was delighted to be able to share the excitement of the wedding preparation.

Regular and irregular calls.

A routine of a regular monthly or weekly phone call can work well. If you keep the relationship flowing by regular contact, your family and friends get to know your everyday routines. You can enjoy small talk with them, rather than being limited to major events. Having a regular call time does mean you have to be ready at that time, or your parents or friends may worry.

Charlotte has a routine of calling on Sunday mornings. Amber's calls are less frequent. Five years after setting off on her travels, and now a citizen of a different country, her contact with her family in England has a vague routine. 'I contact once every couple months. I usually say, "Oh crap, I'd better contact them".'

Irregular calls offer a feeling of spontaneity, but unless you know each other's routines, the call may have to be cut short. With Skype you can arrange a time to be on screen together. Some immigrants text the person first to see if it is a good time to ring. Having a bit of warning can allow you to finish your dinner, pause the movie, get dressed, get the children occupied or safe, and give your full attention to the phone or Skype call.

Time differences mean that when you ring, your time zones are unsynchronised. It may be early in the morning in South Africa or Europe, but late evening or night in Australasia. One person is full of beans at the beginning of the day, and the other is winding down or reflecting on the end of the day. Already the contact is disjointed – it may start jarringly, but with time and practice it usually settles and is rewarding (see Chapter 14).

In situations where there is a significant event, or one of you needs a listening ear, the time difference becomes irrelevant once you are focused on each other. These are often the longer calls, and as Sylvia says, it is worth putting your day on hold and sitting with them, linked by the phone, for as long as is necessary.

It is up to you to keep connected

Don't be surprised if you feel you are the one making the most effort to keep in contact. You are the one who moved. You know their routines, they don't know yours. If you want to keep up the contact, then expect to keep making an effort.

With Facebook, you can keep up to date with many people. You may in fact want to keep connected with fewer. Quality connections are likely to counteract the 'missing'. When Christina immigrated, there was no home computer, so she sent faxes every week. She says she couldn't have survived without that connection at the time. Now she enjoys Skype.

During Monica's first few years, her mother was tearful every time Monica phoned. This made her hesitant to call her mother.

Charlotte's calls can bring mixed feelings too. 'I still feel very connected to the UK. At the weekend, Sunday morning, it's my contact with them. I always phone my family. I try really hard to listen to my mum. I just wish it was two-way.'

Holidays and festivals are good times to make contact (see Chapter 14). If you send bulk emails, personalising them increases the sense of connection. If you send a newsletter, try and give the reader a taste of your life in your adopted country as well as your news.

Sending parcels and presents, especially to younger relatives, reminds them of you. The contents don't have to be expensive. I used to send a small calendar of New Zealand images to my siblings and close friends, hoping that when they looked at it, they would think of me.

Madeleine chooses to hold onto memorabilia: 'I don't throw anything away from family and friends from home. That keeps me connected with them.'

Not the full story

Immigrants can be reluctant to share information in difficult times, because they know that the help they can receive is limited.

Amber usually only talks to her parents when she is feeling good. 'I always feel like I'm protecting them. I am cushioning. I only speak to them when everything is resolved and I am okay, or they worry. I never ring home when the ship is going down. When I had a car accident, I told my mother two weeks after, saying, "By the way I had an accident, but I'm fine now". We can pick up from each other when we are not really fine so I always make sure that I am on top of the world when I talk to her.'

Jessica found that her family and friends knew only half the picture. 'They used to send me letters when I was first here. I was so unhappy, and yet they were so jealous of my life in my adopted country. I felt, if only you knew! I'm jealous of your life in America.'

Conversations without mention of problems may be superficial, but they are a valuable form of connection. Just hearing the voice of a loved one can be enough. I have rung my mother even though I knew she was away. Hearing her voice on the answering service was comforting.

In a non-superficial conversation, Anita tried to relate some of her emotions and worries over the phone to her sister. Unfortunately, Anita's sister misinterpreted her, and instead of the support Anita wanted, her sister reprimanded her for her actions as a parent.

When you don't get the support you need, either from someone in your homeland or from your support network, find other places to go for help, for example community helplines, counsellors or the Samaritans.

You don't always know how a call to your family and friends will evolve. Sometimes a chatty, superficial call can evolve into a longer call, because one of you needs it. As you are physically distant, you can share problems that you perhaps couldn't discuss if you were near to each other (see Chapter 20). These tough times, for you or them, are difficult. The listener can do little to help other than listen and care. Sharing the problem helps. Try looking at this distant sharing in a positive way. Missing someone is all the more poignant and sad when one of you is low, but these feelings are a reflection of the depth of loving. It may be a distant relationship, but it is a loving, caring relationship.

Relationships: grandchildren, nephews and nieces

Jessica: 'I must have been crazy. I've taken my parents away from my children!'

Rebecca: 'I was really close to my grandparents when I was growing up, it is such a different sort of relationship to [the one you have with] your parents. I am sad that my children aren't going to have that.'

Your children are likely to miss the regular grandparent/cousin relationships and connection. However, when these relatives stay with you, or you stay with them, it is likely to be for at least a week, usually more. As an immigrant you have occasional visits for long periods, instead of frequent visits for short periods. In this long period, your visitors will be able to see your children on their best behaviour, and, when the children are tired and have had enough of an unsettled routine, their worst behaviour. In this continuous period of togetherness, there are opportunities for grandparents and grandchildren to delight in the ordinary; reading or telling stories together, or going for a walk; seeing them early in the morning and later at night. They can get to know each other's daily routines and live them jointly.

Relationship building between child and grandparent is enjoyable and usually trouble-free. The relationship can be enhanced by leaving the grandparent and child to get to know each other without you there (see Chapter 8).

Sometimes, with or without you there, there is a clash, as Lena found out. 'I couldn't believe it. A sixty-six-year-old and a four-year-old fighting. I think he wanted all the attention and expected more from her. He expected to be served first. Not in my house!'

The friction turned out to be temporary. 'When we were visiting Germany, my daughter was older and they got on. My father even encouraged her burping at the table and I had to correct it.'

It was Lena's daughter who reminded her that as Lena's parents were old, Lena needed to be more patient.

Olivia is concerned about her relationship with her nephew and niece. She knows her young nephew is more familiar with the people around him than with her. She doesn't want to be a 'virtual aunt'. 'He knows who I am, but he's not going to remember what it's like to be around me. His sister is two years old and doesn't really know me. I am jealous of my sister-in-law's friends who have been around the children. I'm feeling a pulling. I want them to know me more.'

Olivia can be encouraged by Sylvia's experience. Sylvia has found that, even though her children missed time with their grandparents, uncles and aunts, three decades later she has a great relationship with her adult nieces and nephews, who have been to stay with her and kept in contact since.

Key points

1   When you first emigrate, you will be keeping up with many people. This will drop off.

2   You may have to make more of an effort to keep in contact than the people in your homeland.

3   The Internet has increased the opportunities for and quality of contact, for example Skype, Facebook.

4   Time differences can make phone calls awkward.

5   When you phone someone, you may be ready to sit and talk, but they may not be.

6   If you share all your woes with them, be aware that they can listen, but often can't help.

7   Grandparent-grandchild relationships can be built up during occasional but long periods of time, especially if they have time to bond without you there.

8   If relationships with relatives seem weak, they can be built up later.

Strategies

• Set up a routine for contacting people, for example every Sunday night or the first of the month.

• If making irregular calls, bear in mind the commitments of the person you are calling. Give them warning or opportunity to get things arranged so you can have a rewarding conversation.

• When you call, be prepared for a short call or a long call. They might need to talk to you more than you need to talk to them. Be prepared to sit down and enjoy the contact.

• Accept the time differences. If you contact the person often enough at this time, you will get used to the unsynchronised time. Phone when a call is convenient for them too; you are less likely to get an awkward response.

• Find other people to support you when times are tough.

»

»

- If you are going to share your sad or low times, make sure you share your happy and high times too.

- Accept there is a sense of loss at being distant, and that this may be alleviated or highlighted by the contact.

- Often, if you keep in touch with your parents, they will keep you in touch with the rest of your family.

- Use a variety of ways to keep in contact: send parcels, snail mail, email, and use social media.

- You may not know all your relatives, but you are connected.

6 A heart in two homes

Where there is love there is pain.

- Spanish proverb

Distance from family and friends in your homeland is emotionally testing. You miss them and wonder whether they miss you; you are not able to help them in times of need, and you may feel divided loyalties between countries and people. These feelings are uncomfortable and often painful, but if you can acknowledge and accept that they are a natural consequence of the love between you, the discomfort may feel less of a burden.

Abandonment, guilt and emotional ties

When you emigrate, you are leaving behind people you love. You don't intend to hurt them, but family or friends may feel abandoned, or you may feel you have deserted them.

You have reasons for emigrating, but your family and friends may not see these as being strong enough for you to separate from them or leave your homeland. Your loved ones may voice their concerns, and these can be upsetting to hear.

Teresa: 'My sister said I was running away from the family and its problems. I think they feel I have deserted ship, which is hard, because that was never my intention.'

Anne: 'When my parents' divorce was not going well, my sister said, "Why did you go in the first place? We need you here."'

Lena's father thought she was completely selfish to leave her parents behind. It wasn't her intention to be selfish. She wanted to be happy and for her parents to be happy. She says, 'You cannot always do what your parents or your family and friends want. You do have to take charge of your decisions and that may cause hurt.'

Monica married in England and emigrated straight after. In his speech at her wedding, her father, knowing Monica was about to emigrate, said, 'One can't stand in the way of love'. However, his croaked voice and the tears in his eyes suggested that he probably would have preferred to stand in the way of love.

Since immigrating, Monica has found the separation still troubles her. She often says aloud to herself, 'I wish you were here Mum. I'm sorry Mum, I'm sorry I hurt you.'

After a while, immigrants usually find ways to acknowledge and deal with feelings of guilt, or the sense of having abandoned family and friends. Sylvia, now a grandmother, emigrated from England when she was in her early twenties: 'I made sure I did my bit. I kept in contact well. My mother heard from me more than she heard from the others. It worried me at first, so I made an extra effort to keep my place in the family.'

Lena: 'It can't be helped. Telephone as much as possible.'

Yvonne: 'There was some guilt, and I've chosen not to go back. I have feelings of not pulling my weight, but I have to look at why we are here. I have to think of my priorities. If you're continually weighing up whether you should be here or not you may continue subjecting yourself to some kind of guilt.'

Christine: 'I did feel guilty, but my family is my first priority at the moment. It always will be. I will help wherever I can.'

Elizabeth: 'I feel terribly guilty about my mum and it tempers joyous things like my daughter getting a certificate for her art. We did Skype her and hold it up, but I do feel sad.'

Susan realises the feelings of guilt are her own. 'I look at my kids and see how I would feel. I feel guilty I have left my mother. She loves the grandchildren. When she dies I will feel I haven't spent much time with her. I could have been there more. That feeling won't leave me. She has never done anything to make me feel guilty; full marks for that. It is all my own thoughts.'

Do you miss me? Dreams and visions

I have a recurring dream, in which I take a surprise trip to my homeland to see my family. I arrive, and amazingly the family happens to be in the middle of a gathering. Everybody is there, including my late father. I stride into the room ready for everyone to turn their heads, see me, and run towards me with open arms. That doesn't happen. I enter the room, and besides an upward nod, they all carry on with what they are doing. I feel ignored. Of course, I can't accept this; in my dream I have just flown a long way to be with them. So I announce my presence with a vigorous, 'Hello! I'm here!' A few heads turn, there are muttered greetings, but the overriding feeling is, 'You are here now, so what?' I am crushed.

I fear that everybody is over 'there', continuing their lives without me, and not missing me. I fear I don't count in their lives. I miss my large family as a whole and as individuals. I can acknowledge it's a feeling of love – the pain of love – but I don't like that pain.

I'm glad to report that, over twenty years, the recurring dream has returned less. I can't remember the last time it happened. I am less threatened by the fear and feelings behind it. I have become more used to the pain of missing. I also think more practically. My family may not miss me as much as I miss them. They have only me and my family, and now my sister and her family too, to miss. Day to day, with our occupied lives, we do not miss each other too much but sometimes, particularly on special family occasions, I really miss them and want to be with them. The missing is a shame, but that is how my life is, and I have become more accepting of it.

Sylvia often visualises a table with all of her family gathered around, and an empty chair, which is meant for her.

The feeling of missing is emphasised for an immigrant because you are frequently reminded that you are in a different country. Your accent and social blunders are signals that you are away from not only people, but also familiarity. Meanwhile your family and friends in your homeland will miss you, but they are not missing the familiar. You have both to process.

If you want to hear that you are missed, you may need to ask. Those left behind may not realise you want to hear you are missed, or may not feel inclined to let you know you are missed – after all, you are the one who left. They may also be protecting you from reminders of what you are missing, and from making you feel guilty, or guiltier, for leaving them.

Over the years, Sylvia has realised that 'You are part of their lives, they just forget to tell you. You have to drag it out of them.' Recently she spent a length of time in her homeland, and '... stored up lovely memories of being with them.' One such memory was of her family revisiting a favourite place. The vacation was so successful that the family returned to the same place the following year, but this time without her. She was looking forward to hearing how their second trip went: 'No one sent anything. When I finally did mention it, they said, "Oh yes, we missed you so much and we talked about you." I thought, *You could have told me*. Perhaps a little prompting is all that is needed.

 ## Not being there in tough times

In tougher times, family and friends will feel your absence more strongly. When someone close to you in your homeland dies, your absence is felt all the more by you or your loved ones (see Chapter 12). When Jim's mother died, his brother said, 'Now you're leaving me with Dad to deal with this?'

When Hanneke's father died, she could not get back for her father's funeral because she had just started a new job, and her employers wouldn't give her enough time off. She felt disappointed. Her mother was supportive, saying it was very sad but 'That is the way it is.' Her sister was angry. Hanneke said, 'For years I've struggled with that |my sister being angry| because I was angry myself at not going. The family situation comes up all the time, you can be on the other side of the world and it will still affect you. I knew I had abandoned her, but I was surprised that I was such an important person for her. We've never been great friends. Then I realised it is something in her that needed support more than it had to do with me. Later something happened in her life. I realised my gut feeling was right. She had problems. At the time, I couldn't help wondering if I did the right thing. I had to reassess my priorities and realise that my focus was here. I got support from my husband and my daughter. I did feel alone, but I had to go through my own motives, which makes you stronger.'

 ## Pining for home

The grass is always greener on the other side
of the fence.
- English proverb

Maybe your side needs more watering.
- Wise addition (Anon)

If you are continually comparing your adopted country to your homeland, if the missing is too much, then perhaps you should go back. Before you make that decision, though, remember the above saying. Perhaps your life in your adopted country would be better if you gave it more attention and appreciation. Living in your homeland could now be different to how it was before you left.

Many immigrants who go 'home' for a visit are surprised to find how many things they *haven't* missed, for example smaller or larger houses, conveniences, or the pace of life. A visit home allows you to identify what you miss the most, and assess how important those things are You may have been viewing life in your homeland through rose-coloured spectacles. Make sure you get some clear lenses, and look objectively at both living in your adopted country, and your homeland, before you make such a major decision (see Chapter 7).

 ## Where does your loyalty lie?

Five years after I came to New Zealand, people often commented, 'You must be a Kiwi |New Zealander| now.' During that time I thought I wanted to be a Kiwi. To be perceived as such would have been an acknowledgement that I had fitted in to New Zealand. However, being a Kiwi didn't feel right to me. There was always a part of me that not only felt English, but wanted to hold onto my English background. I wasn't a Kiwi, nor will I ever be. I'm an English person who is happy to live in New Zealand, and that is enough.

Olivia: 'I neither feel part of my adopted country nor part of my homeland. I am in this little space, a modified version of something.'

Yvonne and her husband Mark were in their mid-twenties when they emigrated more than twenty years ago. She feels tested when someone makes an assumption about why she emigrated. 'People assume we are here because of the troubles in Northern Ireland. I feel prickly about that. I had a good upbringing, I enjoyed my upbringing. It was a privileged childhood. I feel patronised. It was my choice to come here, I didn't have to come.'

Immigrants often have joint loyalties to their homeland and adopted country. When asked whether their children belong more to their adopted country or their homeland, most of the women interviewed felt that their children identify more with the country they live in – their mother's adopted country. Some felt their children identify with both the country they were brought up in and their parent(s)' homeland.

If their child identifies solely with the country they are living in, some mothers have given an occasional reminder that the mother's homeland is part of the child's heritage too, for example by teaching them the national anthem, getting them to wear the country's colours during an important sports game, or praising great artists from that country (see Chapter 13). Such reminders of mixed nationality may not be welcomed at the time, especially if the children are teenagers and are keen to seek an opposite identity from at least one parent, but at least the children will be exposed to half of their heritage and can explore it later.

Sophie, from England, met her husband Michael when they were both working overseas. They lived in England for a time, but when this didn't work out they went to his homeland 'for a while'. Still there more than fifteen years later, Sophie loves watching sport with Michael and their sons. However, if England are losing, she finds she is the only one disappointed. Michael and the boys primarily support the country they have been brought up in. 'They are actually foreigners to me. I feel a foreigner in my own home.'

Olivia and her husband Stuart emigrated to Stuart's homeland when they were in their mid-twenties. She is not sure what she is going to do when they have a child. She definitely wants to introduce American culture to the children.

Some immigrants have found that holding onto their homeland passport helps keep part of their past in the present. Some hold both passports, although to keep both up to date can be costly and is not always possible. Other immigrants are happy to seek sole citizenship in their adopted country.

Christina emigrated from South Africa with her husband and two young children. She now holds only the passport of her adopted country: 'In my heart I am South African. I don't need that paper to say so.'

Key points

1 Your family and friends may feel you have abandoned them. They may not understand why you emigrated. You have to work through your feelings of abandoning them and any guilt you have.

2 Fears of being isolated from your family and friends may come up in your dreams or thoughts.

3 You are missed.

4 Some people need to go back.

5 You may be seeing life in your homeland through rose-coloured spectacles. You have probably changed since your immigration.

6 Your children may feel they identify more with your adopted country than your homeland. At times you may feel a foreigner in your family.

Strategies

• Acknowledge your feelings of having abandoned your homeland and people you love there. Remind yourself that it was not your intention to hurt anyone. You can't keep everyone happy all the time, and time may reduce the hurt for you all.

• Ask your loved ones whether they are missing you. Drag it out of them, even if asking them seems like you are fishing for compliments. You may feel better when you have heard the words. Put yourself in their shoes. If you missed you, would you say so, and how often?

• Listen to the feelings of those you have left behind. Make your presence felt in their lives by keeping in contact. Do what you can to make up for your absence, for example take up opportunities to fulfil family duties, even if at a distance (see Chapter 20).

• Realise that a person's awkward reaction may not be to do with your 'abandoning' them – there may be other issues in their life that you don't know about.

• If you feel you can make plans for a visit to your homeland, you may pine for it less, even if you don't go in the immediate future.

• Water your own garden – your side of the fence (see Chapter 7). Review your priorities and reasons for emigrating.

• Try not to force an allegiance to your homeland on your children; it may be counter-productive (see Chapter 13). At some stage they may embrace a connection with your homeland.

• Hold onto your homeland passport if it helps, and if you can. Your children may want a passport for that country when they are older. (However, this may mean they end up living there, and then – bad luck – you have to be the parent who has been 'abandoned'.)

7 The settling process

There are steps, it's a process. At first you feel
isolated, and then you get a job, make friends,
get around town. It is all steps.

- Susan

Every immigrant's experience of settling into their adopted country is different.

Often you don't know how settled you are until you consider going back.
Throughout your life as an immigrant, there will be turning points – times when
you realise that perhaps you would not go 'home', even if it were possible.

It may help you to feel more settled if you think about why you emigrated in
the first place, and acknowledge and appreciate the differences between your
life now and the life you would have had in your homeland. By reviewing your
life in this way, you may increase your level of commitment to your new home,
and feel settled enough to be happy to stay.

Recognising turning points

Over time there may be turning points – times when you realise there are fewer
reasons to go back. These turning points may result from an event, or even from
speculating about an event, such as winning Lotto or the death of a spouse.
You weigh up the alternatives, and you become aware that the best choice is
to remain in your adopted country. Even if these are only speculations, the
process of reflecting on what your reaction would be helps you identify how
you are feeling about the bigger picture of being away from your homeland.

Would you go back if money was no object?

If I won Lotto, I imagine I would stay in New Zealand and buy a small property
in England. Some interviewees would pay for a member of their family to

immigrate, or would offer their friends or family, or both, a stunning holiday in their adopted country, all expenses paid.

For Vanessa, any changes would depend on where her children were living, as that is where she would want to be. Having said that, she would probably take longer trips back to England. She has emigrated twice already. When she went back to England the first time, she was surprised at how long it took her to settle. The idea of emigrating again was not immediately appealing.

Other interviewees' reactions were varied:

Olivia: 'I'm not sure. I have my job and I don't think I would go back. Maybe I wouldn't. I would be a foreigner in my own country. For those who have emigrated it may be too scary to do it more than once.'

Nina: 'I would spend some time travelling in India and other countries. I don't think my husband would enjoy going back.'

Katy: 'I wouldn't want to split up the family. Depends what the children are doing. I don't want to be a dysfunctional family with family everywhere.'

Christine: 'I can't see us moving back, the crime is too bad over there.'

Madeleine's children are grown up now, and settled in the States (her adopted country). 'They are still my children, so I don't think I could leave. My parents are getting old and less active, so I should be there to help them. I'm confused as to who I should take care of. Although my daughter has suggested that I go home to take care of my parents, I still believe I need to be here for her and her brother.'

When Lena was visiting Germany, a neighbour told her that she should return to Germany, 'But my Dad pointed out, and I was very pleased to hear, that this is a holiday situation and we don't know what it would be like if I was there all the time.'

Yvonne: 'If my mother was alive, it [going back to Northern Ireland] would be more likely.'

The immigrants quoted here would not go back to their homeland if they had the means. As an immigrant, you have invested, both emotionally and economically, in your adopted country. You need to make a major effort to establish a life in a new place, and to feel connected to it. To leave the life you have established in your adopted country may not be appealing.

As I mentioned in the introduction, the women I interviewed were not refugees. They made choices that led them to becoming immigrants. If they have a good life in their adopted country, money isn't a strong enough reason to return to their homeland.

Would you go back if you became a widow or widower?

Some nights, David would return late from his hockey games. Our children were small, and I had been in New Zealand for more than ten years. As I sat by the fire, I wondered if he was just late, or was lying dead in a country ditch. What would I do if he died? (I was a mother of small children – being on alert for dangers and disasters came easily.)

I want to acknowledge that the reality of being a widow may make me think and act entirely differently. In such a tragedy, I'm not sure whether I'd be able to think much at all. However, as some buy life insurance to ease the consequences of widowhood, I have contemplated where I might live if David died. Around that time there was no question: I would go back. I had a stronger support system in England. The children were small, and were therefore more easily transferable than older children.

Fortunately he didn't die, but he didn't stop being occasionally late, so until I became more relaxed about him being late, the contemplation continued.

By the time the children started school, I had built up strong friendships in New Zealand. I had a good life. If I were widowed, although I would still have stronger support from my family in England, there were other issues to consider. My children would have to move away from their friends and from everything they knew. I would have to learn how to operate as a single parent in England. I would have to relocate us all. The thought of upheaval from New Zealand, relocating and facing so many changes, made my neck tighten and my head pulse.

A turning point for me was to be less certain about going back to my homeland in the event of widowhood. This made me realise there was a connection with New Zealand that I didn't want to let go of.

Rebecca is certain that, if Brent died, she '… would go home straight away. My kids are small enough that they have to go where I take them.'

At different stages of your life, your reaction to the idea of going back is likely to change. Issues that may influence you include the needs of your parents and children, career opportunities, a sense of adventure, or wanting a change. While some immigrants are sure they will not go back, others reply along the lines of 'I'm not sure, maybe not, but I'll never say never.'

Other indicators of being settled

Turning points or indicators may be small and gradual, or powerful and prominent. At the time, a thought, decision or change in opinion may not seem significant – it is only later you realise this was a turning point.

When I realised I would never be a Kiwi, nor did I want to feel almost-a-Kiwi forever, it was a relief and a turning point. I realised it was enough to be an English person living in New Zealand.

A gradual turning point for me was acknowledging that the differences between the two countries had become less jarring. For example, over the years, my spoken language has become a jumble of both countries. To pinpoint which words or expressions belong to which country sometimes takes time. This is especially true when I am in my homeland, or when I have visitors. Swimming togs or costume; Glad Wrap or cling film, Hoover or vacuum cleaner, section or garden, uni or university. If I see raised eyebrows when I use one of these terms, I know that I have used the wrong word for the present company.

As the words and accent of my adopted country have become my normality, the differences between my new and old countries feel less obvious. I see this as beneficial – I am acclimatising. What I say and hear has evolved into an acceptance of both countries. Neither is out of place. I no longer have to listen carefully to ensure I understand what is said.

A variety of reasons have prompted immigrants to notice they are feeling more settled. Sylvia found that having her own house after her separation made her more settled. 'My own house, not a married house … Also having a garden to dig in, having pets and superannuation have all helped me feel grounded.'

Yvonne settled more easily than her husband Mark. She remembers him watching planes flying overhead, wondering if any of them were on their way to Northern Ireland. His homesickness lessened as he became more involved in their children's activities.

Rebecca realised she was feeling unsettled when Brent suggested they get a dog. 'The commitment side of it scared me. Also, when he decided to get a [house] extension, I felt it would use up all our savings for going back to England. It was the same when he suggested doing study. I feel I always have one foot on the plane and ready to go. That's how I know that I am not fully settled.'

Jenny no longer feels sure she would go back if she were widowed. 'I would have to make my own way here before I would default to going home for their support. I would end up being with Mum and Dad and I'm not sure I want that. But I still drive past the local cemetery and think there's no way I'm ever going to be buried there.'

Jasmine knew she had to change her mindset, as 'In the worst times it felt like I was in a cage.' As a new immigrant, she looked after her mother-in-law. 'I coped by trying to be nice to them [the family] and hoping they would reciprocate. They were suspicious of me. I did think, "Why am I here?" Then I had to realise this is life, get over it. Deal with it.'

Elizabeth has always felt very settled. She was clear about who she had to focus on. 'Parents are getting older and are not here forever. We have to focus on our children.'

When Katy separated, she had to consider all parts of her life. 'I would go back in a second, but I have to realise I have children who have been brought up here. I had to look after my immediate family because they are the ones who expect to be looked after. The fact that I have not been a great mum in the last year is weighing on me. I need to look after them. It's easy to say I need to go home, but my children need me more.'

Madeleine's concerns for her children were the decision maker. 'I could go on about those years and the struggle, but the elements of being settled and not settled were the same. I accepted I was where I had to be and got on with it; emotionally I was raw, but the lives of my children were the most important thing to me … I never truly saw returning home to be an option. When their father and I separated, I did not want to separate them from him.' With her children now in control of their own lives, Madeleine now feels equipped to establish her own life in her adopted country.

Elizabeth, Madeleine and Katy were influenced by the fact that they had people to take care of. Olivia, after two brain tumours, was influenced by who would take care of her. The first brain tumour developed while she was in her homeland. She knew that if she had a second tumour, she would not qualify for public healthcare in her homeland. After recovering and graduating, she and her husband Stuart went to live in his homeland. A second tumour developed. 'I was delightfully taken care of by the health system [of my adopted country.] Very blessed. It was a very difficult, different experience, and it made me feel more like this is my home now because they are taking care of me.'

 # Acknowledging the loss

Grieving and loss – you don't get over it, you get more used to it.

For a few months after my father died, I went through a low time. Amongst the grief for him, my loyalty felt torn in two. Should I be spending my thoughts and energy on my mothering and marriage in New Zealand, or on my grieving family in England? I felt I was doing a bad job of both. Feeling stretched over the two was more than I could handle, so I sought help through counselling. I made the first appointment after throwing the Denby cup on the concrete (see 'My story' at the beginning of the book).

In one of my sessions, the counsellor invited me to place two cushions on the floor, one being New Zealand and the other England. I had to stand between the two of them and talk to each of them. Talking to the New Zealand cushion, I was aware there was only David to talk to; there was no one else with whom I could share my feelings. I spoke to him, via the New Zealand cushion, of my feelings of isolation and loneliness. It hurt that there wasn't anyone in New Zealand besides David who was listening or who could appreciate how I was feeling. That was part of the isolation.

When I spoke to the England cushion, I remember saying things like, 'I miss being with you. This is a terrible time. I can't make it any better. I am sorry that I have left the country. I'm sorry you are not in my life more. I'm sorry that I'm not in your lives. I am sorry that I have made these choices that have made us apart. BUT life isn't bad to me and I may have made a different choice, perhaps a wrong choice, but I am living with it and I am trying to get used to feeling okay about being apart from you.'

In the sessions, the counsellor suggested I was feeling a form of grief, not only for the loss of my father, but also for the loss of my country and the freedom to be with the people there.

I warmed to the analogy. With my father recently dead, I knew a bit about grief. I knew that grief can grab you when you least expect it. Grief comes in all forms: involuntary tears, numbness, sadness, gut-wrenching sobbing, anger and raw reactions, cutting comments to and from friends and strangers. I have felt this, albeit on a smaller scale, as an immigrant. When dealing with grief, there is a saying, 'You don't get over it you just get more used to it.' This is true for an immigrant. I no longer try to get over the fact that I'm away and apart from some of the people I love. They are not accessible to me and I am sad about that, but I have become more used to their absence. I am more used to the goodbyes and the visits over there and over here. Immigration takes its toll emotionally. I know I am not the only one who feels the need to acknowledge and accept the loss.

Katy: 'My husband made the comment that I'm a very different person in my homeland than I am here. I know there is an element of truth in this, but the fact is, when I am here, I feel the loss, the homesickness ... My feeling of homesickness will never change. I may learn to accept it more and feel it less often, but the feeling of loss will never change. I thought ten years ago that I would stop being homesick. But it's impossible.'

Anne feels it is never fully resolved: 'You are living in this bittersweet in-between place.'

Rebecca has had time to know it is a process. 'I didn't realise it would be so hard. There is a conflict here all the time, one foot here one foot there. But you do get more used to it.'

Sophie bottled up her emotions about being an immigrant for so long that there came a time when she had to seek help. 'When I had that breakdown, I was depressed. My hormones were at that stage too. It was a whole build up. I didn't have anyone to talk to. Michael doesn't know how to deal with it so he doesn't want to listen. This made me bottle it up even more. Quite possibly the turning point for me was when the doctor had given me anti-depressants. I was so sick [from them] I vowed never to take them again. A friend suggested I went to a herbalist. I did. The herbalist was also an immigrant. She gave me the rbals, but it was the talking to her that helped. I talked for an hour and a half. I saw her a few days later and talked again. It was most definitely the turning point, to be able to open up.'

By acknowledging that there is a sense of loss, you can nurture yourself accordingly. Give yourself a hug. As you become more used to the fact that there is a sadness, you can learn to live with it, rather than allowing it to take over a major part of your life.

Amber feels you can do things to help yourself. 'So avoid holding onto things which make it difficult for you – "Move on from the Marmite".'

 ## Rationalise - Why did I come?

Reminding yourself why you came can help you feel more settled. Rebecca suggested that to go so far away was an adventure, and at the time she had wanted to leave England. Elizabeth was happy with getting away from family pressures and crime.

When you are unsure, try a SWOT analysis. Write down the Strengths, Weaknesses Opportunities and Threats of life in your adopted country.

You could consider getting theoretical, as Vanessa did. 'Another way of looking at the decision to move to another country, which affected both times we came to New Zealand, was that our decision was based more on a feeling rather than the logic. I think some of our biggest decisions are not based on logic; a bit like the desire to have children. It is more feeling or perhaps a human programming or instinct rather than logic. My theory is that it [immigration] is a way of mixing the world's gene pool, allowing humankind to survive in the world in spite of natural disasters or famine in some areas. The human race needs some people to stay where they grew up, where they know best how to live and survive there. It also needs others to move to discover other places that can support life and to mix the gene pool. As with the desire to have children, we need both people who have children and people who choose not to. This theory has helped me accept and understand my own immigration. It has helped me feel more settled in unsettled times and has helped me accept and appreciate the diverse opinions and feelings of family and friends back in England. It has helped me see settling into a new country can be difficult, but it doesn't mean it was the wrong decision or that it was wrong to have a desire to move.'

 ## Reasons you left

We just wanted a better life for the kids.
- Elizabeth

Joint choice. I wanted Sydney, he wanted New Zealand. I lost the argument.

- Charlotte

When I asked the interviewees why they left, some of them felt it was not a conscious decision.

Sylvia: 'It was the old-fashioned way, I met a man. We met in September and in October he said, "I'm emigrating to New Zealand, so either we finish now or we get married and emigrate to New Zealand." So I said, "Yes! Where is New Zealand?" I didn't make up my mind to emigrate, it was more a decision on getting married. We married in December. I came out with someone I really didn't know very well. We had been married a week when we arrived on New Zealand soil. It was a huge change to be married, let alone to move somewhere else. I'm confused about which one was affecting what. It was a crazy decision. I thought through it all, **Yes, let's go, how exciting!** I later said to my parents, "Why didn't you stop me?" and they replied, "But what could we say?" My friends were torn between supporting me and saying they missed me. It was such a fast thing. The wedding invitations were out so fast I didn't have time to think about it. I think it was more my husband's decision than mine. In truth, I was in La-la land.'

Anne: 'I think I was happy to get away from my parents' divorce. It gave me freedom and to be away during the process of healing.'

Monica: 'I was on my way to Perth, and then I got a niggling idea of following up on the man I had met in New Zealand. To see him, I had to detour on my ticket. I remember the travel agent said, "It will make your ticket go anti-clockwise. It will cost a lot of money. I hope he's worth it." But I felt I had to do it just to find out. I went back, got married, had my daughter nine months after that. It's all been nothing but life's realities since then.'

Jenny: 'I didn't think about it thoroughly. I thought I could wing it. I didn't think of the big issues of the security of the family. It wasn't until we got married that it was a conscious decision to be here.'

Monica: 'At the time of leaving, my parents were in good health, and I also thought my sister could come out as well. But she can't get citizenship.'

Vanessa: 'We were interested in emigrating. Our passports came through that week so we thought that would be a good place to go.'

Emma: 'It was a conscious decision to leave. One Sunday we drove in the park. We came to an intersection. It was a shambles and there was rubbish on the road. I thought, in a few years, my son would be amongst this bad life, so I decided to leave [Germany]. We came here [to New Zealand] on holiday, we loved it. When we returned home [after the holiday] we knew we were emigrating to New Zealand. We had moved in our hearts already.'

Rebecca's husband Brent had family in their adopted country. 'In England his passport was burning a hole in his pocket. We were living in London and when I brought my [new-born] daughter home from hospital, I suddenly felt the dirt and grime. Everything changed from a wonderful, multicultural, exciting city to hideous and dirty. We looked at where we could move to in London, but we couldn't afford anything. We could sell our brick terraced house and buy a four-bedroom house with a garden in a boutique suburb by the beach in the Antipodes. We thought it would be an adventure.'

Charlotte and Mitchell had each worked overseas before they decided to emigrate. When they met, they knew there were alternative places they could live. 'Once I saw other people's lifestyles in my twenties, I decided life in the UK wasn't for me. We thought that with children we would have more outside life in the Southern Hemisphere. It seemed so far away. It was an adventure.'

An adventure

Some people come for a sense of adventure. Jessica, whose first husband had died six months earlier, was ready to get away from everything and thought emigrating would be an 'interesting little adventure'. In retrospect, she would advise, 'Don't do it. It was a bit of love and romance. I must have been crazy. My children didn't have easy access to my parents. I have lost much of my sense of cultural identity.' However, with time she feels 'I have come far enough now, though, that I would think, Oh well, that is how it is.'

Jessica mentioned that her young adult children might also have a mixed marriage. 'You don't think things through when you're young and in love. My mother knew. She tried to warn me, she said, "It's so far away". And I thought, *What's that got to do with anything?* She saw the potential and she saw me living away. It was easy when my parents were healthy because they visited us. It is not so easy now.'

Madeleine: 'Adventure; the remoteness and wilderness appealed to me. Our cultural backgrounds could not have been farther apart.'

For Charlotte, the feeling of adventure was short-lived. 'Now you are here it's just life. It is just life without things that make your life rich, therefore it is empty.'

Other reasons

One of the reasons Olivia emigrated with Stuart to his homeland was because, after a series of illnesses, her homeland did not provide her with healthcare.

'I didn't really want to be in a place where they didn't take care of me. I was a taxpayer; there was no healthcare for me. Nothing my parents could do could help me.' She was bitter and cold towards her homeland at the time of leaving. This helped her to go – she was emotionally disconnected.

Elizabeth: *'With my family there was pressure, which was unhealthy. We needed to get away from my family and have our own life and make decisions about work and better education and better lifestyle for the children.'*

Anne: *'I came here as a university student. I loved my university experience so much I just wanted to stay.'*

Acknowledge the differences

If you can identify and acknowledge differences between your adopted country and your homeland, it can be easier to see these objectively – neither better nor worse, just different.

When I arrived in Auckland, most homes were single storey with a large garden. In London they were two storeys or more high, with a smaller garden, but there was always a public park and a pub within walking distance. The two ways of living were different. Each had advantages and disadvantages that could be discussed at great length depending on your point of view.

When Rebecca arrived as an immigrant, she looked for people similar to those with whom she identified in London – but they weren't immediately obvious. 'Male culture is more macho here: sports clubs and pubs, and nice sherry for the ladies. There are no North London Guardian-reading liberals.' Her search for like-minded people was part of trying to find reference points so that she and her husband could avoid social blunders or offending people. Features such as the dress code could be confusing: 'You go to a drinks thing, a barbecue, and the men are all casual in jeans and shorts and the women are really dressed up. Are you going to the same event? I find it quite strange.'

When you are a new immigrant, the differences are distinct and often jarring. As you become more familiar with your adopted country, you will find people you can identify with, but you may need to broaden the places you search for them.

Rachel knew she would initially feel and be considered different. 'That's what happens when you move.' She said if she had stayed in Britain and moved to another district, she would still have been an outsider to those who had lived there all their lives. 'I just moved on a macro scale … It doesn't worry me being an outsider. I would never win *Who wants to be a millionaire* here, but I might in Britain. Even after fifteen years here, I still don't know half the characters here and yet I know the British. I must have learnt it by osmosis.'

Rachel's immigration involved changing from a city environment to a rural environment, and this has added to her 'outsider' experience. She was limited in conversation topics, as she found she was not fluent in rural-speak. 'No, I haven't made my chutney yet. I thought that was for grandmothers and people in the nineteen-fifties.'

From the first day Olivia immigrated to a seaside town in her adopted country, she felt like a 'pampered American' who did not fit in. The differences were too great for her to be comfortable. Then she and Stuart moved to a small city that was perfect for her. 'More people my age, more opportunity of getting involved in the community and feeling you are part of something. Here, there are more ways to feel connected.'

If the differences are too much to live with, you may have to act as Olivia did and move.

When Jessica was a new immigrant, she struggled with the differences, but for a long time was unable to talk about how she was struggling. Two conversations within a short space of time made it clear to her what she needed to do. The first was with someone from her adopted country. 'She suggested that I, being from America, must notice the difference [in living]. I was relieved that somebody finally understood that I was living a different world. But before I had time to reply, she said, "It is so much better here. That smog there is terrible. You must be pleased to be here." It was a huge lesson for me. From her perspective, she didn't really want to know what was different and she didn't really want me to say whether it was better or worse. That was a real turning point for me. Even though I had only been here a few months, I knew I had to get on with it.'

Jessica's second conversation was with someone from her homeland, which helped her move on. 'A short while later I talked with a fellow American who said, "Don't you just hate it?" I almost felt like bursting into tears. At last I was able to think, "Yes I do hate it" Since then I have been able to find things I can appreciate here.'

Assumptions are made that countries with the same language have similar cultures. New Zealand and England speak the same language, have a similar government structure and have four seasons, but are culturally very different. England has the influence of Europe and a history spanning thousands of years; New Zealand has had humans living here for seven hundred years, and is influenced by the Pacific Islands. They are on opposite sides of the world, and the people in each country often have very different ways of thinking.

Sophie has become used to people in her adopted country assuming she should think in the same way that they do. She was once asked, 'Why don't you think like we do?' It was many years before she was confident enough to say what she thought.

You need tact when stating your own opinion. Hearing a tourist loudly criticising the country they are visiting is a bitter experience for someone from the host country. A criticising immigrant could be seen as that negative tourist who has stayed too long. If you can state your opinion in a way that points out the advantages and disadvantages of the differences, not only are you less likely to offend and more likely to be listened to, but you have mentally gone through the process of seeing and communicating the differences as neither better nor worse, just different. The more you can acknowledge that they are differences rather than one better or worse, the more you can appreciate what the differences have to offer.

Appreciate the differences

Jenny: 'Different, but I like the differences.'

Sylvia: 'When they were young, we lived in a place which had a swimming pool, beaches, safe rivers to play in. It was a lovely upbringing for them. We felt that we had given them the best we could.'

Emma: 'He loves fishing, barbecues, sitting outside, going to the beach, having a meal [there]. My daughter walks around in bare feet. I think I'm more relaxed here. I think I'm more giving here.'

When I was first in New Zealand, I enjoyed the differences in lifestyle and the freedom to be who I wanted to be. I did things I'd never thought of before, such as commuting along a beautiful coastline and sharing a house with a swimming pool, and I loved that I never needed a coat. I found myself going to woodwork classes and swimming in a river clean enough to drink, and I loved the fact that I could go on a four-day walk and not see a car.

Differences which are jarring at first often become acceptable once you realise the reasoning behind them, or their advantages. At first, Olivia was frustrated by the limited shopping hours in her adopted country. By the time her mother visited, Olivia could see the reasoning behind the shorter shopping hours. She explained to her mother that one of the benefits of limited shopping hours was more family time. In hearing herself, she noticed she was defending her adopted country. It was a pleasant surprise, and a revelation to Olivia that she was not only embracing the differences, but also forming a loyalty towards her adopted country.

When Elizabeth and her family decided to emigrate, her parents were not happy about them leaving. However, when Elizabeth became sick, her parents were surprised at the support she received and they could immediately see some advantages of their daughter's adopted country. Elizabeth said, 'I'm happier than I ever thought I would be. I am more settled; I can't imagine being anywhere else.'

My experience in a New Zealand rural community is that people turn up with a meal at challenging times. Maybe people give food due to a lack of nearby takeaways, but this was a characteristic of rural New Zealand that I appreciated enough to try and implement in my homeland city community. When my father was dying, I returned to the family home. My mother was camped at the hospital, and the rest of the family would come and go from the family home on their way to and from visiting him. When members of the community called around and asked if there was anything they could do to help, I was ready with a response. 'Bring an expandable meal please. We never know how many people are going to be here to eat.' Food offered with love is the best comfort food you can have at difficult times.

 ## Having family here

I am very fortunate to now have my sister and her family in New Zealand – they arrived nearly three years ago. Since their arrival, my sense of loss has lessened. It is the day-to-day things I notice most. When I phone my sister, we are chatting in the same time zone; we can talk about New Zealand issues. I don't have to explain to her what's going on with the politics, education, climate or social situation before I make a statement or give an opinion. The fact that my children have cousins here from my side of the family feels wholesome. We can share celebrations, as well as distressing and ordinary times. When our family and friends visit us, they can be with two families.

When my sister came here, I realised what a large task it is building a life in a new country and establishing a new network of friends. It made me realise how much I had already made New Zealand my home.

Interviewees who had someone from their pre-immigrant days or from their extended family living in their adopted country spoke of how much they appreciated this. Jenny, from England, met her husband Colin through his sister, when Colin and his sister were doing their 'overseas experience'. Colin needed to return to his homeland, and Jenny went with him. Later, Colin's sister returned too. 'My sister-in-law knew me before I met Colin. So she knew me before I was a wife and a mother. All my time here, everyone has only known me as a wife.'

Madeleine has an uncle in her adopted country. He lives many kilometres from her, but although she has had little face-to-face contact, she can talk to him for hours over the phone, because they have a mutual understanding of the country's current affairs.

Anita's mother lives with Anita's family. 'It is often the Indian culture to have your mother staying with you; my mother is here and that's a luxury. I know my husband gets lonelier than I do because he doesn't have his mother here. The children are my centre and with my mother here, I have made peace.'

 ## I'm committed! How committed are you?

Your ability to feel settled in your adopted country will depend partly on your commitment to being there. Yvonne said she always felt settled, as 'It was a committed decision to be here.'

Putting your adopted country 'on trial' for two to three years gives you the freedom to leave, but you may become less involved than you would if you knew you were moving permanently. Being 'on trial' may be the right way for you, but the settling process, and the growth of a sense of belonging, may take longer than if you considered your immigration permanent.

Going home for a visit increased Elizabeth's sense of commitment. 'I recognise that the first time you go back, it's a kind of test … You then know whether immigrating was the right thing to do. Within a few days of arriving [in our homeland], we knew. It was good to go back and get homesick for my new [adopted] country.'

Sylvia's commitment to living in New Zealand was more about being married than being in the country. 'I think it was more the fact I was getting married than emigrating … My husband completely cut the ties. He said if you go back, you go on your own. I had to make it work.'

I came to New Zealand as a traveller. I chose to stay a bit longer. It wasn't a conscious decision to move here, but it was a conscious decision to marry David and stay committed to him. Over time I could see that I was okay in New Zealand. I liked aspects of the lifestyle and the opportunities living in New Zealand gave me. I was unsure how David would cope as an immigrant in England, and I didn't like the idea of us going to and from each country on a semi-permanent basis. My commitment to New Zealand probably happened when we became parents. I wanted to make a home for our children. Once we found a place to live, making our home and starting a business was enough effort. I put down my roots. I intended to be here for a long time and make the most of it. My unstated commitment to be here had evolved.

Amber wanted to go back to see her parents after she separated, but she wasn't prepared to do so until she had a job to come back to. She was afraid that, without a partner or job, there would be no commitment to her adopted country. If she went back to England, where she would have the support of her family, she might have felt tempted to stay with her parents even though she knew this was not what she wanted long term. Once she had secured a job in her adopted country she felt she had a commitment there. She could see her family knowing she had to return.

Nina went to her adopted country with her husband and their two-year-old son for a two-year working holiday, and later decided to stay. In the first year, they made few non-Indian friends (see Chapter 2). They still had ties to India – they could have gone back to their jobs and picked up where they left off. 'That stopped us being committed to our adopted country.' They discussed going back, but when a job opportunity came up in a different city, they saw it as a fresh start. In the new city they made a conscious effort to become more integrated into their community, and have now decided to stay.

When Hanneke immigrated with Arie and their teenage daughter, Hanneke and Arie were committed to their new country. 'As a parent I was so enthusiastic about it all and determined to find a job.' Her daughter was not committed. 'I was, in her eyes, overconfident. She was still in denial.' Hanneke continued to regularly point out the beauty of the country and the new opportunities her daughter would have. 'If I did it again I would let her find her way in her own time … I was overexcited about the place. But she did adjust pretty well later, in her own time.'

Madeleine: 'At the beginning of my life here, I felt very unsettled, but by having children, I knew I'd made roots. I had to do that to feel at home, but it took me five years before I could genuinely call here home.'

Key points

1   Reflecting on the idea of going back might make you realise you are in the right place.

2   Recognisable turning points in feeling settled as an immigrant may be influenced by the needs of your parents, children, and/or your career.

3   There will be times when the idea of going back becomes less reasonable or less attractive. This may be an indicator of how settled you are.

4   If you were to go back to your homeland, it is unlikely that your life would be the same as it was before you emigrated. You will have changed, your homeland may well have changed, and your views and perspectives will be different, too.

5   The sense of loss from lack of regular access to your family or friends can be viewed as a form of grief.

6   There has always been migration and exploration.

7   Differences that were initially jarring may evolve into characteristics of your adopted country that you like.

8   Your priorities are likely to be different to those of your family and friends in your homeland. For example, you may have wanted a different life for your children, while family and friends may have placed a higher importance on keeping the extended family together. The differences in priorities may be part of the reason you left.

9   Commitment to your adopted country comes in different forms. It may be marriage, work relationships, children, or sticking to your decision to make the best of living in a new country. Being committed to your adopted country will help you settle. However, though you may feel committed, your family members may not feel the same way.

Strategies

•   Talk to your spouse about going back or not. What would you do if you received a huge sum of money? Doing this allows you to explore your feelings on living in your adopted country.   »

»

- Appreciate the life you have created here. Do a SWOT analysis.
- If you are visiting your homeland, remind yourself that living there is different from visiting.
- Recognise that migrating back to your homeland is not easy. You may have to recreate your life over there.
- Acknowledge the adjustments you have already made, such as when accents or language become blurred.
- Allow the process of grief at the loss of access to your country and loved ones to happen. Nurture yourself so you can appreciate the country you are living in more.
- Accept that the grief may not get any easier; you just get more used to it.
- Even if you are feeling settled, there may always be sense of discord. *Yvonne*: 'You are neither Martha nor Arthur.'
- Support your partner, and ask for their support to appreciate your adopted country.
- If you are struggling with the micro reasons for emigrating – the 'What am I doing here?' – then consider the macro reasons. There has always been exploration and immigration.
- Identify the differences between your homeland and adopted country, and be aware how these impact on your life. These differences may annoy you, especially at first, but then they may grow on you. Approaching differences positively, and appreciating what they can offer you, can increase your sense of belonging in your new environment.
- If you immigrate as a family, allow each member to settle at their own pace in their own way.
- Your sense of commitment may be strong at the beginning or may evolve over time due to life stages. Recognise the changes in commitment and in feeling settled.

8 A visit 'home' - practicalities

Immigrants put a great deal of thought into visits home, in particular wondering when the next one will be and how it will happen. Non-immigrants may consider a visit home an extravagance rather than a necessity: 'She's not going to England again. All that money!'

During a visit home, you need to consider your hosts, and your children, if you have them. Sometimes it's more realistic to go without your children, or without your husband, or both.

A visit home is a cost on your annual leave, time and finances – how can you manage that? Do you plan the itinerary in detail or not? Finally, have you ever considered a surprise visit?

 ## A necessity?

I asked the interviewees whether they viewed going home as a luxury or a necessity. Most considered it a necessity and described how, every few years, there is a pull to go back.

For me, the pull starts with an itch. At this stage I tend to warn my husband, as I know that within the next year or two, or maybe three, the itch will develop into a full-blown scabies attack and I will have to go.

A trip back rejuvenates and replenishes me. It is soul food. I need it for my sanity. If I can't go, I struggle. This struggle sometimes evolves into focusing on the negative aspects of being in New Zealand: lack of access to family and friends, missing events, realising how many adjustments I have made to fit into New Zealand life. Fortunately, David acknowledges my need to go as a priority and is supportive. I have been able to go back on average every two to three years.

Olivia: 'It is pulling on me that I want to go and I do miss my friends, and since the recent death it is pulling me too. It is time.'

Lena: 'I needed her to see her grandparents and for me to check out my parents. I hate to leave here. I go into a panic beforehand.'

Vanessa: 'Maybe every three years, as long as I've got it somewhere on the horizon. It is necessary for me to do it.'

Rebecca: 'I needed to go back. It was the right thing. I want to go back more than Brent.'

Charlotte: 'I feel like I need a top-up of my family. It is where I fit.'

Sophie: 'It is like taking them to see my [other] home. I feel I have two homes. It is so familiar. I was brought up in the same house [my parents live in now]. I go down to the town, M&S in the same place, bandstand at the other end of the high street. I am showing my kids "my home", this is home for me too.'

Charlotte recognises how being unable to go can affect her relationship with her partner. 'I just feel I want to be with my mum and dad. The cost of going on holiday is not so different from a trip to home. I feel like I'm running on low. I need to top up. It's overdue. When you get to that stage, then you should go, or you end up bickering.'

Emma weighs up the options: 'I would have to make every effort to go. I have to go, especially when my parents get older. My husband said I could return every year, but that would take up all my annual leave. I have to spend some time with my family here.'

When Sophie heard her two sisters were meeting up for the first time in ten years, 'There was no deciding. I had to go.'

A holiday?

A holiday usually means time off work, too much money spent, a change of environment and a feel-good factor. A trip home covers all of these – but immigrants don't always see it as a holiday.

Elizabeth: 'You have to visit everybody. It is not a relaxing holiday. You have to go here, there and everywhere. You are trying to make everyone really happy. It was hideous.'

Jenny: 'It doesn't feel like a holiday. I enjoy it, but it is not a holiday.'

Rebecca: 'I did it as best I could. When I came back, I needed time off. It was every day. I went home for three-and-a-half weeks and saw thirty-two people. When I think about it now, it's not a vacation or holiday, it is work!'

A feeling of being rushed is common. You may be visiting many people, and they are only getting you as a visitor. They may not appreciate the effort needed to visit several people in a short time. This can be frustrating when you are trying to plan visits to them. If you feel they don't appreciate the effort, you could be right. Remember that those in your homeland are not intentionally being unsympathetic to the effort you are putting in, they just don't realise how much effort is involved, because they haven't been an immigrant visiting their homeland.

Not every trip is the same. Anne says, 'Depends on the visit. Last year it was a holiday with Andrew. The year before I went by myself, it was family issues. When Andrew is there, it feels more balanced.'

You can make a visit feel like a holiday, even if only for part of the time. When Jessica went with her children, she would stop off on the way there or on the way back. Susan would always include an extended stopover on her way back to her adopted country. She said this made the leaving easier and the trip more like a holiday. Others see the holiday potential:

Yvonne: 'It's great to be a tourist, to reconnect with all the people and introduce my children to their heritage.'

Amber: 'I tend to go when there are things to do. For example, my brother said there was a show that sounded really interesting. I like to go back when things are happening.'

Vanessa: 'The focus is really on seeing people rather than seeing sights or doing things. So, it is kind of a holiday experience rather than "chill out" time.'

Christina: 'We see it as a holiday. We have enjoyed it every single time. They [our family] have spoiled us rotten and made us feel special.'

Consider your hosts

If you are likely to be staying with one person or family for the whole length of your stay, it may be tiring for them. Your hosts will be happy to see you and have you stay with them, but your stay will temporarily disorder their lives, so communicating with them about your plans and wishes will help.

Their expectations of the visit may be different to yours. Jessica found that, while staying with her parents, seeing other people was tricky. 'We would go off and see friends and my parents would want us to stay. I felt tremendous guilt. They would say, "When are you coming back? Should we have dinner ready?" If I could go back and stay for weeks that would be great, but we always have limited time.'

On a subsequent visit, to avoid leaving her now-widowed mother, Jessica adapted her pattern, asking friends to come and see her at her mother's. Unfortunately this didn't work out either. 'We didn't anticipate how it would affect my mother, having people coming and going so much.' What works for one visit does not always work for the next one.

Consider the wise saying, 'Fish and family, out after three days.' Monica always takes off to visit a friend for a few days to give her parents a break.

If you can afford it, you could consider other accommodation options. When Christina and her family visited South Africa, they rented a house a few doors down from her brother.

Hanneke and Arie are retired. They have no dependents, and they wanted their recent trip to feel like a holiday. They found a place to house-sit for free. The house-sit wasn't near to family and friends, but Hanneke and Arie had a base. From there, they could travel to family and friends as they pleased. This gave them a sense of holiday and space.

Consider your children

Children, particularly younger children, may not be on their best behaviour during a visit. You want to show them off, but they need to get over jet lag and culture shock, and find the familiar. Their routine, their environment and the attention they are used to receiving will have changed. Your children are not used to you being a daughter, sister or aunt.

Some immigrants choose to have a longer visit so that children have time to settle and naturally reveal the more enjoyable sides of their personality. Adults are more practised at being charming when they might not feel like it; children often use up their limited charm earlier than adults would like.

When our children were younger, some of the easiest times were travelling from one house to the next with just our immediate family in a rented or borrowed car. In the car, there was a sense of normality for us all. We could regroup and get back to familiar family dynamics. David and I would judge how they were coping. If there was the usual sibling bickering, I welcomed it as a sign of their normal behaviour. I do remember a feeling of unity and relaxation at not being 'on show'.

Having a holiday activity or a treat or two during the trip helped, as there was something more tangible than visiting relatives and friends for our children to look forward to. A theme park usually did the trick. Nine years later, with teenagers, having an activity that teenagers could get excited about needed a bit more work. A few months before we were due to go, we asked our teenagers for suggestions and then adapted them to our budget. A weekend in Paris changed to a picnic in Paris. A day return meant we could enjoy our own bananas and muesli bars on the Eurostar. The made-the-night-before burrito wraps on the steps of Sacré Coeur may have been soggy, but the busker's song and the Paris vista kept us enchanted. We walked Paris, were warmed by the *chocolats chauds*, and came home with photos, memories and a bagful of Eiffel Tower keyrings for the teenagers to share with friends. The month we spent was a mixture of time with family and friends and doing tourist activities. We packed a great deal in. The trip was exhausting, but great.

During your visit, if you can leave your children with your parents or a sibling for a while, you provide an opportunity for the grandparent-grandchild, aunt/uncle-nephew/niece bond to grow. The dynamics can be quite different without you around. This also gives you time to catch up with other relatives or friends, or even to take a break for yourself.

 ## There goes my annual leave

An immigrant's reality is that much of your annual leave will be taken up in maintaining the connection with family and friends from your homeland. As most of my trips last from two to four weeks, my annual leave is often used up. In the years I don't go back, the leave may be used for welcoming guests from England.

Many immigrants find that, as so much of their leave is taken up with visits or visitors, there are few opportunities to holiday in their adopted country. Before Rebecca and Brent emigrated, they had spent years visiting and hosting Brent's family. By the time I interviewed her, they had had twelve consecutive years of either going to visit family, or family coming to visit them. As these visits dominated their holidays, they recognised the need to have one holiday as a family unit. It was 'absolutely wonderful'.

I have always welcomed visitors and taken time off work to be with them. At one stage, after a run of visitors, there was a further request. We didn't want to say no, but felt we needed a holiday with just our family, so we suggested that rather than spend the whole time with us, they spend some of the time touring New Zealand. This worked well as they toured New Zealand first, which meant that when they saw us, they had stories of places they had visited which we could relate to.

 ## financial implications

Trips back to your homeland will have considerable implications for your family budget. Yvonne described these as 'crippling', but 'Ultimately, it is more important to sustain family relations than be mortgage free. You have to know your priorities.'

I heard of an immigrant who didn't buy a house for eight years, as she thought it was more important for her children to stay in touch with her homeland. Having access to her homeland also helped her settle in to her adopted country. She noticed that other friends were less able to make a trip to their homeland once they had bought a property.

In addition, Vanessa said that she would much rather have a humble house and be able to go back to visit.

Katy and Jessica have watched friends go on holidays to exotic or popular destinations. Katy said, 'You would love to take your children there, but you can't because you are always going home. I feel going [to my] home is what they need.'

Jessica's family's overseas trips have all been to her homeland.

I find I am reluctant to consider a loan for car buying, renovating or investing, as the priority is always to have money accessible for the next trip. Resources for a trip back, even if these are the ability to get a loan, are a must-have. Anything else is a nice-to-have.

Plane tickets aren't the only cost involved – you need to consider the expenses while you are there too. Monica became resourceful in spending less money. She thought she would take a few days out from her parents to spend time with her children. They could afford the train fare to Edinburgh, but they couldn't afford the entrance fee to the castle. They did manage to see the Edinburgh Military Tattoo for free, and on the train 'sneaked into first class until they chucked us out'. The trip to Edinburgh was a success.

Charlotte has found the expense of going to her homeland difficult to include in their budget. 'We used to make sure there were enough savings in our account, now we make sure there's enough room on the credit card.' She considers the future implications: 'Part and parcel of living in another country is that every couple of years you have to go back. Holiday money – gone. You have to make it happen. You have to wonder whether, with children, it is still affordable.'

My opinion is that, even with children, a trip back is still affordable. It has to be. You make more sacrifices, and try to make the trip a holiday too. You either save furiously or accept the prospect of debt.

To lessen the financial strain, you could put aside a percentage of your income. Good luck with that. Like Charlotte, most of the immigrants I have talked to intended or started to put money aside, but were unable to keep it up. Which would be easier to save for – two weeks on a beach, a ski holiday, a car, or a trip that may or may not happen in the next year or two or three? When you are tucking money away for the soul food of a visit to your homeland, does part of you wish that money was being put towards a relaxing cruise or adventurous holiday, a house renovation, or children's needs? Keeping money aside for trips to your homeland can be dull, especially if you don't know when you are going. When there is a definite reason for going, such as a wedding, there is a deadline and therefore greater motivation.

Unanticipated trips may blow your five-year plan, but the expense is worth it. The fulfilment of spending time with people you love is great value for money. If you have to rush over for sickness or death (see Chapter 12), perhaps only one person, or part of the family, could go to lessen the cost.

Going solo or with part of your family

When calculating the cost and logistics of a visit, there will be stages where you can contemplate some alternatives to taking the whole family.

I have gone twice on my own and twice with two of our four children. I have enjoyed my time on my own and as a temporary single parent. David has been to England five times. He has less pull to go there, and is able to care for the remaining children when I go, which has worked out well. However, after nine years of going without David, I felt my family had become used to seeing me without my 'virtual' husband. We knew he should be included in the next trip – I wanted my family and friends to get to know him again and to see me with him.

Christina found that 'If you go on your own, you are still worried about your family. Your heart and mind are still with them.'

When your children are older, going on your own is more acceptable, as your children can take care of most of their own physical needs. One of my easiest trips was when I went back for a week, to help my mother move out of our family home. My brother was there to help with the physical move, but, as he put it, 'not the emotional stuff'. The move was to happen in September – the beginning of the school year in England, and two months after a sister's wedding that I had regretted not going to. The pull to go back was strong. There was going to be a big gathering to say goodbye to the Victorian house that had been our beloved family home for more than forty years. Although I had said a goodbye to the house every time I had been back there, I knew I would miss not being at the final gathering of friends and family. I visualised adults standing in the family room recalling memories while they ate buffet style, trying to manage wine glass, fork, best Wedgewood dining plate, serviette and occasional parenting. The children and teenagers would either be playing soccer on the lawn or watching *Star Wars* in another room. There would be many laughs and a reluctance to leave the home.

As my mother's move drew nearer, I devoured each of the group emails bouncing around the family. I watched them set daytime rosters to be with Mum during the moving process. Then, hooray for David who suggested I go for the 'moving' week. It coincided with a New Zealand school holiday, and I would only be away for twelve days including travel. As I would see everyone at one event, there would be minimal cost besides the airfare. The family was pleased that the rosters could be abandoned and I could look after Mum for the moving week. I was pleased to do so. I could give a hug and a kiss to all family members and I was fulfilling a need for the family and for myself. The trip was short, but precious.

Going with your spouse could make you feel you have an extra person to consider, especially in a mixed marriage. Monica is used to travelling home by herself, but now that their children are older, her husband is considering going with her. 'Going back, no, it's not hard work; it will be if he goes. When I am on my own, it's fine.'

Jenny said that when Colin goes with her, 'I feel torn in the roles I play. It's easier when Colin doesn't come because it's less people to look after. If Colin is there it's hard to cater for him.'

Jasmine's husband Jack says that when he returns to the Philippines, 'There's nothing to do except listen to the chickens.'

 # A shorter trip

Even if you are travelling across the world, you don't have to spend a long time away. If you are going only to see people, or for an occasion, a shorter trip can work well.

The precious trip to help my mother leave the family home gave me only a week there, yet I received as much soul food and energising as during a three-week trip. I was able to say to my friends, 'As I am only here for week, this is the day we can meet. If you can come, lovely, if you can't, see you next time.' After a week, I was not drained, exhausted, or over the time differences. I was back on the plane ready to get back to my family and pick up where I left off. I arrived back in New Zealand on my daughter's birthday, equipped with a luminous green handbag for her – the latest fashion from Singapore Airport's shopping mall.

 # To plan or not to plan?

There is never enough time.

- Anne

Whether it is worth planning the details of your trip depends on your circumstances. Over the years I have planned some trips but not others.

Planning has its advantages. You are more likely to have a say in what you would like to do, you can let your hosts know what is happening, and you give friends and family the opportunity to make time to see you.

If you are staying in one place and/or have only a few people to visit, then planning may not be necessary. But for more complex trips where you want to see many people, or keep your children entertained beyond 'drinking tea with old people', you will need to do at least some planning.

When I first started going back, arranging to get there was difficult enough. I would leave it until I arrived to contact people to arrange visits. By the time I had recovered from the travel and time differences, precious days had already disappeared. People I wanted to see would say, 'just ring when you are ready.' However, from the day you arrive, your time there is on a countdown. As I usually want to see many people, fitting them all in is a logistical nightmare. Ringing them later, can be too late. Often on the days when I am available, they are not. Amazingly, the world doesn't stop when you arrive in your homeland. People there still have commitments. You have to fit in with them.

I found I was more relaxed once I had mapped out my stay. However, arranging to see people a few days into the trip was often a squeeze, an effort, and when I could not meet people, a disappointment. There was barely any downtime, and although I would come away feeling that I had soaked everybody up, I was weary from the gluttony of visiting. If you have ever been on a compacted tour you will know the feeling: Monday, Eiffel Tower; Tuesday, Leaning Tower of Pisa; Wednesday, Rome ... By the time you get to Thursday, Parthenon, you can barely absorb the wonders of the place, let alone take a photo.

During a trip to your homeland, visiting people every day from breakfast to dinner is exhausting. It is wise to plan some down time; have beans on toast, an early night or two. Refresh yourself every few days so you have energy for fulfilling visits.

Our trip in 2009 was a big one – probably the last we would choose to do as a family. There were six of us, so I figured I had to be organised. I wanted to minimise the last-minute decisions. We planned beforehand what we were going to do: the must-dos, the maybe-dos and the days off. I let people know the timetable framework, tried to confirm as much as possible and then emailed the final itinerary to the people I was visiting. Being that structured may not be your choice, but having an itinerary worked well for us, especially for our teenagers. They knew what we were doing and where the spaces were to do other things, have drop-in visits or just relax.

Planning lets people know in advance where you will be and when. When Christina was planning, she made sure that she was seeing everybody for an equal amount of time so that there were no quibbles over who she was spending the most time with.

Lena's last visit was a great success. Her planning included looking up activities in Germany that would show her daughter the differences between Germany and their host country. They went to a festival on 60 km of closed autobahn, which had more than 20,000 stalls. They also went on a train, a first for her daughter. 'For a while she didn't want to be German. Now she is pleased.'

Emma's mother plans for her. 'My mum does a lot to make it easier for me. She has my schedule quite tight. The visitors are easy; they're just dropping-in sessions.'

Planning suits me. I like to be able to see my large family and a few friends, and to do this I feel I have to give them plenty of warning of the times I am available. If we turn up and expect them to drop everything to fit in with us, I feel we are setting ourselves up for disappointment.

Jenny's comment echoes frustrations I have had in the past in trying to make the visits happen. 'My expectation is that everyone will want to see me, but they are in their normality and busy working. They don't realise what a strain it is, what we have to forego to come.'

Their reasons for not being able to see you, or fit you into their busy lives, may seem petty and irrelevant, especially as you have travelled so far to see them. Their lack of enthusiasm to see you may hurt. The reality is, they don't know how visiting your homeland is for you, and they won't know unless they become an immigrant. Try to appreciate their point of view. There may be events happening in their lives they have not shared with you. It could be that they need time to get into the idea of seeing you and weighing up whether or how they can get out of their routine. They may not take on the reality of the limited time you are in the country. They may not like the idea of planning ahead or short-notice visits. If none of the above reasons apply, perhaps they just don't want to see you enough. Hopefully, there will be others there who do.

To get to see those who are keen to see you, be clear on the times you are available and your reasons for committing them to a time. This is where planning does help. You may not be a planner, but the people you want to see may be, or vice versa. You are giving them the opportunity and advance warning of readjusting their schedules, reducing the disruption for them. Seeing someone who begrudges your visit is not a good start to the event.

Trips without plans

A visit where you turn up and 'go with the flow' can work well, especially if you have a long visit, are based in a place where people are happy to come to you, or if you have few people to visit, which is true for Monica: 'I don't visit anyone else, only my parents and my sister.'

Jenny found you have to be adaptable. 'I used to plan, but I try not to now. I like to go and be, rather than do lots. Enjoy time with the family. This may change with the children's needs.'

Amber has changed her approach to visiting: 'I tell my friends that I'm here and if they want to see me they can. I used to travel around, but it was too hard. My best friend comes and finds me wherever I am. I did do a bit of family |visiting|.'

Emma gave her family and friends a clear idea of what would work for her and why. 'At first I went back to try to see everyone. That was hard. Last time I said, it is my annual leave. I want to hang out with my parents at night, do enjoyable things. I'll go out for coffees, but not meals and late nights. Some were annoyed with me, but I would say, I'm just too tired.'

Katy is happy to stay in one place and soak up any time she can with her family. 'You burn it because you want to burn it. You *don't* not do that. You want to get every hour of the day. If I still think someone is up, I stay up or get up.'

Your situation will determine whether you should plan or not. I would recommend putting some thought into planning because, if nothing else, it's part of preparing for the trip and can be fun.

 # Surprise!

I have fantasised about turning up on my mother's doorstep. It could be great. I imagine the shock of seeing me on her face. Then insecurities take over and I fear that the shock will give her a heart attack, or maybe the shock will be mine when I find she's not there, or is ready to go away on a three-day trip I didn't know about. I have also thought of turning up as a surprise for a wedding or a birthday. It's a nice idea, but I would worry that my arrival would distract from the focus on the key person's day.

Surprise visits can, however, be very successful. Sophie's sister's fortieth birthday was approaching. 'My brother-in-law wanted to give Sarah the supreme gift at her fortieth. He said there was nothing more she would like than to have both of her sisters there. My other sister, Sally, was already coming from the States. He sent money for my sons and me. He picked us up from the airport, unbeknown to Mum and Dad, who were on the way to the airport to pick up Sally. We had to stay low in the car in case they saw us crossing paths on the motorway.

'He dropped us off with our suitcases at the back of my parents' house, and after thirty-three hours of travel, we changed into different clothes. Dad arrived first with Sally. We were hiding at the back of the house. Dad had the most beautiful huge hanging baskets, so I hid behind them. He was getting the key into the door, and I said, "Hello, hello, hello," which is our standard phone greeting. He froze, his hand on the key still. He couldn't work out where the noise was coming from as it sounded as if it was from the hanging basket. I popped my head around and he said, "Oh my goodness me." There were big hugs all around with him and Sally. Mum turned up five minutes later. Dad was in the kitchen, putting the kettle on. I sat down in the chair because I was so tired. Mum came through the door, she sort of looked and then looked away and then suddenly looked again. I thought she was going to have a heart attack because she was so shocked. I vowed then I would never do it again. It was lovely though.'

The next night was Sarah's birthday. At the party, there was a huge box in the middle of the floor. Sally and I were in this box. She thought it was a sax. She opened the box and we jumped up with, "Surprise!" It was just amazing. It was fantastic.'

Jenny decided to surprise her dad for his eightieth birthday. 'It was very last minute and lots of fun planning it. Going with no children, I could be there for Mum, Dad, and family. It felt wonderful. Dad was in the pub with Mum and my job was to wait outside. As I went past the window, I thought he saw me, but he didn't. I walked over to him at the pub and said something like "Happy Birthday, Dad".'

Jenny did point out that you can only surprise once. She is concerned that her parents will always be wondering whether she is going to turn up and surprise them again.

Monica surprised her mum on her seventieth birthday. 'The surprise trip was the most brilliant. Even my sister Carol didn't know. Carol's husband met me at the airport, stuck me in the lounge and I waited. I could hear him say to Carol, "Part of your mum's present has arrived, go and have a look." He videoed the whole thing. I can still see her coming out with a dressing gown on and seeing me. That first sight, it's all in the video. "How did you get here? Wow." And then we screamed and jumped up and down. It was just fantastic. This was three days before Mum's party. The idea was that Carol was going to put on a surprise meal for Mum. Of course Mum didn't know that I was going to be there too. They had to keep me a secret. The three days before, I had to stay in a bedroom with barely any windows and keep hidden in case somebody from "up the road" saw me. I remember Dad popped over for a coffee pot, and I could see him from the window. I wanted to call out, "Dad, I'm here". They nearly wanted to tell him that I was here, but they didn't. The day came for Mum's birthday. The idea was that Mum was going to go and have fish and chips with her friends. Carol rang her up and said, "Pop in and see my new placemats because I'm having friends round for dinner." Mum has hip and leg pain, and, while I was hiding up in the room, I could hear her getting out of the car moaning and groaning, "Oh I've got to go in there and see this table." She went into the dining room and all her friends who had been hiding surprised her.

'No one had known about me except Carol, her husband and their daughter Ruby. I was still upstairs, shaking like a leaf, thinking I could really use one of those drinks they were having down there. It's a family tradition to have a table present at the beginning of the meal. I was going to be the table present. As I had been stuck in this room for three days, with barely any daylight, I'd sorted out Ruby's toy cupboard. In there was a wand that made a tinkling noise. Ruby and I decided that she would wave the wand and I would come in with sparklers.

'I could hear them eating the starters. I thought, *I'd like some of that, and a stiff drink.* Halfway through, Carol's husband said, "Now to the table present" and turned off all the lights. Ruby came in, waved her wand and I followed with sparklers flaring in front of me. Nobody could see my face because it was so dark, other than the sparklers. Eventually they saw me. Watching the video later, I could see her expression, part surprise, part giggling. It was brilliant. I stayed a couple of weeks after that.'

Key points

1 Whether you consider a visit home a necessity or a holiday, there will be a pull to go back to your homeland to visit.

2 Going back to your homeland takes up a substantial part of your annual leave.

3 Your visit may feel more like work than a holiday, but sometimes holidays are exhausting too.

4 Your children will be disorientated, and probably not on their best behaviour for a while. Remember your homeland is familiar to you, but not to them.

5 Going back to your homeland is a financial burden. The trip usually costs more than you thought. You are likely to have to compromise on what you spend your money on in your adopted country.

6 Different combinations of people make for different trips. If you go without your spouse, you may need time out, especially if you have children with you.

7 It is exhausting trying to be nice the whole time.

8 If you go on your own, you may miss your family and friends in your adopted country.

9 If you go on your own or without your complete family, your holidays will be divided.

10 If you go with your spouse, especially if you are in a mixed marriage, you may feel you have to look out for an extra person.

11 You can plan your itinerary down to the last detail, but it still may have to be changed. Alternatively, you can choose not to plan and go with the flow, in which case you may miss seeing some people.

12 Everybody may not be rushing to see you. They are living their own lives, and some may find it is an effort to find the time to see you.

13 People in your homeland may not consider how hard your trip can be for you. Why should they? They probably perceive your visit as you being on holiday while they are in the routine of work/life.

14 Make sure you have help with a surprise; it is difficult to organise on your own.

15 Enjoy the planning, enjoy the event.

Strategies

- Be prepared for the pull to return.
- A trip to your homeland may not feel like a holiday, but it is a change and you are away from the routine of life. Relish that change from routine.
- Know your priorities concerning a trip to your homeland. Communicate with your spouse, and know you are matched in your priorities.
- Accept that you will use up a significant portion of your annual holidays seeing your family and friends.
- If you are feeling deprived of a holiday for you or your immediate family, then it is probably time to take time out. Have a holiday!
- While visiting, take time out from your hosts to give them a break.
- Include a couple of days or tourist trips to make the visit feel more like a holiday.
- Allow your children time and opportunity to bond with their relatives.
- Make extra room on your credit card, or put a percentage of your income aside to save, or both.
- Have cheap holidays in your adopted country in-between times.
- Give your children the time and space to settle down. Take one of their favourite books or toys with you (see Chapter 1).
- Give yourself a break; time on your own is important.
- Consider a short trip – it can be just as fulfilling as a longer trip, and less strain on time and finances.
- If you have children, consider taking just one or two of them. This will be a great experience for them, and will also give you some precious time with them on the way there and back.
- Consider planning. It may make you review what you want to get out of your trip.
- Don't forget the delight of impromptu visits while you are there.
- Independence and mobility help. Consider renting/borrowing a car, or for a longer stay, buying one. With no mobility, you are more of a guest. If you are travelling with a family, independent mobility can give you a sense of regrouping.
- Be prepared for tension as you arrange visits to people. Some may expect to see more of you. Explain that you have limited time, and that you need to spend more time with particular family or friends.
- Give people options for days to visit or plenty or warning of when you will be around.

9 A visit 'home'– an emotional roller coaster

A visit home. Excitement. Gulp; mixed emotions. The idea of going to your homeland *is* exciting. There is the anticipation of seeing family and friends; then the pleasure of being with them, combined with the sadness of knowing you cannot see them more often. You relish the prospect of a hug and a chat with those you love, and enjoy the familiarity you have missed.

However, you may find that once you get there, not everything is familiar, and sometimes the familiar is jarring. Your family and friends don't always want to hear about your life in your adopted country, and there may be comparisons, which can get uncomfortable.

 ## Mixed emotions

Sometimes it's better not to go, it stirs up all the
emotions. But we must.

– Sylvia

When I'm away from England, many of my loving feelings for family and friends hibernate neatly in an imaginary golden syrup tin with a tight lid on. I keep this tin somewhere deep in my body archives. I put the tin there because to live with a constant awareness of the missing is too upsetting. I can't miss the loving on a day-to-day basis. When I get to England and I see people again, the tin pops its lid off, the loving bursts out and overwhelms me. The loving feeling is great, but questions nag at me. 'Why am I so far away from these people I love? Why aren't these people in my life more?'

The ease of home

Jenny: 'The feeling of – aah, familiarity.'

Yvonne: 'I cry on the plane when I see the coast of Ireland.'

Madeleine: 'I always love to go home. I get the feeling that I am myself again: it's a feeling I never feel here, although I don't think about it until I'm back there.'

Going home, with its feeling of familiarity, is like sitting in your favourite old armchair. Home is familiar, warm and cosy. As you sink lower, your bottom nestles into the worn indentation of the chair. Home is where you fit. You can sit there and be. You don't have to explain yourself or your history to anyone. This is where you have spent your formative years and have a shared history. Being home can give you contentment.

Rachel: 'I enjoy the familiar, getting to Heathrow, realising how hectic it is compared to the other airports. I feel a sense of coming home.'

Emma: 'I can blob. I get the food I am used to.'

During visits to my homeland without my husband, I have often sunk into the familiar so easily that I feel as if I've lapsed into my previous life – life before immigration. Rebecca and Jenny have found that, too:

Rebecca: 'You just slot into your life as it was before. I had this whole conversation with someone in Wales, and I said I lived in London, forgetting that I'd emigrated.'

Jenny: 'I feel I revert to the person I was. I often forget that I am a mother.'

Seeing your homeland through different eyes

Anita: 'When you are away from a country, that country changes a lot.'

You may be surprised to experience a degree of culture shock, especially if you have been viewing life in your homeland through rose-coloured spectacles. For Madeleine, the surprise was the new demographic in her old familiar landscape – she was taken aback to have a Russian show her how to use an Oyster card (London's travel card).

Culture shock is not necessarily a negative feeling, but it can be disorientating and give you a sense of disconnection. It may take a day or two to get used to the differences. You are not used to this country; you have been living a life elsewhere.

Experiencing the once familiar with a new perspective, you may be more aware of things like the different foods, the beauty (which you may appreciate more), the cultural diversity, the conveniences, or the long or short history. If you have children, you watch them experience the differences between your homeland and your adopted country. If you speak a second language in your adopted country, you may enjoy speaking your first language again.

Hanneke: 'This time I felt more Dutch than ever.'

Rebecca: 'When I go back to London, it is always nicer than I remember it. It is greener. I love the theatre and cultural stuff.'

However, while sinking deeper into the old armchair of home, surrounded by warmth and familiarity, you may feel a snapped spring poking through the worn upholstery – features of your home that you are now uncomfortable with.

When Lena took her daughter back to Germany, she noticed the police were wearing guns. As a child, Lena was used to police with guns, but now, as a parent who lives in a country where police don't wear guns, she is uncomfortable with seeing them.

Jenny was used to dealing with bombing in London before she emigrated. When she went back for a visit, there had been recent bombings. Now a parent, she was uneasy that she had taken her children from the safety of her adopted country to one where there was danger.

Olivia had not realised how commercial and materialistic her homeland was until she had been away. She realised she enjoyed her adopted country's laissez-faire attitude, and that, since immigrating, she had focused on what she now thought were more important issues. When she went back for a visit, she felt disorientated and disconnected with her homeland. Her change in perspective made it difficult for her to function there in the same way she had previously. Using an electric clothes drier when the climate was suited to drying clothes outside no longer made sense, nor did being able to shop late into the night. 'Even the differences in food – when you go back to your homeland you have to readjust to their diet and their type of food. That can be overwhelming.'

With new experiences, new environments and time as an immigrant, you have moved on from life in your homeland. Realising that some features of your homeland are familiar but no longer comfortable can make you feel disconnected or distant to this home, this place you have been excited to reconnect with. You start to feel more than one broken spring in the old armchair. They begin to poke into you.

Disconnection can also come from small incidences. You realise you have forgotten basic phone numbers, such as directory assistance (used often before the Internet). When Jessica returned to California to look after her sick mother, she realised that she was no longer familiar with the health system – it was no longer ingrained in her.

When Sylvia first went back to England, 'I certainly felt a guest there and I didn't feel I belonged to the country because there were things that were familiar and not familiar. The TV was different; in the sports teams I didn't know anyone that played, I didn't know anyone in politics. It was only the family and friends I felt I had the connection with.'

These feelings of disconnection can make you feel you don't belong there as much as you used to or expected to … which poses the question, where do you belong? Is it your adopted country or your homeland? Some people find trying to identify which country they belong to difficult, and may end up feeling disconnected from both. Anne points out, 'Over there I have an accent; over here I have an accent. It's very weird. It's being in between … I feel I will never fully be one or the other anymore. I am neither completely from here nor American.'

Nina, who goes back to India at least once a year and sometimes twice, suggests that this culture shock, the feelings of disconnection and disorientation, lessens the more frequently you visit. On my visits home, I am now more prepared to feel the soft armchair's broken springs poking at me.

Feelings of disconnection from both countries are a challenge to get used to and accept – this is one of the main emotional challenges of being an immigrant. Time, experience and acceptance help the feelings to be less jarring. You may not feel you totally belong in either country, but, as an immigrant once said to me, 'Why not think of yourself as lucky to be loved in both places?'

Do you want to hear about my new life?

You are back in your homeland. You have arrived with baggage – a suitcase full of stories, comparisons, ideas and observations. But if you think that your host will welcome you tipping out the contents onto their lounge floor, then think again.

Consider your host. Consider their point of view. They may be interested in hearing about your experiences, but not all at once. For them, seeing you face to face and seeing that you are well is enough. It may be wise to unpack the information at their pace, to allow them to share with you what has been happening in their lives, even if, to you, the latest events in *Coronation Street*, or Fred and Fiona getting engaged, seem less important than your new life experiences.

There needs to be time for you, the immigrant, to settle into their ways and routines. After a while, they may be more interested in your new life. If you feel they are not interested, or not interested enough, then maybe they feel they don't need to hear, they don't want to hear, or when they do they can't relate to what you are telling them.

Hanneke suggests they don't need to hear. 'If you evoke happiness, then maybe your friends in your homeland don't need to ask you about your adopted country because they see that you are happy there. They don't need to solve a problem for you.'

Lena found people near her didn't want to hear. 'I am really surprised that the neighbours invited me to dinner, but they asked me nothing about my adopted country. They didn't want to compare, they know their place is better and they do not want to hear of any other places. They feel they are complete.'

Charlotte found that her parents haven't accepted that she has emigrated: 'They don't ask about New Zealand, which is sad. I've been away two years and they're not interested in my other life. It feels like stepping back into a time warp. Dad has never really asked about my life here. I talked to him about it and he just tells me a neighbour baked a cake. It's not really very nice that the relationship is on their terms. I have to fit back into my life with them, rather than them participating in my life. It can't go on forever. We will have to have a conversation where they face what we're doing. When I left this time, my dad thought it was just another trip again. We need to talk about it.'

While Hanneke was visiting friends in her homeland, she would complement their home, for example 'That is a lovely bookcase.' The bookcase was something they could look at together. But when she tried to talk about her teaching in her adopted country, her friends couldn't relate to her experiences. 'It doesn't click with them because it is so different.' Hanneke calls the strange feeling of being unable to share your life in your adopted country with family and friends in your homeland, 'Immigrants' baggage.'

You are the one living in 'two homes'. How much do you need them to know your way of life? You don't have to sell it to them. For them to appreciate what you are talking about is difficult if they have never been to your adopted country. You are there to reconnect with them; let that be enough. Perhaps if you drip feed the information incidentally, you will stir their curiosity, making them more receptive to hearing about your new life.

The New Zealand calendars I sent to my family every year (see Chapter 5) were to remind them where I was – to get them thinking of me and make them curious enough to consider visiting. Was it an attempt at manipulation? Maybe, but whatever their reasons for coming, I'm delighted to report that during the two decades I have been here, all of my siblings have visited. Knowing that they know more about my life in New Zealand has helped me feel more settled here.

Levels of engagement

One of the main motivations for going to your homeland is to have quality time with the people there, to be with them and converse with them, to engage with them. These engaging times don't all have to be deep and meaningful, they can be superficial. Each has a time and place.

The initial conversations when you first meet up are usually icebreakers, easing you back into your face-to-face relationship. The icebreakers are typically the journey, how you are, how people are in your adopted country. I did hear of an immigrant being greeted at the airport with, 'Hello. Julie has anorexia.' The usual, less intense icebreakers prepare the way for more settled conversation, or deeper conversation, if the need arises.

If the deeper conversation – the 'heavies', such as Julie having anorexia – starts, be prepared to listen well. The issue is on their mind, and they may have chosen you to be the listener precisely because you are not usually there. You have a limited, if any, influence on the situation. If you are relating *your* 'heavies', be honest, and savour their caring, support and love.

Anne pointed out that 'heavies' are better face-to-face, as the personal contact gives you the chance to follow the whole body language. Over the phone or Skype, the 'heavies' can seem like dumping and are often avoided. Face-to-face you can read the situation more accurately and can respond with a comforting touch or hug.

I appreciate both the heavy and lighter levels of engagement; both are times when I feel glad to be with the people I love. The variety is important too, as astutely pointed out by Anne: 'There is a catching up and then there is what is really going on. How much of that you want to take on depends, as it can get really testing. Sometimes it is appropriate and you get the visits where all the crap comes out. Then there are the visits where it is: no, we're just gonna hang out and get to know each other on a different level. If you make it so you get all the heavy stuff every time, that's really strange, and they may dread you coming |to visit|.'

 ## Changing friends

After a few visits, you may find there are some friends you feel you have less in common with than before. You are not sharing each other's lives. It is natural for friendships to decrease in intensity, and sometimes drop off.

Jessica: 'If you're only going to see them for lunch every two years, is that really a friendship? I let people go. It was something I had to do.'

Anne: 'I've disappointed people by not seeing them. I made an appointment to see an old high school friend, trying to pack it in. I couldn't keep the appointment. I've never seen the person since. It is frustrating.'

With the Internet, it is possible to keep up with 'friends' on Facebook or other social media. The bond may not be as strong, but you do have a way to see what your friends are doing. Realising friendships in your homeland have lessened can stir a sense of loss. By building up face-to-face friendships in your adopted country, the feeling of loss may lessen.

Comparisons - East vs West, which country is best?

Jessica: 'We would like to go back and just enjoy it, rather than constantly say it is much better here because of this and that.'

You may find there is a sense of point scoring between your homeland and your adopted country. Naturally, people in each country want to hear their place is the best. For those in your homeland, the fact that you have left suggests you think there is a better place to live than your homeland. For those in your adopted country, by immigrating, you are suggesting their country is a better place to live. Perhaps for you, your adopted country *is* a better place to live. That doesn't mean it is a better place for everyone. I find myself voicing the diplomatic phrases, 'They are different. Each is better in different ways. Neither is better overall.' Or if that doesn't work, then the swings and roundabouts analogy: the time you gain on the swings, you lose on the roundabout, but you can't do both at the same time.

As an immigrant, you are in a position to compare the education, politics, cultural diversity and lifestyles of the two countries. You may find such comparisons helpful, or a hindrance. By acknowledging the beneficial things in both places, you make the listener more interested; they can appreciate that both countries have great things, but different great things.

Immigrants who have made a few trips back to their homeland deal with comparisons in different ways:

Jessica: 'They ask, but I don't say much. It's too hard to explain. On an emotional level, I would never compare. They don't want to hear. I love what America offers, the most complete [wide variety of] food, etc. I don't compare back here either. If I do, I may only say the good things.'

Anne: 'I am constantly comparing countries. I know this whole different world. Sometimes they [family and friends] address that and sometimes they refuse to.'

When your family and friends have seen you in your adopted country, it helps, because there is less need to compare or talk about the differences. As Katy said, 'Not any more. Many of them have been here. It's not new to them.'

If your family and friends are not reconciled with you being an immigrant, they may only see the negative side:

Elizabeth: 'They see it as, "Why would you leave a good job where you were doing financially well?" They don't get it. This is the best decision we made. It's our lifestyle. Mum gets really embarrassed when friends come to see us because Mum thinks, "What would they think, when they see your house?"'

Jenny: 'I feel I have to defend our position here. They have no idea what it is like. Older people think it is like pioneering days, still clearing forests by hand. Younger ones assume we are in a backwater with no culture.'

Lena: 'Last time in Germany, they said "I think you should come home." They haven't seen my adopted country, and yet they are telling me that I have everything I need in Germany. If I had to go back, I would miss all the things. I love the space, the peace, the light here.'

If people are bluntly comparing countries, choose your replies carefully. As Jenny said, 'It depends who's saying it. I may let them get away with it. If it's someone I respect, then I may point out the differences.'

Comparisons can be uncomfortable for an immigrant. They make Anne feel in-between and sad: 'You can never have both, you're always missing something. If you grew up in the same place you wouldn't miss what you didn't know.'

In my early stages of being an immigrant, when I had small children and my family knew I was going to be here for a while, conversations with my parents seemed guarded. I found myself telling them only the disadvantages of New Zealand, and relishing the advantages of England. I found this exhausting and disloyal to both my husband and my adopted country. If I was continually highlighting the deficiencies of New Zealand, what was I doing here? I couldn't maintain the divided loyalty between two countries. I wanted to be true to myself and to the new place I was living in. I had made choices that led me to be in New Zealand and with David. I needed to let them know how I was feeling. I needed to grow up a bit. I wrote to my parents saying that I needed to be fair to New Zealand. I needed to be able to criticise New Zealand without a feeling of point scoring. I needed to be able to talk about the benefits of New Zealand, and hopefully to share my joys in this place without feeling disloyal to my homeland. I wanted my parents to believe I could have a worthwhile life here, because if they didn't, it was more difficult for me to believe I could. We had to change the focus of conversations from point scoring to relishing the good and accepting the bad of each country.

The letter was hard to write. I was nervous during the two weeks it took to get to England, snail mail only. But as soon as my letter arrived, my parents rang me to let me know that they understood, and reminded me that most importantly, they wanted me to be happy. They promised to support me more in my choice of being in New Zealand. They followed up the phone call with a letter that I still treasure.

Key points

1   A visit home can produce mixed feelings.

2   The familiarity is comforting, but there may be features that no longer work for you.

3   You may feel discord, feeling somewhere between the person you have become and the person you were. You may feel like a foreigner in both countries. You notice the changes and sense of disconnection.

4   Your hosts may not want to hear about your life in your adopted country. You go over there to connect with people. Do not expect them to feel a connection with your adopted country.

5   Comparisons are often made. It is natural for you to compare; you have been exposed to two lifestyles. Be prepared for the difference in your perception of your homeland and the reality of it. Everybody wants to hear that his or her country is better. People can take offence if you tell them that their country is not as good as yours.

6   Be aware that the systems in your homeland may no longer be familiar to you.

7   Levels of engagement vary with people, places and pertinent times.

8   You may find you seek out your close friends less.

Strategies

- Be prepared for the mixed feelings.
- Recognise the changes and look for the positive.
- Be ready for the culture shock as well as familiarity.
- Acknowledge the differences by identifying them, and writing about them in a journal or discussing them with other immigrants. See them as differences, neither better nor worse. Find the advantages in each country. Share them with the people who live there. Be tactful. Having an insight into both countries allows you to compare each objectively.
- Drip feed information about your adopted country, or find ways to make your family and friends curious.
- Let your family and friends know how comparisons make you feel.
- Be ready for a variety of conversation.
- Lighten the intensity – do things together, even sedate activities such as watching TV.
- In 'heavy' or pertinent times (for you or them), allow time and space to talk face-to-face. This can make for a heavy visit, but can be a fulfilling form of engagement. Accept that sometimes, your time together has to be that way.
- Give yourself time out.
- Relish the shared experiences you had.
- Embrace the fact that you have family and friends in two countries.

10 family or friends come to visit

If they make an effort to come here,
I will do everything to be the best host.
Make sure their room is perfect, do things.
Try to fit in as much as possible.

- Anne

News of family of friends coming to visit will bring excitement and maybe a little apprehension. If you live a long distance away, or the visitor is a close family member or friend, the visit is likely to be a long one. This is the time to show off your adopted country. You are the host. The prospect of a visit may urge you to block out your diary, inspire you to research activities, and motivate you to consider spring-cleaning your house. It's all go. Don't forget that within the visit there should be time to relax and relish the smaller pleasures of being together.

It's important

Visits from family and friends are important – they increase your sense of belonging in your adopted country, and decrease your sense of detachment from your homeland. When your visitors go home, they can chat to others about where you live, what your life is like, and how you are: 'They seem to be happy there' (hopefully), and more generally: 'The food is cheaper/more expensive', or 'It's so much colder/wetter/drier/hotter.'

This process of reporting from first-hand knowledge gives your family and friends a chance to become more accepting of you being in your adopted country. Their report may also convince other family or friends that a visit would be worthwhile, because they can see you will be there for a long time, if not forever.

Anne's suggestion to 'Let them meet the people here' is invaluable. Later you can have conversations about people they have met in your life. My mother will often ask about my neighbours or friends. When she comes over and sees them again, they greet each other with affection and enthusiasm. I watch the connection with an indulgent smile. They have a shared interest – me. I am the link to each of them; also they have built up a history of caring about each other.

After my mother's visits, conversations with her have more meaning and are more engaging for us both, as she knows the people I mention. The more engaged the conversation, the more there is a feeling of connection with both the people in your homeland and the people in your adopted country.

If your family has not come to see you yet, keep hoping and encouraging. Charlotte's parents have found excuses, such as they can't come until the dog dies. Her attempts to get her mother and sister out have included giving flight details and offering to make arrangements, 'But they never get taken up. It is upsetting. They think I will be back home soon. They're in denial.'

Time to put on the travel agent hat

'We want to see where you live, but we want to do a trip too. Can you arrange things?'

Once the arrival dates are confirmed, most immigrants have the visit in the back of their mind. It is exciting. My preparation for visitors includes collecting information on activities we can do, and thinking about how I can make their stay better. I want to share the great features of the country I live in: my favourite bush walks, a drive up a dormant volcano, a swim in hot pools, and on at least one day, fish and chips on the beach.

Assuming your visitors are happy for you to guide them, make sure you give them choices rather than an itinerary. If they have plenty of brochures and Internet access, they can choose the activities and then savour the success of their choices more.

When you are browsing for things to do, try to include some that are new to you too. This way you can share the excitement of discovery. Be aware that the more diverse the group, the more diverse the needs. Be prepared for child-friendly, adult-friendly and aged-friendly activities.

One of Sylvia's visitors asked questions such as, 'How many people are there?' 'How many big cities?' Sylvia had a list of answers ready so she felt knowledgeable about the place she was living in.

A number of visitors in a short space of time can be challenging. Olivia considers herself lucky to have had many visitors: 'I wouldn't have it any other way'. However, the issues of time and money are real: 'Sometimes it is frustrating … as soon as somebody says they're going to come here, I already know the touristy things I'm going to have to do which can cost a hundred dollars. I guess it's the same anywhere. People want to do the fun things. It's a shame you have to pay for them.'

Your visitors' enjoyment becomes your priority. 'When you do have many visitors, you want to take time off work to make them feel welcome; even though you only have limited leave, somehow you have to cope.'

 ## Length of visit

With distance and work leave in mind, a visit is likely to be for a minimum of two weeks. For immigrants with retired parents, the length of stay often has a pattern. Jenny's parents usually stay for five weeks: 'Long enough that when they come here you are not feeling that they are going to go. After five weeks they're ready to go.'

Emma mentally prepares for having someone in the house for a lengthy visit (usually six weeks). 'Once, my parents stayed in the house. Sometimes I felt I couldn't breathe, but overall it was good. Another time they rented a house. We would share cooking, go to the beach, they got to know my life.'

Nina regularly has visitors. 'My sister comes every year; my parents have been here once. We do the touristy things and arrange our travelling to be when they are here. My sister stays five weeks; my parents stayed a few months.'

Rebecca's wit helped to keep the visit realistic. 'I told my mother-in-law that, as she was staying here for the whole month, it was impossible for me to be nice the whole time. After all, she was staying through my whole menstrual cycle.'

 ## As we get older

My mother has made eight trips to New Zealand. She has aged beautifully. More recently has been less inclined to go off on her own or hire a car as she used to. What works for one visitor or visit won't necessarily work for another. Time differences and tiredness will impact more on visitors as they age. They may already be tired from just the *thought* of: leaving their home, getting out of their routine, travelling, being in an unfamiliar place, time differences and living with you, let alone actually doing it all.

Once they arrive, allow them recovery time and be prepared to adapt to their needs, or there may be friction. When Jenny's father was younger, he helped out on the farm during visits. Now he is older he makes mistakes, which can be costly if they involve machinery. 'My husband doesn't believe he can have a go at my father about it', but he makes sure Jenny hears all about it.

The longer you are an immigrant, the older your parents get. There will be a finite number of visits.

Sophie:	'When they first came over they were in their fifties, there was a lifetime of them coming over. Now they are nearly in their eighties. They are often having surgery or treatment.'
Lena:	'When I first came here, I thought my parents could come every other year. Then I realised they have turned seventy and I have to get over myself.'

Older family and friends may want to travel with a companion; if so, welcome them, too. My mother has travelled with my aunt twice. She has been a lovely guest, and her stay allowed us to get to know her better. During their visit, however, I did request a mother and daughter day. Mum and I ambled along the coast, took our time in shops and cafés, talked and enjoyed comfortable silences.

In a mixed marriage, you may need to remind your spouse what an effort a visit is for your parents. Lena found her husband was keen to show her parents all around Auckland when they had only just arrived. 'He didn't appreciate they were jetlagged, tired, and just wanted to go to bed.'

Three generations in the house

When your parents come to stay, they get to see their grandchildren in their own environment. Unlike when you visit your homeland, the children are not tired and jetlagged – although the grandparents may be. The children can play in their familiar space and surroundings. The children will notice the different dynamics in their home, but it is *their* home.

Relish seeing your parents and children spending time together doing ordinary things, even if your children are not well behaved all the time. Jenny says having plenty of space helps: 'It can be hard with the children because you really want them to bond and be well behaved for the grandparents. We're lucky that we have a big enough house.'

For children there is prestige in having grandparents around. As Elizabeth said, 'Children love that it is their grandparents who pick them up from school. Most days, it's only me that picks them up. In fact, they have often vetoed me picking them up.'

Allow your children to be with their grandparents or relations; give them time together without you, so they can bond. This will also give you a breathing space.

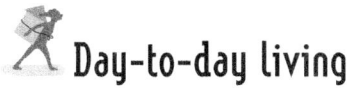

Day-to-day living

With my super girls, even the supermarkets are precious shared time.

- Margaret Baker, my mother

Much of what your visitors experience will be alien, and they may seek out the familiar. You may be the only familiar part of their visit. They may not want to be tourists, feeling that to see and be with you is enough.

Others, however, enjoy the novelty. Even routine activities, such as going to the supermarket, will be interesting for your visitors.

Katy: 'Realise that everything for your visitors is new and exciting. They don't need to be doing a lot to be stimulated. Simple is enough. Even the way the mail happens. The letterbox is different. They may not be ready for the touristy things. They may just want simple.'

When your visitors are more settled, you may find that they are ready to explore a little. If not, then accommodate their needs. By communicating well, you'll be more in touch with what they'd like to do, which will help make the visit a rewarding one. It isn't always easy – as Lena said, 'You have to keep everyone happy. The more people there are, the harder it is.'

When Jenny's parents come to visit she looks forward to having three-generation family time. This doesn't always work out, however. 'While I'm enjoying time with Mum, Colin feels that, because I'm happy, he can work more. I would like him to get to know my parents more. I have to think of organising things which Colin will want to come to so we can have time together as an extended family.'

With visitors there is a change in dynamics in the house, which may cause tension.

Elizabeth: 'My rules go out the window. My parenting is overridden. Jim and I have fights about it. I'm expected to let the boundaries go, but then I have to deal with the behaviour when the visitors are gone.'

Boundaries give children a sense of security. The house will operate differently, but keeping some of the routines in place, especially for small children, will help. Where possible, involve your visitors with the children so that the children don't feel they are losing out on their usual quota of attention. Encourage your visitors to read to the children or play with them.

Just as routines are important for young children, so they often increase in importance as you age. Since retiring, my mother has her main meal of the day at lunchtime. My family is used to a quick sandwich. During earlier visits, as lunch loomed, young and not-so-young hosts hovered to see if there was a sandwich on the menu. Being the food director, I had to decide who was going to feel most put out; my mother or the five others. My mother is an easy guest. She had flown a long way to be with us. I wanted to accommodate her needs more than the others', but I didn't want resentful family members sulking across the table each lunchtime. Being summer, I was able to compromise with food that could be either. On the table I laid out medium-sized plates with a knife and fork, and a range of food such as cold meats, bread, salad, fruit, peanut butter and jam.

When her mother stayed for a few months, Olivia had to return to her normal work routine; meanwhile her mother would go off and entertain herself. 'This time, she really got involved in all the community clubs and she had a blast. She liked the fact that she got to know people in one group and then saw them again in another group. Some people she has met over that time have become our friends. It is almost as if she has started a social network for us.'

Sylvia remembers how, when her parents used to visit her, they would be happy to try and fit in. 'Mum and I would make jam and Dad dressed like a local civil servant of the time with walk shorts and long socks. Unfortunately his winter-white legs made him stand out a bit.'

Be aware that you may need space from each other, especially if the visitors are living with you for a long period. Maybe go for an early morning walk or spend time alone in your room reading a book. If you have your space, they have licence to have theirs. Time with them is precious, but you don't have to be together constantly to make the most of their company.

They can help

It is great when your family and friends can come and help you.

Madeleine: 'My parents came every summer for a three-year period to help me when I was divorcing and I had to work. My mother was amazing. She would do laundry and cook, and my dad would play with the children.'

When Olivia was sick, 'My mother was here for me when I needed her.' Olivia's mother had been out previously and was used to staying a long time.

The first time my parents came to visit us, we had two small children. My parents wanted to contribute to the house finances because they saw us struggling. I wanted us all to have a great time. I knew they would usually go out for dinner a few times on their holiday, but that dining out would be difficult for us to afford. I was keen to put their offer of a contribution, towards something more appealing than house finances, so I suggested to them that while homegrown food from our lifestyle block would feed everyone well during their visit, a real treat would be for them to take us out for a meal one night. They did. Later, when I continued to be surrounded by small children, nappies and budgets, I could recall the memory of the meal with white linen tablecloths, matching non-chipped wine glasses, and great company.

Enjoy them

Lena: 'At the airport, seeing the big eyes looking around [for] the first three days.'

Amber: 'Going to places is cool, I was still exploring.'

Katy: 'Real buzz going to the airport and picking them up, seeing them come off the plane. Even the downtime is good, sitting around and seeing them absorbing your [adopted country] life cultures.'

I love showing off my favourite parts of my adopted country and discovering new places. I agree with Katy that even the quiet times are great. You can reminisce, remember and relive your pre-immigration life. You can have conversations around a shared history.

Monica's best friend from England visited and took Monica to a city hotel for the weekend. 'We went to a revolving restaurant and left our bags on the window ledge which didn't revolve. Found them again once we had done the whole circuit. We lost each other in the separate lifts. It was a weekend of non-stop laughing with an old friend.'

Sometimes opportunities fall on your doorstep. Sylvia was living on a berry farm. During her parents' visit, Queen Elizabeth was going to be driving past their house. 'I said to them, "Let's go see the Queen." The children jumped out of the swimming pool and, still in their swimming costumes, stood on the fence to wave to her.' Sylvia threw back her head in laughter as she told me, "Mum was horrified that we were waving to the Queen without the right respect. We were the "terrible colonials".'

Your pleasure at being with family and friends may be hampered if they struggle with enjoying the country you have chosen to live in. Perhaps coming to see you is enough. They may be not interested in seeing another place, or can't get beyond the fact that you have left them.

Elizabeth's parents are negative during their visits. 'You have to prepare for that. It is very hard to show off the country to them.' They toured 'from one end of the country to the other, and there was nothing they liked.'

If your visitors don't like your adopted country, or parts of it, try to understand that their opinion is valid. If you allow them time to voice their opinions, they may be more open to hearing your views on the advantages and disadvantages of you living in your adopted country. One country doesn't have to be better or worse, the two are different and suit different needs.

It is great if everyone in your household enjoys your visitor(s). Susan's husband says he considers himself lucky as, having a mother-in-law overseas, he only has to enjoy her company for two weeks every few years.

Some husbands find even this too much of a challenge. Monica suggested to hers that he should be on his best behaviour when her family came to visit. His idea of best behaviour was different to hers. With a week left of their visit, he refused to allow Monica and her parents to use his car, even though Monica had arranged alternative transport for him. The refusal caused a standoff, and Monica's mum wanted to leave straight away. The dynamics changed in Monica's house. '[My mother] was just hanging around that week. He did apologise, but they [my parents] didn't accept the apology. They have been at loggerheads about it ever since.'

Katy welcomes younger adult guests, but is afraid of them finding a future partner during their visit. 'I love having people to stay, but the golden rule is that any visitors don't pair up with the people in this country.' This is, of course, impossible to enforce, as young people – as many of the interviewees were when they emigrated – are not aware of the possible future conflicts. Katy's rule reflects an elder's wisdom.

Do as I say, not as I do.

- John Seldon (1584-1654), English jurist

When younger people stay for a while, the communication channels need to be open or there can be problems, as Emma found. 'Sometimes when younger people come, I don't enjoy it. They expect me to do everything, including making beds and feeding them all the time. I feel a bit used. Some people are so generous, others aren't so good.'

Yvonne's experience reflects this too. 'Young people can be good visitors too, as long as they pull their weight.'

Many family and friends may visit only once. As your parents age you may be concerned that this is the last time your parent(s) can visit. You never know whether your visitor is going to come again. A great reason to do all you can to make the most of your time together.

Key points

1   Having visitors uses energy. You will probably put extra pressure on yourself to show them a great time.
2   You can have a great time.
3   There can be tension during the visit.
4   Preparations are needed, physically, emotionally and strategically. Work out with your partner/children what is okay.
5   Be ready for many questions. You are far more knowledgeable about the country than they are.
6   You may need space.
7   Be realistic. The visit can't be all euphoria. Your visitor may be experiencing tiredness and culture shock.
8   Your guests may want to contribute; you may want your guests to contribute.   »

»

9 Not all visitors want to be tourists.

10 Downtime for your visitors is necessary. Age may restrict what you can do.

11 Your visitors have often come primarily to see you.

Strategies

- Be aware that your visitors' trip to see you is likely to be a holiday for them, whereas your trips to your homeland are likely to be harder work and more complicated. Your visitors usually have just you to see.

- Prepare yourself for having someone in your house for a long period.

- Enjoy the excitement of preparation in arranging things you might do with them. Gather brochures, car hire prices and trip details. This is a great excuse for a house spring clean or spruce up or both.

- Be patient with the visit. Adrenaline will have been pumping around before they come. Allow things to settle down in the first few days.

- Showing off your country is a great feeling, and if they enjoy your country too, you feel more reconciled with being in your adopted country. This is usually the time when they are interested in the country you are living in. Tell them about it.

- If they are not interested in your adopted country, let them complain, let them compare. However, allow yourself time to point out your perceptions of the differences, good and bad.

- Visitors often cost money, especially if you want to give them an entertaining and enjoyable time. Prepare for this in your finances, or suggest activities that fit your finances. If they offer to contribute, allow them to do so in a way that is comfortable for you both. Enjoy the simple things: a cup of tea or a walk in the park.

- Be aware that some visitors are harder work than others. Communicate your needs to each other.

- If your visitor has returned a few times, be aware of their changing abilities and requirements, and accommodate them.

- Be prepared to take time off work.

- If your visitor is here for a long time, introduce them to the life here. Get them to join clubs, play golf, etc. If your visitor wants to 'rearrange your cupboard', let them, if it makes them feel useful or gives them purpose. You can always change the cupboard back when they have gone.

- Know that when visitors are in the house, the house dynamics and routines will be different, especially if there are small children involved. It can be worth tolerating minor issues during the stay. If the issues feel major, communicate with your family about the change in dynamics and

»

» the consequences of those changes. Try to involve the visitors in the discussion, especially if the children are young.

- If you are the main connection with the visitor – their daughter, mother or friend – try to go away and have a blast with them. Give your own family a break from you and your visitor(s).

- Give yourself time apart. If your visitors are able, encourage them to go on a trip, even a short one, by themselves. It will give them something about the country to share with you, and it will give your household a break. If they are not able to, be sure to include time alone in your day – take a walk, meditate, or go to bed early.

- Have brochures ready so they know what the country offers. Involve them in the activity choices.

- Prepare for the micro features, for example biting insects, and the macro features, such as climate, roads. Do what you can to make their trip as pleasant as possible.

11 Goodbyes, and life just after

Parting is such sweet sorrow.

William Shakespeare (1564-1616), *Romeo and Juliet*

At the end of a visit to your homeland, or after having visitors, there are the goodbyes. 'Hard', 'hideous', 'horrible', 'I blab like a baby', 'I cry my eyes out' – just some of the interviewees' descriptions of these difficult farewells.

It is comforting to remember that the pain of leaving is a measure of the love you have for the person you are saying goodbye to. There are ways you can make the departure and the build up feel less daunting, and we'll look at those in this chapter.

After a visit, while you are readjusting to life without your homeland family and/or friends, you may find yourself sullen or touchy. This is 'the grump'.

Anne was a teenager when she first said goodbye. More than a decade later she feels that goodbyes have become harder. 'It is a bittersweet feeling. I know so much more now. What it is like to say goodbye and what that means. When I first left, it was for a year, no big deal. I was excited. Now |when| I say goodbye to family members, I know what that means and know it could be a very long time until I see them. It gets harder each time.'

The goodbyes are more upsetting if you are leaving behind a loved one who is sick or elderly, as this may be the last time you see them. Departures are also distressing if you leave on unpleasant terms. During one visit, Lena had not got on well with her parents, and was depressed for months after they parted. The following visit was a more harmonious one, and the goodbye was easier.

Jenny keeps the days busy in the last week because she knows the goodbye is imminent and hanging.

The hanging goodbye and PLT (pre-leaving tension)

The goodbye feeling lurks in the back of my mind as soon as I decide to make a trip. I know I am going to have to go through the routine of getting all the loving back in the imaginary golden syrup tin and putting the lid back on (see Chapter 9). When friends and family come to visit, or when I go to England, there is always what I call a 'hanging goodbye'. This is like a dark cloud that hangs over you during the visit, reminding you that your time together is temporary.

Rebecca's mother came over for two weeks, '… which wasn't long enough. I just couldn't get into it. I felt sad the whole time. I couldn't be happy. I couldn't enjoy the moment of her being with me. I just felt sad all the time that she was going to be going.'

Over the years, I have tried to focus on the present rather than the hanging goodbye. I try to create tangible memories we can look back on when we are apart: a special day out together, a lovely meal, or playing together. This works for me until the departure approaches and I am hit with PLT, pre-leaving tension. PLT is the beginning of the leaving. For me, PLT takes the form of anxiety and often tears, which, like PMT, pre-menstrual tension, is usually three days before the event. I become aware that we have only two or three more breakfasts together, and that, when meeting others, there are now going to be more goodbyes than hellos.

In England, I start thinking about the final load of washing, the last trip to the shops; about how many hours before the flight to leave. I know we still have time together, but it is finite. This is the time when my clenched fists wipe away involuntary tears. I scream inwardly as I yank open my empty suitcase and start the next stage of the leaving process. By the time I get to the airport I am sad, but part of me has already said goodbye.

 ## Ways to soften the blow

Sadness is an indication of the love you share, so instead of denying these emotions, try to find practical ways of making the departure easier. Jessica said, 'My mother says she looks forward. She counts the days until I return. We stay positive.'

Sophie has adapted their way of saying goodbye. 'Goodbyes have become harder. My mum would sometimes rather not come than have to say goodbye. We used to have something to eat at the airport and sit around, now we just drop off.'

Emma is familiar with goodbyes. 'Once my parents and brother have got out of my sight, it is fine. It is the leading up to it that is so upsetting.'

Once you are on your own, you may feel this is an appropriate time to feel sad. Jessica said, 'I cried all the way to the airport. Two-and-a-half hours' drive. I was on my own and it was terrible, awful. I hated leaving. It was really hard.'

At the airport, getting passports, tickets and departure cards ready can distract you from the sadness. I take solace in the prospect of a long journey ahead where, in the confines of an aeroplane seat, I can be sad if I want to. Allowing time for sadness seems to make some of the sorrow drift away. As

Rebecca pointed out, 'I usually feel fine once I get that far. The flight is so bloody long that you can't possibly sustain that sadness. You just have to get on with it.'

Rebecca found that visiting people twice helps to ease the blow of goodbyes – not having to say both hello and goodbye in one sitting. There was a space in between.

Sylvia has been an immigrant for nearly forty years. 'I know it's going to be sad, but that is okay. Leaving is such a sweet sorrow. We had a great time and we'll see you again.'

Susan always includes a few days stopover on the way home. 'It helps me to not think about it. It gets easier as time goes by, you have more to come back to. I have my few days holiday to do. It breaks the leaving there and coming here.'

In-transit

For Charlotte, who has only been back once, the plane journey was a time to think. 'Sometimes on the plane there were mixed feelings such as, should I be there or be here? Why am I here for my family, what about my |extended| family? Why do my friends and family have to be so far away? All I have here is sunshine, and it's not enough. It's not a good reason to be so far away.'

I hope I have had my worst return journey. It was after six weeks of being with my family. My children and their English cousins bonded well, and we were able to have a white Christmas together. David had to return early so I had four children under twelve to get across the world. A doable task evolved into an endurance test when the four-year-old and one-year-old had copious sickness and diarrhoea during the flights. If I wasn't in the toilet with one of them, I was wishing the seat belts sign would turn off so that I could rush them in there again. As I cleaned projectile vomit from the toilet walls one last time, I was relieved the journey was near its end. Strapped in as we descended into Auckland, I thought, *I don't want to be in New Zealand. What I am doing here? Why am I so far away from so many of the people I love?* The thoughts were so intense that I looked at the children to see if I had spoken out loud. The sick two were fast asleep, and the older two were too engrossed in stuffing their in-flight treats into their backpacks. No one heard, no one knew my thoughts, which was just as well, as I still had baggage, customs and an enthusiastic husband to process.

Settling back into my life took me longer that time than it had after previous trips. My thoughts on the plane haunted me for a while. To be with David again was soothing. Watching my children relish being with him and in their home helped me to adjust. I knew I had to focus on my immediate family and put aside resentment at being away from people I love in my homeland. I had to get on with my life.

Seeing off visitors

When visitors leave, you have to get on with your regular life. It's easier doing so after having visitors than when returning from a trip to your homeland – you are saying goodbye to fewer people, and aren't leaving that special place.

The goodbyes are still distressing, though, and again I recognise a pattern of emotions and behaviour. The knowledge of this pattern can be a comfort in itself. First, there is PLT, then the journey to the airport is dotted with pleasantries: 'It's been a great stay.' 'Send them all my love.' 'What time do you arrive?' 'Have you booked a seat?' If we have had icebreakers at the beginning of the trip, perhaps these are ice-restorers.

At the airport our coffees taste bland, we fiddle with our watches and then, with a synchronised sigh, we drag cabin baggage to the 'Passengers only' departure gate. There, bags are parked at our feet while we use our free arms for last embraces. Words of love become choked. We pull apart and I watch them enter the gate, and stay watching for a few more seconds after they disappear, in case there is one last wave. I turn away, wipe tears and fumble for tissues and the parking ticket. A quiet journey home, and soon after arriving at the emptier house, I go to the room they were staying in, lie or sit on their bed, and soak in the smells and memories until I am ready to take a deep breath, strip the sheets, and start to get back into life without them.

 # After a trip to your homeland

Rachel:	'Coming back to my life is quite a nice feeling.'
Amber:	'I'm more excited about returning here than going home. It's my space.'
Elizabeth:	'It was good to have routine.'
Emma:	'It is good to have my husband to come back to.'
Sophie:	'It is good we have a busy life.'

Even for a more seasoned immigrant, returning to your adopted country can cause mixed emotions. You may be happy to be back where you have established your life, but the love and memories of those you have just seen are still fresh, they are rumbling in the syrup tin.

Immigrants have found that the more established they are, the easier it is to get back into things.

Madeleine:	'As my life has become more established here, I think coming back has become easier. If my trip back there has been fulfilling, coming back is easier. My most recent trip back during the summer of 2010

was so exceptionally good and I went by myself and went back for longer than I have in the past. I was ready to return to my own life here. I wasn't sad. In fact, I felt very good. It was nice to come home to friends and my partner, all who had missed me and wanted to hear about my trip. In the past, it was harder, especially going through a divorce over a five-year period.'

Jessica: 'I appreciate the different things when I get back. I take a deep breath and the air is just great. Then we have a drink of water. When we turn on the tap, aah. The air and water are the things that make me feel so good. Our life seems ours again. I am happy to be home.'

Emma: 'Being in your own bed, reuniting with your family, having your husband spoil you. These are some of the pleasures of getting home.'

Some interviewees also said that although they miss their homeland family, there is a relief at not being so intimately involved with them.

 The grump

Rebecca: 'Took me a long week, poor Brent copped it. It wasn't his fault. He just happened to be married to me — this fire-breathing dragon that was very sad to be here.'

You need to adjust when you return. Not only do you have time differences, tiredness and post-holiday feelings to deal with, you are also grieving for the absence of your family and friends. This post-visit collection of emotions and behaviour is 'the grump'.

Rachel: 'I'm grumpy for two weeks. Peter knows that.'

Jenny: 'A week of misery and then life takes over. Colin knows it's going to happen.'

Monica: 'If I am bad when I come home, too bad. It's the price they have to pay. He didn't get a wife from his country.'

The grump may show itself in a variety of ways, such as not wanting to be sociable, wanting to rearrange the world or house, being angry at the person responsible for you living there, or having a criticism crusade. When Brent brought Rebecca home after a solo trip to her homeland, he said, 'I spent ages cleaning.' 'Oh,' she replied, looking around her. Then, 'Were you cleaning someone else's house?'

On one occasion when we returned from London, it was great to experience the clean air and the calm again, but the pleasure disappeared when we arrived at our house. Our concrete driveway seemed to have more cracks than before, the leaking sunroom appeared to have new splits in the glass, and the spouting had another piece missing. Within a couple of days of returning, I said to David, 'We've got to do something about the house.' This wasn't a suggestion. I had come back with a different perspective. I was living without my family and friends, a major compromise. I needed something to make me feel that my life here was going to get better, and I probably needed a project to distract me from being away from my homeland.

Goodbyes, and getting back into your life in your adopted country, is a journey in itself. The demands on you in your adopted country can be a welcome diversion from the feelings of sadness until you become more settled and reconnect with your everyday life.

Key points

1   Goodbyes are demanding. The level of demand is a measure of your love for the people you say goodbye to.

2   You may experience hanging goodbyes; the thought of the goodbye before it even happens. This may jeopardise some of your time together.

3   Coming back from a holiday is never easy. Coming back when you are leaving many of your homeland family and friends can be distressing.

4   Feelings may be mixed as you transfer yourself physically and emotionally from your homeland back to your adopted country. You have exposed yourself to experiences outside your normal lifestyle. To have a different perspective on your life in your adopted country is natural.

5   The more established you are in your adopted country, the more things you have to come back to, and the more exciting coming back may be.

6   There may be a grump.

7   Getting into the routine of your daily life is a necessity and a help.

Strategies

- Keep yourself busy in the last few days of a visit.
- Allow yourself to cry. The plane journey can be a private place for sadness. Ponder on your feelings; journal them.
- Try to arrange a time to see friends and/or family again – even a vague time.
- Look forward to having your own routine/life/family unit back.
- Be aware that the longer you have been an immigrant, the more you have to come back to in your adopted country.
- Consider the ways in which you will be happier in your adopted country.
- Allow the grump to work itself for a while. Communicating with your spouse beforehand on the possibility of this and what may help is a wise idea.
- Appreciate you may be very tired. Fatigue heightens emotions.

12 Births, marriages and deaths

Those significant events that make you glad or sad – births, weddings, important birthdays, illnesses and funerals – are likely to make you consider visiting your homeland. News of these events sends me into a state of turmoil; should I go or should I stay?

I have never regretted choosing to go. Sometimes I wish I had gone. Other times there is no pragmatic choice; the heart takes over: 'Dad's dying. If you are going to come, you have to come now.'

 ## Weddings

I love weddings – the excuse to dress up, and to be there to toast a couple who publicly announce their love and commitment to each other. I love the opportunity to see distant family and meet new people.

The announcement of a wedding causes excitement. If it is from England, by the time I have put the phone down or finished reading the email or invitation, I have already started thinking, 'Can I go?'

My eight siblings have all married. Two weddings took place before I left England, and I have gone back for two. To be part of the four weddings I attended was great – even the one where my three-year-old daughter, who had developed sickness and diarrhoea the day before the wedding, projectile vomited down the wedding reception venue stairs and then over the bride's wedding dress. (Yes, the same daughter who had decorated the airline toilet two years before.)

My reasons for missing my other four siblings' weddings were variations on the theme of being too far away. In retrospect, I'm not sure I had good enough reason to miss any of them, but I made those decisions based on the situations at the time.

Deciding not to go was a burden. I ached to be there – for myself, for the couple getting married, and for my family. I haven't worked out yet whether or not you should always try to attend family weddings. The reality is that, for an immigrant, a wedding takes longer than a day or a weekend. You need to consider time off work (often more than a week), the finances involved, care of your children if you are a parent, and the likelihood that you are not going to be able to go with your spouse.

For siblings' weddings I haven't attended, I have tried to mark the day in some way, not always successfully. On one occasion David and I dressed up and took ourselves to an expensive restaurant, where we wined and dined in wedding style and toasted the happy couple. On another I rang the reception venue and, although I was able to congratulate the bride and groom, my sitting room and sofa seemed very dull, empty and quiet during the phone call. For the third missed wedding, David and I took the children out of school and went to New Zealand's only theme park. The children loved running from one queue-free ride to the next. David and I sat on wooden seats, under a grey sky, nursing tepid cappuccinos in paper-cups. He tried to comfort me, but my hurt, my missing, was deep. As much as I rationalised that not going to the wedding was the right choice, it didn't feel right. The sacrifice of not being there for the sake of our finances and family well-being was piercing, and a moroseness started which lasted longer than the happy couple's honeymoon.

The fourth sibling wedding I missed was less painful, as my brother opted for short notice and a very small wedding, with only my mother and one sister invited. He rang me on the day. I could hear his exhilaration; I congratulated him and was relieved not to be missing another major family celebration.

When Hanneke's daughter announced she was getting married in The Netherlands, Hanneke had already used up all her work leave on her daughter's recent visit. She couldn't go to the wedding. Her husband, Arie, went. On the day of the wedding, a friend had invited her to dinner. 'I came home and I sat on the sofa on my own with a glass of wine. I was quite upset. All I could do was toast my daughter with a glass of wine. It wasn't easy at all. Later I got the photos and heard the stories from Arie, but it was a hard situation.'

Anne got married in her adopted country. 'My family didn't come to my wedding, partly because I was so far away and also because of my parents' divorce. They were at a stage where they couldn't even be in the same room as each other. I think if they'd been there, I wouldn't have had such a good day. Father wanted to come over, but I put my foot down and said I need you to either both come or not, because if one of you is there, then I will miss the other too much. On the day, I focused on our wedding. It felt right. People still expected all the family would have come out, but my parents were unable to be there as parents, as they were so focused on their own issues.'

Skype, mobile phones and the internet can help you feel more included. Christina was not only able to watch the women prepare for the wedding in the dressing room through Skype, but as the wedding photos were quickly put on a website, she 'could see them straight away rather than waiting for them to be mailed.'

Sad times

Sickness and dying - to go or not to go?

Dealing with death and dying is never easy. When you are a long flight away you have to make some big decisions and be reconciled to them. After my father was diagnosed with cancer, we (David, the children and I) visited twice. The first time was for my parents' ruby wedding anniversary – a poignant celebration night for family and friends. We visited a second time, almost a year later, because he was reasonably well. Then, eighteen months after diagnosis, the fight with cancer was almost lost, and my sister telephoned to let me know this was the time to come. I am very grateful I had someone to put me in the picture. The phone call could not have been easy for her, but with the information I had choices: to try to see him before he died and/or be there for the funeral, or to not go.

The call came on a Friday night, and on the Monday morning I was at my father's bedside. My mother woke him from his stupor and said, 'John, John, Eleanor is here.' He stirred and replied, 'Oh. Am I that bad?' My arrival was the 'near-death' indicator for him. He died ten days later.

While I was there, my mother didn't leave his hospital room. She had a camp bed set up and, as I had no one else to care for, I was able to bring her home-cooked meals and comfort packs. I was glad to be there not only for the funeral, but also immediately after, when the gaping void in our lives made every action or decision feel like something out of a bad dream (see Chapter 20).

Katy had been back to her homeland often, especially when her children were all preschoolers. As they became more involved in school and sport, the three-month visits became less frequent.

Her father had often been sick, and during visits home he would suggest she should not rush back for his funeral. Her light-hearted reply was always, 'I'm not rushing back for your benefit, because you'll be dead.'

Katy hadn't visited her homeland for a while when she heard that her father had gone into hospital again. This time he chose not to have any treatment. Katy's sister-in-law rang to tell her he was dying and that Katy needed to come over quickly. Katy's travel agent gave her a choice of two flights: the first was that day, in which case she needed to be at the airport in two hours; the second was a few days later. Katy lived more than an hour's drive from the airport, so she had less than an hour to get herself and her three children ready. While her husband and friends collected the children from primary school and preschool, '... I gathered passports and went to the clothesline with an empty suitcase, as I figured if it was on the line then it would fit them and they'd be happy to wear it. The car had a flat tyre. We borrowed a friend's car and managed to get to the airport in time.'

Katy remembers being on the plane, looking at the children's muddy knees, her oldest son still in his rugby shirt and the rest in play clothes straight from a morning at primary school and preschool. A motley collection of clothes worn on bemused-faced children. She thought of her usual trips to her homeland, where the clothes picked out for the plane ride would have been part of the planning and preparation. Children would have their 'plane clothes', comfortable enough for sleeping in, and she would be trying to settle them while twitching in her seat from excitement. This time she was in a daze. 'We managed to phone from each airport [before mobile phones were common]. They mucked up our flights. I was on the phone trying to get it sorted while my brother was getting a phone ready in the hospital so I could speak to Dad. When the phone was ready in Dad's room, we were on the plane. I didn't get to speak to him. My sister-in-law met us at the airport. She drove down the freeway fast, smoking and speeding. I sometimes wondered whether we would get there safely. But we did and Dad was still alive. I was able to spend forty-five minutes with him. Then he died.'

Katy said she wouldn't have changed anything, except perhaps to have got there a bit earlier. She was able to stay another three months, and she put together a journal of her time there – the funeral service, the emails and her thoughts. She said this helped her later in her grieving when she was back in her adopted country.

Anne happened to be back in the States when her grandmother died. 'It was good to be there for her. We were a support network. We look back on that time – it was a bad time, but we got through it together. Andrew got to know my family from the first-hand perspective; he saw all the raw stuff.'

Susan saw her father six weeks before he died. She had already decided not to go back for the funeral, and at the time was quite pragmatic over her decision. Now, she regrets not being at his funeral, and feels she didn't have closure on his death. She realised this when she went home to celebrate her mother's eightieth birthday. 'All the family gathered around and they talked about the last time they all got together, which was my father's funeral. I realised then what an important occasion I had missed.'

When Emma's grandmother was dying, Emma spent many evenings on the phone with her father. She was able to use her nursing knowledge of palliative care to help her family.

Christina's sister had a brain tumour. Christina visited her three times during her illness. 'I had said goodbyes to her and thought I'd finalised it. The last time we were together, we cried an awful lot and we apologised for the things we did wrong to each other. So it really was a finishing time for the two of us. She gave me an old wedding band. There was closure. She knew I wasn't intending to come to the funeral. We used to joke about what she was going to do when she got to heaven. We had tears in our eyes. That for me was the final goodbye. The memories of the last time we spent together. Now, I know she's not there. It doesn't bother me, but I don't regret anything because I did everything I possibly could. If I hadn't done that then I would have had a lot of regret. When the time for the funeral came, I did have my passport ready, just in case.'

If you don't go, figure out what you can do to acknowledge the death. Emma had plaques made for those who died, and lit a candle. 'I planted a tree and put the plaques on the fence for the grandparents who had died.' Jasmine and her sister paid for their father's headstone. Other people have gone for a walk or taken a day off to acknowledge the death. Make time to cry. You could hold a memorial service or ask people to pray with you or stay with you while you commemorate the death in some way.

Madeleine was unable to go to a friend's funeral. To mark the occasion, she collected the letters, pictures and even a petticoat her friend had given her, and put them in a small box.

Hanneke had insufficient bereavement leave to go to her father's funeral. She felt guilty, but knew that when she saw her relatives in her homeland face-to-face she would be able tell them the reasons why. She asked for support from her husband and her daughter, as she wanted reassurance that she had made the right decision (see Chapter 6).

Olivia struggled with not being there when a friend died. 'I felt like a failure as a friend. I couldn't be there. It's hard to explain to someone "I'm on the other side of the world. I can't be there." They just don't get it.'

If you can't go, communication from you may be a breath of fresh air to those who are in the fog of grieving. You are someone else to share the grief with. Through Skype you can talk to and see your family and friends. They can go through the funeral plans with you, which may be comforting for both of you. You could ask if anyone would be prepared to take a few photos or set up a live link to include those who can't go. (If there is a group of you, or you don't have access to a computer, libraries, community centres and immigrant 'drop in' centres have computers available for public use – you could Skype your family and friends from there.) Any of these – or even just a phone call – may help you feel included. Jenny rang her uncle's mobile at the reception after her aunt's funeral. She then spoke to many of her family, and felt like she was part of the occasion.

Whether you are able to go or not, the grieving lasts past the funeral. Allow yourself time to grieve. You can't predict when the sadness and tears will come, but when they do, know that it is part of loving and being loved. You are not likely to get over the loss, but you may get more used to it.

Plans change

When you hear that someone in your homeland is seriously ill, you may think, 'I'll go when they're alive, then if I miss the funeral it'll be okay.' This was Elizabeth's and her husband Jim's plan. They had emigrated only the previous year. Her mother-in-law, Judy, had been unwell when she visited them and had deteriorated since her return home. Elizabeth and Jim decided to take their children and visit before Christmas, while Judy was still relatively well and walking. They expected that she still had a few months to live. Unfortunately, Judy deteriorated rapidly. They were there for four weeks, and Judy died on the day they were due to fly home. Fortunately, they had an open ticket, but when they came to rebook, the only options were a flight in six weeks' time, or an airport stand-by. They felt they needed to get home, so decided on the latter. Straight after Judy's funeral and wake, they left for the airport. 'It was incredibly emotional, but there was never going to be a good time to say goodbye. We left, and luckily we got flights soon after. Jim's father and brother were very upset with us doing this, but in retrospect, they did say it was the best we could do.'

When Sylvia immigrated, '... my husband and I made the decision that if someone died, we couldn't be there for the funeral. But when Dad died, I knew I had to be there. There was no option. I was pleased that I was there, for my own sake. It was good because, as I was jet-lagged, I was awake at 3 a.m. and Mum wasn't sleeping, so she and I would have a cup of tea together in the middle of the night.'

Rebecca and her family had booked a trip to England for Christmas, and were due to fly out on 19 December. Her father died unexpectedly on 18 December. She was there for the planning of the funeral. 'It felt good to be there.'

As funerals, sudden deaths or serious illness can be so overwhelming, consider discussing beforehand with your partner or your support network what you might do if you suddenly need to go back. Who will be going over? For how long? Will you be able to go at short notice?

Yvonne and Mark established who would go for each situation. Four children meant usually only one of them could go 'It made it easier, being slightly prepared for it.'

Preparation includes having the money available or access to funds/credit cards. Your support network can help with the practicalities: watching out for your spouse or house while you are away, childcare, picking you up from the airport, being a willing listener. Do not be afraid to lean on people when you need to go, and if you are not used to asking a family or friend to help, then perhaps this is the time you need to ask. Most people are glad to help. They can share your burden of grief, and knowing people are there for you may enrich your sense of belonging in your adopted country.

Sudden death - my regret

I had been travelling and working in New Zealand for a year when I got a phone call at work from my father telling me my brother Eddie had died in a motorbike accident. At the time, my sister Vanessa and her husband were living here. We immediately left our work places to meet up.

We had to tell our relatives in Australia the tragic news. I remember sitting on the edge of a double bed as we made the sad phone calls, slumping back and involuntarily saying, 'I just want to be at home.' I knew I had to go.

There was a complicating factor, as one of our sisters was due to get married in seventeen days' time. Vanessa already had a booking to fly out in a week. She had not been back for three years. As I was still travelling, I hadn't booked to go back for the wedding, but because of Eddie's death I was now going to be there anyway.

If we wanted to be there for the funeral we could bring Vanessa's flight forward, or we could keep Vanessa's existing booking and I could go with her. We asked around for advice, and although my father used to say 'Never take advice,' we did. We went with Vanessa's original booking, which meant we weren't there for Eddie's funeral. In retrospect, I feel I let my head take over my heart. I have few regrets in my life; the biggest is not getting to Eddie's funeral. I should have been there.

There was a further complication. As we waited to catch the flight, my father let us know that his own father didn't have long to live. I hadn't been aware of how sick he was, perhaps because my parents hadn't wanted to worry me, knowing there was little I could do, being in New Zealand. Our grandfather died the morning we arrived. We managed to see him an hour after his death. Two funerals and a wedding in two weeks. It was a death-wedding sandwich.

At my grandfather's funeral, I wanted to hear more mention of my brother because I needed closure of his death. I sat in the front pew of the church that my grandfather had attended all his married life and heard the prayers for him, but there was no mention of Eddie. I wanted to be brave enough to stand up and say a prayer for my brother, but I didn't. I tried to convince myself that the prayers and thoughts going through my head were enough, or that I was too jetlagged to have the energy to say something. But more than twenty years later, I still feel a gap. I still wish I had been there for Eddie's funeral. I learnt that for me, there are times when I have to go back.

 **Births**

The hot news of a pregnancy, the freshness of a birth; milestones of life. At these poignant times you may miss being with your family and friends, as Elizabeth found out when she was a new immigrant. 'My sister-in-law got pregnant and she rang and said everyone was so excited. But I felt that sickly feeling. It was jealousy. I didn't like that I wasn't there, I almost didn't want to hear.'

When Monica had her children in New Zealand, she found that she missed her parents: 'I wished my mother would surprise me with a visit so she could smell her new-born grandchild. It's one thing seeing photos, but there's nothing like the smell of a new-born baby.'

Lena was very keen to show her baby to her parents. This was their first grandchild. Her parents said they would come in a year, which was too long for Lena to wait, so she took her baby to Germany at five months old.

Jenny's three children were born in her adopted country. The first was born with Down's syndrome: 'I was glad that my parents weren't there for the birth, because dealing with everybody else's grief, as well as my own, was too much.' She felt her parents could deal with their grief at home with the support of her brother. 'I was so engrossed in what was happening with my baby I didn't pine for them. I was able to put blinkers on.'

For the next child, the plan was for her parents to be there for the birth. 'Mum and Dad came out beforehand because they didn't want to miss the birth. They went on a trip and I thought the baby was about to be born so they shot back, but she wasn't born until three weeks later. They said, "Get out there and walk around the paddock because we're going home soon and we don't want to miss it."'

They didn't miss the birth, but for the third child Jenny suggested they came once the baby was past the fragile first few weeks so she could enjoy her parents being there more.

Olivia is not a parent yet, but is already contemplating life with children: 'My mum is not going to see me have her grandchild? Is she going to be here? This evokes a lot of emotion because I am missing that. I'm missing that connection of my mother and the delivery room and my mum at key points in my life.'

When Yvonne was pregnant with her first child, she felt she would miss her family at the birth more if she was in a ward with other mothers. She imagined other parents saying, 'Ooh and ah, what a clever daughter' and thought she would feel devastated. She knew that parents tend to focus on their own child, whereas friends focus on the baby. To avoid this, she requested a single room. That way she felt she would miss her parents less. This worked well, and by the time she had her other children she was no longer a 'new mum', and had her immediate family around to support and congratulate her.

My first child was born in England at seven in the morning. My parents individually raced from work to be at the hospital that afternoon. When my mother saw my father, she said, 'What are you doing here? You didn't tell me you were coming.'

My father replied, 'Same as you. I had to see my newest grandchild as soon as possible.'

My other three children were born in New Zealand, and I made a point of calling England as soon as possible after the births. My second daughter was born at three o'clock on a Monday morning New Zealand time, which was three o'clock on a Sunday afternoon in England. I eagerly rang the numbers I knew by heart, but everyone was out visiting their mothers, as it was Mother's Day in England. As a result, the first person to learn about the birth was a schoolfriend's ex-husband's father. He gave me tentative congratulations and promised to pass the news on. I ran out of phone numbers and energy and fed my one-hour-old baby until I could try again when they came back from their Mother's Day visits.

My parents may have not been there for the New Zealand births, but they saw each baby before it was six months old.

 ## Celebrations and relations

As parents reach the big decades – sixtieths, seventieths, eightieths, ninetieths – celebrations are likely. We can't always be there. However, we can do other things. Madeleine, unable to go to her father's eightieth, made a PowerPoint presentation of her father's life, which was played at the party. 'I included pictures of him from when he was a child; his career, his family. It helped me and they appreciated it.'

My mother's seventieth inspired a visit. I let my siblings know that I was coming over for her birthday with two of my children. The occasion hadn't been announced or arranged at that stage, but I guess this prompted the planning. My siblings put on an excellent lunch for her. A visit can be a catalyst for a family get-together (see Chapter 20).

Figure out ways of celebrating your own significant birthdays. Get creative, think outside the square. For my fortieth I jumped out of a plane; for my fiftieth I had a hat and high tea party with theatre sports; in between the two I had a dinner where guests were asked to come dressed in black-and-white.

Anita had two separate birthday celebrations in her adopted country: one for her Indian friends, and another for everyone else.

Finally there is always the surprise option. Sophie, Jenny and Monica organised surprise arrivals for their family members' birthdays, which were a great success (see Chapter 8).

For your children's important celebrations, extended family may not be able to be there. This is normality for the children. You may miss their grandparents and relatives more than your children do, especially when the children are young.

Your children are unlikely to have the strong bond with their cousins that you may have had with yours, although social media sites make it easy for cousins to connect and stay in touch. Your children may rarely talk to their cousins, but they often have a good idea of what they are doing and being family, there is a connection (see Chapter 5).

As your relatives' physical attendance at celebrations is usually not possible, invite your good friends and their families instead. Consider them your substitute family. For your children, this will be normality.

Key points

1   You and your family and friends in your homeland will miss each other's happy and sad milestones. The times you can be together will be treasured.

2   If a family member or friend is terminally ill, it is difficult for someone in your homeland to make the decision whether or not to suggest you should come back.

3   When facing the death of a loved one, you may feel isolated, as the people around you probably do not know the person who is dying.

4   Sometimes there is no choice. You have to go back. Other times it is not so clear. You may make mistakes. Don't be too hard on yourself.

5   As births are often unpredictable, a visit from your parents 'for the birth' may not work well. Some immigrants' parents may have to return home before the baby is born; some mums-to-be may consider an induction to make sure the baby is born in time.

6   The first few days or weeks with a new-born can be daunting and disordered; this may not be the best time to have a 'guest', even if the guest is your mother.

7   If there has been a death or divorce in your homeland family since your last visit, things will have changed. Be prepared for these changes next time you visit.

Strategies

- Identify the occasions that would compel you to be in your homeland. Have tentative plans in place. Discuss with your spouse who may go over for a significant event.

- Have an emergency fund to use for happy and sad times. If this isn't possible, consider a credit card or a loan and your ability to pay it back. Try to avoid finances being too influential on your decision. If you can't go, try to set up an Internet link such as Skype for a short time during the occasion or the time before/after, so you can feel included.

- Leading up to and during a significant event, keep up contact with the people in your homeland. Talk to them often; know what is happening and how it is/was for them, find out how people are feeling. Let them know how you are feeling. Remember they will be sad you are not physically there to share the experience with them.

- Acknowledgement is important. If you can't be there for happier occasions, try to celebrate the event in some way. Commemorate deaths. Allow yourself time to grieve. »

»

- If you have a terminally ill family member or friend, and intend to see them, let those in your homeland know at which stage or stages you want to visit. Ask them to keep you up to date on the person's progress, and to let you know whether this is the time to visit.

- If someone close dies, share your sadness with the people in your adopted country. They can sympathise with you, even though they may not have known the loved one.

- If you can't attend a significant event, send something that will help you feel like part of you is there, for example a PowerPoint slideshow or a poem someone can read on your behalf.

- In giving birth for the first time, you are starting a new generation. You are no longer the child, but the parent. Put your energy into the child and relish the intimacy of your new family.

- Enjoy the rollercoaster ride of your new-born.

- Consider a surprise visit for big birthdays.

- For your milestone celebrations, invite your friends as your substitute family.

- If you want to keep relationships with friends and family in your homeland strong, you may have to work at it more than them (see Chapter 5).

13 Where are my roots?

Yvonne: 'Children have asked, "What am I?" I reply that if the Irish had been grown green, then you would be green, but you are citizen of here with an Irish heritage.'

Emma: 'Coming here, you shift your focus onto pure survival and maintain a lifestyle, but after a while the importance of your nationality comes back.'

By finding ways to acknowledge your cultural identity, you can lessen the feeling of disconnection with both your homeland and your present environment. All over the world, immigrants find ways to continue and celebrate their homeland's culture, for example Chinatown areas in major cities, and St Patrick's Day celebrations all over the western world.

A wide variety of cultural festivals are now celebrated in public domains, as are country of origin international sporting events where fans often choose to support their homeland or the homeland of their ancestors.

People, places and experiences influence and shape us. These influences are strongest in our formative years – the first twenty years of our lives. In this time we learn how to operate as a human in a specific environment. Whether the environment we learnt in is India or Indiana, that is our 'normal'. Our normal also includes our cultural identity, roots, heritage, origins – the abstract or spiritual part of us, and the foundation of who we are. Our cultural identity includes the way we greet each other, the density of population we are used to, the humour, food, family structure, songs, clothes, entertainment, faith and climate of our homeland, and more. If you stay in the environment in which you grew up, you will probably be oblivious to the characteristics you are continuously exposed to. You know you belong there. An immigrant, or someone who moves away from these norms, will be aware that there are differences. At some stage you may miss some of these features – it may be something as small as missing a particular flower or a type of food. The absence of all or many of your norms may make you feel disconnected from both your homeland and the environment you are in. If you give time to your cultural identity, you can reduce the feelings of disconnection.

Giving time to your cultural identity

When my children were at preschool, I became aware of the dominance of New Zealand culture in their lives. Around that time I realised I would never be a 'Kiwi'. I thought it would be good for my children to know what 'being English' meant. They weren't going to pick this up through their environment, so I would have to point it out to them.

An English friend felt the same way, so we decided we should celebrate our nationality in some way. Each year on 23 April, we gather and 'think of England'. This is St George's Day, St George being the patron saint of England. Coincidentally, it is also Shakespeare's death-day.

Our informal annual gathering has been running for more than fifteen years. We invite English immigrants and play the games of our English childhood: egg and spoon race, soccer, cricket or netball. We are happy to make fools of ourselves bobbing the apple or playing English trivia. We dress up in red and white, and chat over tea and cider. For dinner everyone brings their favourite English food. The table is weighed down with Yorkshire puddings, bangers and mash, peas, and lashings of Bisto gravy. For 'afters' we feast on trifle, jam tarts and finally a lovely bit of Wesleydale cheese.

Our non-English spouses put on their tolerance hats for the day. They talk of prospective and past English visitors and visits. They laugh at our jokes whether they get them or not, and enjoy us enjoying the English indulgence. I see them looking at us and I wonder if they are thinking, it's only once a year, I can put up with that. I like to think the occasion reminds them that there are differences, and if they are uncomfortable with those differences, too bad – this is what we are feeling for the other 364 days of the year.

On St George's Day, we can be loud and proud to be English. This is an indulgence and it is liberating. Liberating because we can acknowledge there are differences and we have to make compromises – but the compromises are probably worth it.

Immigrants inject their heritage in all sorts of ways. Rachel downloads *The Archers* from BBC Radio 4. Olivia listens to country music, '… which is weird, because I didn't listen to country music in the States. I put on my country music and it brings out the hick American in me, the patriot in me.'

If your homeland's culture is very different to that of your adopted country, you may find it difficult to ignore the contrast, warns Nina: 'Even if we are citizens of another country, the Indian roots are so strong and we are so culturally different it is hard to cut off. Even if you do try [to ignore it] it will come back to haunt you. It is best to keep [a connection with your culture] going alongside.'

Denying your homeland culture may take more effort than acknowledging it. You can acknowledge your heritage with small fulfilling actions. You could use occasional phrases from your homeland. When my maternal grandmother was a child, her family migrated from Germany to London. When my mother is asked the time, she will sometimes use the German sentence structure in her reply: five and twenty to nine, rather than twenty-five to nine. My mother also still uses German phrases she was exposed to in her childhood: *machen sie das licht aus* (turn the lights off), and *Schlafen sie gut* (sleep well). I use these phrases too, and I have heard my children using them. I'm not sure our pronunciation is correct – we are probably saying something nonsensical. This doesn't matter too much, it's the gesture that counts.

food

The food you eat is probably a combination of the cuisines of your adopted country and homeland. Your idea of comfort food is likely to be associated with your homeland. For me this is steak and kidney pie, and bangers, mash and baked beans. For Olivia it's Mexican food, '... even though that's not American, but I would go and buy American products like Heinz ketchup. Food does that, it brings you home.'

Madeleine was missing the family Sunday lunch she used to have in her homeland, so she has adapted it. 'Although I haven't done Sunday lunch as such, I have been very consistent with family dinners. I'm a big cook. My children and all their friends love to come to my house to eat. We are quite formal, all sitting around a large table.'

Language and children

Language is a way of keeping your cultural identity. Lena speaks German at home, and therefore her daughter is bilingual. At first, Lena's ex-husband was annoyed by this, but now he sees it as an asset. Lena's daughter took a while to consider being bi-lingual as an asset. She was teased at primary school as 'the German one', which wasn't easy for her. Most primary-school-age children don't want to be different. You need to be aware of peer pressure your children may suffer at school (see Chapter 3).

Hanneke and her husband left The Netherlands more than three decades ago. They speak English in their English-speaking adopted country, but within their house they usually revert to Dutch. Hanneke, an established writer, recently wrote an article in Dutch, but the article was returned to her with grammatical errors to correct. She was surprised that although she speaks and reads Dutch regularly, she had lost the skill of writing in Dutch.

If your adopted country's language is your second language, it will be easy for your children to absorb both languages. However, they are in a different country to the one you were brought up in. Their norm can be a mixture of both cultural identities, but they will have more exposure to your adopted country, and so they may absorb only a limited amount of *your* cultural identity. Nina described a friend's experience: 'Mia, who's been here since she was five, had parents who kept up their Dutch habits. Mia found this very confusing. She felt she was not sure where she belonged.'

At the other extreme, Nina warns that if immigrant children aren't exposed to the cultural identity of their parents' homeland, they may find connecting later, as adults, more difficult. 'As children they are fine, but as adults they are drawn back to their roots. With no or little knowledge of their homeland roots, they struggle to connect. I have seen it. I have actually experienced it with some of my cousins, they can't make that connection. Those who have been in touch, it's like normality. They are able to bridge that gap.'

Your children will probably see you as different to their friends' parents. They may see your differences as awkward, or a disadvantage. They may not willingly embrace your cultural identity, and indeed you may not be keen to share parts of it; those parts could be the reason you migrated. However, there are probably aspects you expose your children to without even realising. When the children become adults, they may want to connect with their heritage. This will be easier if they are aware of it.

Celebrations, cooking and language will give your children knowledge of your heritage. Immigrants have found other ways to include their background in their children's lives. Yvonne found that giving her children an awareness of her homeland widened their perspective of the world. 'Teachers have commented on how rounded the children are because they have another heritage, and that gives them a point of difference.'

For a bit of fun, Vanessa introduced a version of a feature from the London Underground. The family used the Underground regularly while they lived in England. In some stations a recorded warning, 'Mind the gap', repeatedly warns passengers of the space between the platform and the train doors: 'We drew a yellow line on the edge of the deck, a *Mind the gap*, just like being in the Underground.'

Anita toys with an idea for her daughters: 'One day I would like them to know how to wear a sari, because it is quite glamorous.'

Susan brings South Africa to their home: 'We have books on South Africa they enjoy reading, as well as furniture and art work.'

Children love to hear stories of your childhood. Jasmine finds this can be an opportunity to illustrate the differences between her own and her children's childhoods. 'I tell them stories of my childhood, like the fact that the only toy I had was a rubber band.'

Anita's husband sings songs to their children. Jenny watches *Outnumbered* – an English sitcom based around children – with her own children. She hopes this will show them how children live in England.

When my children were preschoolers, we exchanged tapes of our children's idle chatter, with their English cousins. This allowed the children in each country to hear the accents and colloquialisms.

A grandparent often welcomes the chance to pass on their heritage to the grandchildren. Hanneke occasionally speaks Dutch to her grandchildren; Sylvia asked her mother to record stories on tape. Sylvia's children would listen to their English grandmother with her English accent, telling stories. 'The children loved hearing them, especially when they were sick.'

Society is becoming more global. Countries are multicultural, and this is acknowledged and celebrated. As Nina pointed out, 'The school has asked me to come in and talk about the festivals.' On our primary school nationality-dress-up days, my children have worn Union Jacks and bowler hats. Nina found her son was keener to take on his heritage than other Indian children they know. 'My son is eating more lunches that are Indian. I was giving him sandwiches, but he has been asking for Indian food. His friends that are Indian have said that they don't like having Indian food in their lunch boxes because it makes them stand out. My son is the other way. I send sandwiches because it's easier. When they have a shared lunch, he insists that his contribution is Indian. He is the only Indian in the school, but he is quite accepted by everyone.'

You never know which identity teenagers will take up. When her children were studying European history, Emma, originally from East Germany, wasn't worried at the lack of interest they showed in the Berlin Wall coming down: 'When they're interested, then I'll tell them.'

Jessica's children have experienced anti-American attitudes. 'They don't advertise they are American.'

When Sophie watches sporting events with Michael and their teenage sons, all the males cheer for the country they live in, and she cheers for England. 'I feel like a foreigner in my own home.' (See Chapter 6.)

Whether your children embrace your cultural heritage or not is their choice. However, exposing them to it will do them no harm. Exposing them to your heritage is an opportunity to acknowledge it yourself.

 Trips 'home'

By visiting your homeland you can reconnect with some of your cultural heritage and, if you have children, they can experience this for themselves. I enjoy seeing my family experiencing the wealth of London history, and the beauty of the English countryside: a walk along the Embankment or through one of London's many parks; a drive to Roman ruin, a lager in a three-hundred-year-old pub. They get to know this is where I come from, and where many people live a happy life.

Rachel:	'We wanted to do the cultural thing. They saw a Scottish wedding with whiskey and kilts. I was glad to expose them to that part of [their] culture at an age where they could appreciate it.'
Sophie:	'I wanted to show them the Tower of London, St Paul's Cathedral, Buck House [Buckingham Palace], Big Ben. I thought they would connect with London more if they had some of that history inside of them.'

 Exposure through media

Olivia reads and watches the American news before that of her adopted country. 'I look at the paper and see what's going on over there. When I go online, my homepage is all-American.'

The media enables immigrants to keep up to date with events in their homeland. Sharing their events, for example an election or the latest flood, has become progressively easier with the Internet, cable and satellite TV. I have found that the longer I have been in New Zealand, the less I feel the need to know the politicians, celebrities and latest news from England. If there is anything major, I will hear about it.

Key points

1   Your cultural heritage will be within you; denying it may take more effort than acknowledging it.
2   Your children could be interested in their cultural heritage now or later.
3   As a parent, you pass on features of your own upbringing. It is natural to pass on parts of your cultural heritage.
4   You will probably pass on your cultural heritage without realising it.

Strategies

- Allow the passing on of your cultural heritage to come naturally; do not force it.
- Point out the differences when there is an opportunity.
- Have a national day of celebration. Invite like-minded friends.
- Connecting with your heritage could take a variety of forms: food, artwork, songs, news watching, a TV series, magazines, comics or other media.
- If you want to support a sports team from your homeland, this offers your family two options to choose a winning team.
- Find opportunities to combine a trip back with a cultural event or place that exposes them to your heritage.

14 Surviving Christmas and other cultural celebrations

Christmas, a time for family

Any festival that marks a time to celebrate with family will be challenging for immigrants. Part or all of your family are in your homeland. They are not with you. Trying to repeat the event as you remember it – the traditions, the build up, the child-like excitement – may be unrealistic in a different country. You are living with a different culture, people and climate. You may need to prepare for a feeling of 'missing' and/or longing for the occasion as you recall it. You can try to find ways to compensate, and to connect with the people you miss, but the event won't be the same and there can be sadness. The missing can lessen once you accept there has to be a change. You have to adapt the way you celebrate the festival, from your pre-immigrant-memory of it, to one that works well in the environment you live in.

Coping with phone calls

New immigrants often try to include themselves in the festival taking place back in their homeland. Olivia wanted to be in contact with her family when they were opening gifts on Christmas Day. It was four o'clock in the morning for her, but the call made her feel like she was there. The following year she decided not to get up so early, and Skyped later in the day. She said it felt voyeuristic, but it was good to see her family in their living room. To try to compensate for her absence, she sends packages of presents, often choosing novelty gifts that represent her adopted country. This is her way of saying, 'Remember I'm here. You have a sister out here.'

When Christmas cards were the popular way of keeping in touch at Christmas, I used to include a small calendar of New Zealand with the card I was sending home. I thought that my family and friends would enjoy seeing parts of New Zealand, and I hoped that perhaps, when they changed the month, they'd think of me.

Presents, I often say, endear absents.

- Charles Lamb (1775-1834), English essayist

At major festivals, such as Christmas, contacting family and friends on the day or day after feels like dancing out of rhythm. The time difference means that, whatever time I phone, they are doing quite different things to me.

On Christmas morning, when our celebration day begins, theirs hasn't started. Here in New Zealand there is excitement. Amongst the mess of discarded wrapping paper and empty stockings, I cradle a cup of tea, wondering if the weather will be too hot to eat Christmas dinner outside. Meanwhile, in England, people are full of anticipation as they sip Baileys by the fire.

Christmas evening, and our feast is nearly over. Around me, bodies lounge like Roman emperors, wondering whether they have the energy to chew through more meat, let alone barbecue it. In England, they are sipping their morning cup of tea and contemplating the dinner preparations, wondering if it will snow today.

On Boxing Day, I am usually busy storing leftover food away from the summer heat and the flies, while those in England are probably lounging like Roman emperors, throwing the last of the Quality Street, usually caramels, to each other, deciding it might be just too much effort to find hats and coats for a walk in the late-afternoon darkness.

Atmosphere is difficult to share with a time lag. They say, 'Did you have a good time?' while you say, 'Hope you have a good time'. Over the years my phone calls have shortened. The reality is, I am not there, and I don't want to amplify the fact.

Festivals can be a time of heightened emotions: excitement, expectations met or not and fatigue. It is a time when Katy says she feels the missing more. 'Sometimes I struggle at Christmas, because I know everyone is having fun without me and that's a real downer. I have hung up the phone a few times. There is a lot of jesting in my |homeland| family. They tried to do that on the phone to me one time and I couldn't handle it. I hung up. I wasn't in the mood to be teased. I was more vulnerable. When I got off the phone, I was angry. Angry at everyone in the house |I was in| because it was their fault, especially my husband's, because if it wasn't for him I wouldn't be here.'

When I was a new immigrant, I had long phone conversations at Christmas, but the calls were too absorbing. They highlighted all the things I was missing about Christmas in England. If I didn't cry during or after the phone call, I was holding back tears. I felt mismatched to the people around me celebrating. I felt alone. But I didn't want my Christmas to be lonely, so I began adapting and shortening my phone calls home.

When we became parents it was easy to focus on our children. Older children were excited for every part of the day. Babies and toddlers chose the wrapping paper rather than the toys to play with, scrunching it up, waving it around, even wearing it. I became busy making sure the children had a good Christmas. There was still something missing, but with more distractions and shorter phone calls, I was touched by the love of family in England, rather than absorbed by it.

Sad tales

It is a great art to laugh at your own misfortune.

Danish Proverb

When new immigrants try to celebrate festivals as they remember them, but in a different environment, this can lead to a slapstick-style disaster.

In our early days, in an attempt to make Christmas different, David and I went camping on Christmas Eve and on Christmas morning went for a walk before joining his family for Christmas dinner. The path was soggy, and I couldn't hear the birdsong above David's sour mutterings about being deprived of his traditional Christmas morning surf.

Sylvia and her husband also tried camping in their early years as immigrants. 'We decided to go camping and it was pouring. We sat opening presents in a cold tent, rain outside with cold duck and lettuce leaves, trying to be jolly. I thought, *It can only get better than this.*'

Charlotte had to adjust from a winter celebration to a summer one. She laughed as she told me her tale. 'It was the most depressing Christmas I've ever had in my life. We were invited to friends with their family and friends. It just wasn't Christmas. No traditions I knew. I felt so lonely. This was probably the loneliest I've ever felt. It just wasn't raucous like I was used to. Everyone was just too polite. It was horrendous. I was just sitting on an upright chair with a sherry in my hand, thinking this is bad; watching everyone open their presents, the games, the jokes, the food, a barbecue, the sunshine, it was all wrong. It just felt like a wake. I said to my husband later, we are not doing that again. We either go home or go away. It is just too upsetting. One year I hope I will feel glad that people invite me, but now, no. Christmas has changed completely. It is one of those times where it has gone forever. I've mourned the loss of it. To compensate we had a mid-winter Christmas in June; it was cold and lovely. It was really nice.'

Susan was still a new immigrant in John's homeland and was feeling new to John's family. Christmas with them was '… nothing special, just a barbecue in the evening', very different to her idea of Christmas. 'In South Africa we would sit down [with] roast chicken, ham, hats and all.' The following year she considered not going, but that would mean having Christmas almost alone, just her and John, so she invited his family for a large celebratory meal. She bought a huge ham and prepared their house for celebration. However, 'At that stage I had no idea of cooking, and cooked the ham to a shrivel.'

Rebecca has been trying different approaches. 'I loathe Christmas since I've been here. It's not supposed to be hot. Last year we said we would do it differently. We had no family visiting, so we were going to get nice fish from the market and try not to make it something it's not. But it was still really shit. It wasn't Christmas. Every year I embrace "It's not Christmas", it is easier.'

It's the missing

The people around you at a festival may be feeling for you, but unless they have been through a similar situation, they are unlikely to appreciate how you are feeling or how to help.

Katy: 'I remember, one Christmas at my parents-in-law, taking the phone into the bedroom and closing the door, sitting in the corner and hearing my sister-in-law [in the other room] saying, "How are we going to solve it?"'

The solution will be different for everyone, but if you are a non-immigrant in the company of a sad immigrant, I would suggest you allow the immigrant to feel sad. If you deny the existence of the sadness, or try to jolly the immigrant along, it may worsen the situation. The immigrant is probably already feeling a sense of disconnection with the event around them. It is not familiar and they are missing people. If you acknowledge their sadness and perhaps ask them to describe their Christmas or festival you include them in the day and the celebration. The sadness is unlikely to last all day, but while it exists, it is a strong emotion for the immigrant, even though at an unfortunate time. Non-immigrants need to be aware that the issue for the immigrant is not whether the celebration is better in their homeland or adopted country, it's the missing.

Olivia: 'I am the missing person at the Thanksgiving table ... Thanksgiving and Christmas just aren't the same. It's a big time, the family comes together, and that highlights for me I'm not there.'

Madeleine: 'It was hard when the children were young ... It was hard for me knowing that my family would not get to know my children. I'd phone home, get off the phone, and be tearful because I'm not with them. I missed all the noise and activity and the bustling around the house.'

Vanessa: 'I miss people at Christmas; I wonder what they are doing. You ring them up and say things like, "Oh yeah we're having such a good time here on the beach wearing a sun hat." There's a bit of one-upmanship, but the essence is we are still missing them.'

Rachel: 'I really miss the lack of faith in schools. It would be good to have that selfless feeling of Christmas. The idea of slip slop slap of summer [Christmas] doesn't do it for me.'

Olivia: 'Now there is just the two of us, we don't even bother with Christmas. It is just another day. I miss it.'

 ## Creating your own celebration

Jenny: 'At one point, we decided to change Christmas. When the children were one or two, I was getting stressed trying to do it their [Colin's family, my adopted country's] way. So I thought, *Sod it.* I couldn't do my Christmas, I didn't like their Christmas so I have to invent my own Christmas, make it easier and more fun.'

At some stage, you have to let go of your idea of Christmas. You have to make the different occasion work for you. Sylvia and her husband went away at Christmas so they '... didn't have to sit looking at each other over a huge turkey.' By the time the children came, they were used to Christmas being different.

In trying to recreate Christmas, Lena baked cookies as she used to in Germany, but '... it was ridiculous because I had to cook in underwear, it was so hot. In Germany you'd be having mulled wine while we baked the cookies.' Then she went to her mother-in-law's and thought their Christmas was ridiculous too. 'I have given up on it. I did try to celebrate a midsummer festival and put a crown on my daughter's head and we did a dance, but it didn't feel right. We need more people.'

Find out what works for you. A small low-key Christmas can work well. Rachel's extended family hasn't been in England for more than sixteen years, so Rachel's Christmas is usually small. Her idea of Christmas is to keep it small and be able to eat and do what you want on the day.

Elizabeth's children were young when they immigrated. The children's excitement carries the day. 'We always enjoy Christmas, especially when it is just us. We have had two with family here and two without. When the family are here, the children are excited about going to the beach and having a barbecue. It's a nice feeling for them.'

Vanessa points out that tradition evolves. 'Over the years, you may find there are traditions you didn't even realise you had, for example, you may have had a special cereal for breakfast for two years in a row, and all of a sudden your children feel it's a tradition. There is nothing wrong with creating your own traditions. The longer the traditions are around, the more you'll see it as a traditional Christmas.'

Madeleine decided she was going to maintain her (British) tradition of opening presents on Christmas Day, even though Bruce's family's tradition was to open them on Christmas Eve. While Bruce didn't make a big fuss for Christmas, most people in her adopted country (America) did, and she wanted to embrace that tradition. She would have a great feast, which was how she was used to celebrating Christmas in England. Now her children are away at college, '... Christmas and Thanksgiving celebrations are going to be much more exciting because they will be coming home.'

Emma: 'We celebrate midwinter Christmas. I did even go back to Christmas in Germany, but I'd forgotten how cold it was. There is no way I would go back to having it the German way now. We do the Kiwi way. Christmas feels like a Kiwi Christmas. It's what we choose.'

Nina: 'I like it to be just us at home, it is too chaotic in India. There are fireworks, celebration and people everywhere.'

Creating your own celebration that works may evolve through trial and error. Katy is still trying to have more say in how they celebrate. She feels that her husband's family have not always been supportive of her input. 'Christmas is always a chore to make it the way I want to make it. Over the years it has become more and more frustrating.'

Sylvia, an immigrant for nearly forty years said, 'Christmas is the hardest time. It was hard when they were little, and it was hard when I became separated. It's hard now as my children have partners and they may go to their families.' She adds that, once she became more relaxed about Christmas, her adult children and their friends would come to her home after they had done the polite family necessities. 'Quite often they'd be knocking on the door saying, "I'm fed up with Auntie Jill." They would come here and put their feet up and we'd play games. I thought I hadn't created traditions, but my children would disagree. They would say we have a live tree, we share presents out in a certain way and I usually put on old songs.'

Since coming to her adopted country, Nina has continued to celebrate Diwali. She invites friends around to create their own celebration. Her son's friends particularly look forward to it. She says, 'There's no doubt there is less of what we used to do as children. But all you can do is make it as good as you can for them.'

If the celebration is not happening publicly, people around you may be happy to embrace some of the celebrations that you would otherwise miss, as Olivia found. 'My first Thanksgiving, my place of work actually had a Thanksgiving lunch.'

I'm pleased to see that with more global communication, there is a move to embrace celebrations of many cultures. In New Zealand, I have watched celebrations for Hallowe'en, Diwali, Chinese New Year and Eid become more prominent and public. For new immigrants in particular, these celebrations are unlikely to be the same as those in their homeland, but the fact that there is a permission to celebrate openly and collectively is a good start.

Key points

1   Festivals – Jewish, Christian, Islamic, Hindu, Buddhist, Pagan or others – are going to be different in a new country. For the new immigrant, these occasions often provoke a pot pourri of emotions.

2   There will be sadness, there will be missing of family, friends and familiarity.

3   Atmosphere is difficult to share with a time lag.

4   Celebrations and festivals can be a time of heightened emotions and high expectations whether you are an immigrant or not.

5   You can make modifications to compensate for the celebration you are missing.

6   You may have to go through a few 'sad tales' before you get to enjoy the celebration.

7   Celebrations and festivals are a combination of old and new traditions. They do evolve. The celebration should be a combination of your traditions and the traditions of those around you.

Strategies

•   Put the sad tales behind you and create a festival celebration that is going to work. For example, if you have moved from the Northern Hemisphere to the Southern Hemisphere, create your own Christmas so you do not

»

»

have to feel you are trying to fit a square peg – winter Christmas with your family – into a round hole – summer Christmas without your extended family.

- If you are missing family and friends, visualise them getting together, celebrating, conversing. Feel that you can be there too in spirit.

- Include some of your in-laws' traditions; this shows you are willing to integrate and compromise. You may even like some of them.

- Introduce your in-laws or friends in your adopted country to some of your traditions.

- Make a phone call over the festival. If long phone calls don't work, keep them short and tell your family and friends about the day or celebration a few days later.

- Using Skype can help you feel more engaged.

- 'Have a good structure to the day. Surround yourself with people. Keep a positive note. Keep busy.' – *Yvonne*.

- Use your support network (see Chapter 4): 'We invite other families and have substitute families. It was easier to have Christmas with people we have known for a long time.' – *Yvonne*.

- Take on the good parts of the celebration and leave out the bad or sad.

15 Career/work

*If you are facing in the right direction,
all you need to do is keep on walking.*

- Buddhist proverb

The experience of working and/or looking for work is different for immigrants and non-immigrants. Your dissimilar background can work for or against you.

None of the women I interviewed gave career opportunities as a reason for immigrating, but some have been surprised at what they have found in their adopted country.

When looking for work, be sure of your priorities, but be prepared to adapt yourself and your job expectations to the new work environment.

 ## Opportunities or obstacles

Rebecca: *'You have to accept that people don't know you. They do not know the organisations you have been working for. It is hard to get in.'*

The fact that Rebecca had worked in Sydney and London didn't seem to help. 'When I was trying to get any office temp jobs, I was told you need to have experience in this country. "What for, filing? Have you got a different alphabet?"'

Anne suggests you use your difference. 'Celebrate the fact you are an outsider. You are perceived as having an edge.'

Olivia was surprised at the career opportunities she found. 'More opportunities? Hands down. I am good at the job I do. In America there are so many more people with degrees, if I applied for the same job there, they wouldn't have given me a second look.'

Research in OECD countries has found that:

- 'the unemployment rates for foreign-born women are double those of the native born.' (Biffl, Gudren (2008) Thematic Review seminar of the European Employment Strategy), and

- earnings of migrants tend to converge after around eighteen years of residence (Chiswick, Barry R. and Miller, Paul W. (1995) 'The endogeneity between Language and Earnings: International Analyses', Journal of Labour Economics, Vol 13 No. 2:246–288).

Many immigrant women have found they have had to take a side step or back step in their career. Hanneke had worked in public libraries in The Netherlands. Her work in her adopted country began in a school library. The school was delighted they had somebody so highly qualified, and Hanneke was delighted to have a job.

When Lena emigrated, she wanted to transfer her horticultural qualifications and skills, but the process seemed so long and costly that she thought it would be easier to do a similar course again. 'But then I found myself sweeping the floor with a fifteen-year-old. I decided I didn't need it. I knew who I was and what I could do. I didn't need a piece of paper. I just did a few papers I was interested in and left it at that.'

No matter how much research you do, when you actually get to your adopted country, the job or job market may be different to what you expected. Charlotte said, 'The career side hasn't been a highlight. It's more about the lifestyle and family.'

Some qualifications are viewed differently, as Jenny found: 'It's difficult to use my qualifications as they are not recognised at the high level they would be recognised in England.'

To fulfil the requirements of working in your adopted country, you may have to gain extra qualifications. These may be needed to allow you to become a member of a professional organisation, or to ensure you are aware of the cultural needs, sensitivities or protocol which may be specific to your adopted country.

Emma was prepared for the extra work needed. 'When you make a decision to leave your country, don't have too many expectations, as you have to work from the bottom up. We knew that. At some point, it was frustrating. I felt more knowledgeable than the nurses there. However, it gave me determination to go ahead and get my registration. Now I'm up to date, and I'm learning. There are so many courses I have done since being here.'

Being adaptable is important. Hanneke suggests you seek places where you can teach what you love. For her it was art, which she taught part time.

Jessica said, 'Realise what's important, what makes you happy and adapt [your job to fit]. You may try something like running a family business, and it doesn't work out … Once you know the country, you may be better at coming up with ideas for work. Work with your new parameters.'

Vanessa suggests, 'If you're starting a new business, look at the places where there is free help. This will also let you know of a peer network that could help you. Look around and see what other businesses are doing [for example what] foods and brands are available. Fact-finding takes time, but then you'll know the idiosyncrasies of the country and what makes it tick.'

Madeleine struggled, but came through. 'I did jobs I never would have thought about: clearing out horse manure, dog walking, staining logs, cleaning friends' cabins. Humiliating in a way, but necessary for survival.'

When Rebecca, Brent and their children immigrated she secured a job before Brent, so became the main income earner. The original plan was to have Brent as the main income earner. The change caused some stress. They had immigrated for lifestyle. They feel they should have done more research.

As an immigrant, there is likely to be less family support for childcare. This may affect your career and work choices. Family are often the main stand-in when a child or parent is sick or needs support. You may have childcare set up without family, but make sure you can take time off work or have a support network set up well before you actually need it (see Chapter 4).

To get a job, you may find yourself in a *Catch 22* situation. A potential employer wants you to have experience in your adopted country, but you need employment to get experience, as Rebecca found. 'They didn't accept I've worked in international cities.'

Is it better to get the job before you emigrate? Charlotte did, but she found that starting her job almost as soon as she arrived gave her little opportunity to explore the country she had chosen to live in.

 # Priorities

By examining your priorities, you will see a clearer pathway to your career. Sylvia, a teacher, enjoys what she does and says it puts food on the table. Yvonne feels she is career motivated. She was willing to take the lower-paid job in her adopted country to get established, get to know her adopted country and be set up to advance her career in the long term.

Many of the interviewees have changed or adapted their careers since having children. For some that has been a conscious lifestyle choice, for others the career change was because of the circumstances in their adopted country, which were different to what they had anticipated.

Nina: 'When we moved here, we decided I would be at home. My husband and I do the same work, so opportunities for both of us were limited [in a smaller city]. I think my being at home has helped, because I had the time to learn and understand the country. I found most of my good friends through my son. If you are working, you don't have time for that.'

By giving thought to your priorities, you can be happier in your choices.

Lena: 'Mothering is my choice, career is not just moneymaking, it is your path in life.'

Jenny: 'Would I be any different in England? I'm glad to do the children thing.'

Acclimatising to your workplace

Work can help you get to know your adopted county, and knowing your adopted country can help you find work. Whichever you do first, appreciate that the process of working in a different country is going to produce new challenges.

Yvonne: 'I took the job in banking in the city, because I wanted to know how my adopted country ticked.'

Olivia: 'I know more about my adopted country's law than I probably do of my homeland's. It has helped me acclimatise here. It is a priority in my life. I enjoy the people I work with and the people I come into contact with. I've seen so much of this country because of my job.'

Rebecca: 'Being in work you can ask about the country. Who are the politicians, how does the country work? Both Brent and I are quite political so we were keen to find out. I think it is important to know the politics and how the country works or you are not really a citizen, you are just floating.'

Madeleine has met many people through her work in a government office, which has been a great way for her to embrace different social settings and careers. She has a wide variety of friends and acquaintances through her connections with both her career and community organisations. However, there have been challenges: 'The workplace has accentuated my foreignness, more than in a personal setting. Work cultures are different here than in England. I find differences in language to be a challenge, especially in writing letters, however, most of the time, my Englishness is an asset.'

 # Familiarise your family

Family and friends in your homeland may not understand your need to take a career side step, backward step or forward step in your adopted country. They may not appreciate your priorities, or choices that have led to you working longer or shorter hours. If you share your reasoning with them, they can hopefully understand and view these changes in a positive way.

Bear in mind that they are likely to be asked by others how you are doing. Being able to respond knowledgeably will help, especially if they were unhappy about you immigrating. Their answers could be something like: 'She has a good lifestyle over there', 'She's getting to know the place before she commits to a more fulfilling job', 'She's working her way through the regulations', 'She's looking for new opportunities,' or 'She is focusing on getting the family settled.' Any of these would be better than, 'I've no idea what she is doing there.'

Key points

1   As an immigrant, you may have to adjust your career. Be prepared to work from the bottom up. Look out for new opportunities.

2   As an outsider, you may have the advantage of a more global outlook. You can bring a fresh perspective to your employer.

3   Research the idiosyncrasies of your adopted country before you leave, and continue researching when you are living there.

4   An immigrant may have less family support when it comes to childcare.

5   Work helps you acclimatise to your adopted country.

6   People in your homeland may not understand your career/lifestyle choices.

Strategies

- Consider your parameters and priorities and come up with a plan. Consider what is going to make you happy in your work, or what will at least pay the bills.

- Be prepared to start something new. Be adaptable.

- If you do not have a job straightaway, use the time to explore and learn about the country you are now living in.

- If you do have a job waiting for you, allow some time before you start to get to know more of your adopted country (if you can).

- It may help initially to choose a job that not only works well for you, but also lets you discover how your adopted country ticks.

- Let your loved ones in your homeland know why and how you have changed your lifestyle.

16 Marriage

Marriage is a work in progress. At different stages of marriage there are challenges to overcome: parenting, moving house, career changes, in-law differences and others. Hopefully, within these challenges your marriage has more harmonious days than not. The harmony or success of your marriage may depend on both of you being willing to communicate, compromise and be committed to your marriage.

An immigrant's marriage, whether mixed or not, has extra challenges. As a new immigrant your spouse may be the only person you can turn to, so they need to be supportive. Your social circle will have changed. If only one of you is living in their homeland, and it's not you, you may feel you are living a compromise. Any further compromises could be felt as too many. Communication can keep your priorities known, especially if they change or differ from those of your spouse. Having a commitment to each other as well as to your adopted country will help your marriage as an immigrant work.

 Your supportive spouse

Anne: 'They all love Andrew, and that was important. That was good.'

Marriages are easier when your extended family approves of your spouse. If you are in a mixed marriage, your homeland family (and you) will be comforted by the fact that although you are away from your loved ones, they know you are with a supportive person.

Jessica: 'When we go out to California, they love Nick. They think he is
                perfect. I love the fact they think so much of him. He's always fixing
                things for my mother.'

In my mixed marriage, it helps that my family and friends consider David lovely, different and delightful. In contrast, Monica found things difficult while there was a rift between her husband and her mother (see Chapter 10).

As a new immigrant, away from family and friends in your homeland, your spouse may be the only person you feel you can ask for support. Charlotte finds that she depends on her husband for many needs: 'I rely on my husband Mitchell a bit too much. It is just us and he is my best friend. If I have problems, I talk to him. I have no one else as close.'

This reminds me of my feelings toward David in the early years of being in New Zealand. He had to be my mum, my dad, my sister, my brother and my friend, because he was the one there who knew me the most. I couldn't talk face-to-face with any of my family. He was my barometer and my support. I relied on him to be my sounding board and to help me when I was struggling. I'm not sure if it was his friends that helped him, or the 'quick' surfs that would last three hours, or the late nights at the hockey turf, but he carried the burden well. The benefit is that we have communicated often and at challenging times. Although I now have more friends around, I am used to communicating with him first, which I do most of the time.

When Sylvia was both a new immigrant and a new wife, she missed her friends. She would get cross with her husband as she felt she had no one to turn to – no one she knew well enough to be able to cry on their shoulder.

Hanneke knew a few families who went back and two families whose wives went home. She acknowledges it wasn't easy when she immigrated with Arie and their teenage daughter. 'It was all of us against everyone else. We had to stick together as a family unit and make it. We knew if we couldn't stick together, we couldn't make it … You have to be such dependable friends. I need him to be all that support.'

Elizabeth has found having only each other to rely on has been positive: 'It has made us much stronger because we can't run to parents or friends. We communicate more and talk more. Our marriage has just got better.'

 ## Social circles

For some, immigration not only increases the bond between you, but also makes your social circle more balanced. Before immigrating, most of both Nina's and Charlotte's socialising was with their husbands' friends. They felt outsiders in these groups. Their husbands' friends may have taken a while to see them as 'my friend' rather than 'my friend's wife'. Immigrating together, you can leave behind established social habits and make a fresh start.

When only one of a couple is an immigrant, the social circle can seem distorted, especially for the new immigrant. Having a ready-made social circle in your adopted country has advantages, but when it is your husband's circle, it can feel unbalanced. Susan emigrated to her husband John's homeland several years ago, but the memories of feeling an outsider are still vivid. 'It was hard here at first, because John had a routine of the same Mexican restaurant every Friday night. Same people, same routine. I hated Mexican. I felt I was dancing to his tune rather than doing what I wanted to do. It was a compromise all round … When you come into an environment when you don't know anyone, you have to slot in. You have to step into their zone and it is hard work, especially when you have no escape. I couldn't share that with him. I don't think men understand that. It [being without your friends] makes you more dependent on them. You haven't got anywhere to run to … It is better after a time when you can establish your own friends.'

Within a mixed marriage, there are benefits to one of you being an immigrant at times of celebration, such as at Christmas. You don't have to choose between families – there is no friction of whose family you go to or have for Christmas, and you don't have to spend precious time on Christmas Day travelling from one family's Christmas to the other's. For the immigrant, the choice is usually Christmas at your in-laws, with friends, or with only your husband and children (see Chapter 14).

 ## Compromise and sacrifice

Often in a marriage, one spouse's family is socially dominant, that is, the majority of contact for social occasions or family support is with that family.

The family of an immigrant in a mixed marriage is unlikely to be the dominant one. The fact that you, the immigrant, have given up access to your family and friends can cause friction. To lessen the feeling of having given up so much, see if there is something you can hold onto. Before I married, I decided I wasn't going to give up my family name. When asked why, I said, 'I have given up being near most of the people I love and the country I was living in. I feel that is enough'. Holding onto my family name gives me a constant reminder that there was one feature I didn't give up.

The word 'sacrifice' suggests one person giving up something, while 'compromise' suggests two people giving up something. You can decide which term is more appropriate to your own situation. For now, I will stick to the term 'compromise', as it is less harsh.

When you make compromises as an immigrant, you may become more assertive about being happy in other parts of your life. Katy was firm about the quality of her marriage. 'Being over here, the fact I had given up everything, I felt our marriage had to be good. I'm not going to do half measures. I'm not going to give up everything for a half-baked marriage.'

Lena's husband didn't appreciate how much she'd given up to immigrate: '… my family, my job, my friends. He was the only person I knew. He never had any understanding of that. You'd expect [your husband] would be there for you when you have left so much behind. But it was, throw me in at the deep end and do your thing. He made fun of my accent and how I talk. I didn't need that. You need more support. What is a husband for?' Their marriage didn't last.

A new immigrant adjusting to a new environment may see their standard of living compromised. Anne was quite shocked by some of the housing conditions in her husband's homeland. 'I was used to more modern [houses]. There are no fly screens on the windows here, even though we are near a tropical rainforest. Although there are plenty of bugs, everyone seems to keep the windows open. We used to have two fires and central heating in California; here there is often an old fire and no insulation.'

Once you are aware of what makes you feel compromised, you can choose to act on it or accept it. In Anne's case, she could put up fly screens, keep the windows shut or get used to the bugs. With time, the surprising or irritating features of the country may not seem an issue. She added that, a decade after immigration, she sees the housing characteristics differently – it's not so much a different standard, it's just a different way of life. Having identified the irritations as differences, she is freer to focus on the advantages of her life in her adopted country.

The compromises you make come at different times. For many mixed-marriage newlyweds, marriage may not live up to expectations of wedded bliss. As an immigrant, any disappointments in marriage may be accentuated by the compromises you feel you have made. Madeleine was attracted to Bruce's entrepreneurial spirit and was prepared to migrate to his homeland. Her family were concerned. 'I have to say there's no one in my family who didn't question me marrying Bruce in the first place *and* choosing to give up my family, friends and a good career. Most were baffled and worried.'

Once married, it turned out '… he really was not interested in expanding his life. It was not fair of me to expect him to do so, although it was one of the premises of our marriage that we would leave and live somewhere else, possibly England, but we stayed there [his hometown] and still did the same thing.'

The marriage struggled. She had made her home in her new country with her children. Their separation was difficult, but a few years after the separation she was able to describe her life as fulfilling.

You may need to consider the housekeeping expectations of each spouse within a marriage. For an immigrant, differences in expectations could be justified by cultural differences. David once commented that the fly poo need cleaning from our ceilings. I craned my neck upwards. He was right. I replied, 'We don't have so many flies in England. It's not my culture to clean ceilings.' I did clean them eventually, only because from then on I started noticing the dirt.

David also tried an avoidance route, when we were living at my parents'. My mother was lining up a small painting job for him, so he told her he was allergic to paint. He hoped that, as he wouldn't be living in the country for much longer, he wouldn't be found out. Once back in New Zealand the allergy magically disappeared.

Sophie was clear and brief about her compromise. 'In some ways I gave up everything so he could keep up his [homeland].'

Communication and priorities

Christine: 'We had to make it work ... We had to have lots of communication.'

Rachel: 'As soon as I have an argument with my husband, I think, "I'm on the first plane out of here."'

Good communication is essential in any marriage. Homesickness, going back for a visit, or even the possibility of returning 'home' are pertinent issues which need to be aired in an immigrant's marriage. Immigrant couples may understand and empathise with each other's homesickness more than mixed marriage couples, but they may not both feel the same.

Whether you are an immigrant or mixed-marriage couple, discussing going back for a visit can highlight feelings around being an immigrant, what your priorities are as a couple and individual, and what is possible.

Yvonne's husband Mark gets more homesick than she does, but '... we have never fallen out over the issue of going home [to visit.] We both had a high priority on family. Shared commitment to family.'

Rebecca and Brent have more than homesickness and visits to talk through: 'I didn't anticipate Brent would love it and have no desire to go back. When we got to the three years being here, I wasn't prepared for him to say, "I don't want to go back." I thought, *What do you mean?* We have some big challenges ahead.'

Charlotte also has different ideas than her husband Mitchell on staying. 'Citizenship is his dream. Something he wants to achieve. For me, it's not, but I do think, once he has it, then maybe we can go back ... Whenever we argue, the ultimatum is, "Right, I'm going back." That's my card, he will listen then ... He takes me seriously then. I don't say it that often.'

Communication stops blind speculation, married couples included. Whether a mixed nationality couple or not, it is likely you will have different feelings about homesickness and visiting your homeland. It is worth sharing these feelings, as it is often difficult to guess or speculate on what your spouse is feeling. If a spouse is not an immigrant, homesickness, needing to visit and the reason for these feelings can seem foreign. All the more reason to be clear on how this is affecting you and how it is important to you. I often dread the heavy talks over homesickness and needing to visit, as it usually involves finances and admittance that what I have around me is not enough. However, these discussions are usually worth the effort. Questions arise such as, What is more important – for me to go home for a visit or for us to go on holiday? Sometimes I know I have to go home. Can we take out a loan so the whole family can visit? What are the pros and cons of going on my own or with one or more children?

By including all the doubts, concerns and feelings, the decision we come to is more informed and decisions feel easier to make. Communication is an effort, but an essential part of committing to the best marriage we can make.

Commitment

I have heard of parents warning their children not to marry someone from overseas as the trips back home cost too much money. That is true, but many people do get married to people from overseas, and relationships do work. However, there has to be a commitment to each other and to having a good life in your adopted country (see Chapter 7). As Jessica pointed out, 'When we changed businesses and changed direction, I didn't see it as a sacrifice. I saw it as a commitment I had made to my husband.'

Rachel and Peter had been working overseas for many years before they started living in Peter's homeland. Buying a property in his homeland committed them to living there at some stage. They moved there ten years later, when their eldest child was nearly five. Rachel wanted to make sure their children had a sense of a permanent home. She said that immigrating to Peter's homeland not only provided them with a sense of adventure at starting something together, but she also felt her immigrating nurtured their marriage. 'I don't think our relationship would progress if I hadn't been prepared to come here … Peter is supportive, but he is also very lucky I came.'

As Elizabeth points out, marriage means work. 'We've been together seventeen years. Not many people we know have been together for this long. We just worked harder [at our relationship].'

Olivia has a mixed marriage, and married young. She often thought: *Right I'm going home now.* But then they would remind themselves that they were young and they needed to work through their problems, which is what they have continued to do. She jokes that the commitment to their marriage has recently been increased, not by renewing their vows, but by her having her dog imported from America. 'My husband calls the dog his insurance policy. He thinks, "Well she ain't going back because she won't pay another $7,000 for it to emigrate." I hear him talking to the dog saying, "You have to stay really healthy and don't die." When I went back to the States a couple of years ago, Stuart gave me a card to open on the plane. It said, "I love you honey and remember I have your dog here, so you have to come back."'

Key points

1   As an immigrant, you may rely on your spouse more than you would if you were in your homeland. If you have immigrated together, you may feel a degree of 'Us against the world'.

2   Having family and friends know that your spouse will be supportive and loving helps your marriage.

3   Social circles can become more balanced for newly immigrant couples, but may be initially unbalanced for mixed couples.

4   When you come out to your spouse's homeland, you may give up plenty: your family, your friends, even your name. With honest communication, your spouse can realise how much you feel you have given up.

5   An immigrant is likely to feel the pull to go to their homeland.

6   Your priorities and feelings about being an immigrant may change.

7   A commitment to your marriage and adopted country will help. Expressions or thoughts of, 'What if I went back?' or, 'I'm on the first plane home' are natural in confrontational times, but they should be used with caution.

8   Marriages are work and pleasure. Compromise, communication and commitment help to keep a good balance between the two.

Strategies

- As a new immigrant, explain to your spouse that he or she is your main or only support.

- In a mixed marriage, make friends of your own (and introduce them to your spouse), as well as mutual friends.

- If you both immigrated, make new friends together and individually.

- If you are feeling over-compromised, find something you can hold onto or aspire to. What will make you feel less compromised? Join a new club, put money aside for a trip back to your homeland, put up fly screens.

- Regularly communicate your thoughts about visits to your homeland.

- The more hurdles you work through together, the stronger and better your relationship will be. If you are both committed to the relationship, there will be a strong foundation which will help you through the hurdles.

17 Separation and divorce

Madeleine: 'Someone told me once, before we separated, that when or if you do, you trade one set of problems for another. This is true in any divorce, but it is particularly hard when you are in a foreign country. It is extremely important to be very sure you are making the decision which is right for you. It's also important to have at least a couple of friends who support you, to be financially independent and try your best to be a reassuring, loving parent to your children.'

If your marriage runs into trouble, you may miss the face-to-face support from family and old friends that would have helped you work through those problems. If you do separate, you miss this same support as you go through the separation.

As I have not been through a separation, I can only relate the tales and emotions of those who have. From what they have to say, there is a desire to return to your homeland. Whether you do or not, you have to get on with your life and believe that you can set up a life that has sufficient good moments to carry you through.

Telling family

When Katy decided to separate, she initially had mixed feelings about telling her family in her homeland. She wanted them to know, but didn't want them to have the burden of worrying about her. She felt she needed to be taken care of, but her family and friends were too far away to be able to nurture her. When she did tell them, there was little her family and friends in her homeland could physically do except listen. Katy thought of asking her mother to come over, but her mother's own health needs made it impossible. Katy realised she would have to go through the separation on her own. She said that in retrospect, separating without her mother near made her stronger and more adult. She would still like to sit down on her mother's couch and feel safe, but she knows she made a decision to be in her adopted country, and she has to live with that decision and its consequences.

When Sylvia separated, she missed her family. Her friends in New Zealand were supportive, but her reaction was that she '… just wanted to get home and get away from everyday life … If my parents were here it wouldn't be the same. It is so hard to compare. I don't know if it would be better or worse. I remember ringing my mum and I don't know whether it was a reaction [to the separation], but my daughter had been caught shoplifting. I cried for half an hour. It must have been hard for her to listen to. I can't remember what she said, but she must have listened very nicely. It was hard telling them that this is what was happening.'

Later, Sylvia did go back for a year. 'I had sorted the children, but I needed nurturing and to do something for me. I stayed with my brother, as he thought my parents were too old to take on my sixteen-year-old and me. It was a lovely time of reconnection with siblings. There were two weddings, two nephews got married, Mum was eighty, big celebrations that I could go to.'

When Amber considered separating, she felt she couldn't leave her partner until she had somewhere else to stay. 'I don't like leaning on people and I didn't have my parents around, so I couldn't stay there. It may have been an earlier split if my parents were near.'

She was reluctant to tell her parents that she had separated, but on the day she moved she was so upset, she rang them and let them know. This was one of the few times she wasn't on top of the world when she rang them. After a few months in her new home, and with a new job in the pipeline, she went to see her parents for a holiday. She felt she needed to go home and show everyone that she was okay.

Lena knew the separation was coming. She had thought about leaving Ben several times. Still, it was a shock when he left two weeks before their baby was due.

Madeleine: 'It was pretty hard as I had no one, no support group. My husband Bruce and his family were rude. They ignored me. They practically spied on me. I lived for five years in our house behind the store [shop] and the only way in or out was going by the store. For a while, my parents disowned me, I'd "made my bed and I should lie in it." My father told me he would do anything he could to keep the marriage together, and nothing to help end it. We didn't talk the month I was at my lowest. One night my furnace broke. It was so cold I had to take the children to Bruce's place. He refused to help. I slept in the house midwinter and forty degrees [four degrees centigrade] in my coat, gloves and hat. A friend's husband came over the next day to fix it. Eventually my parents came out to help me. Once here, they could see the situation for what it was and understood why I had left

Bruce. They have supported me ever since. I have realised that my awful situation was incredibly stressful for them because they couldn't do anything. However, their moral support and encouragement was enough for me. It meant more than anything.'

Lena and her ex-mother-in-law are still on good terms. 'Since the divorce, we are better. She bought me a car when we divorced. She is good. I see her a few times a year. We get on, it's acceptance. She also drops things off now when she passes, although she often doesn't stay around long enough to see her granddaughter.'

Before Katy and her husband separated, they had spent long periods in her homeland. However, with separation and a divided family she felt restricted in taking her children back for long periods, as they would be without their father. 'The hardest thing about separating was the fear of losing my family, because now I have to stay here [in this adopted country]. Before I was married, and even when we were separated initially, he did say he'd come to my country for a while. Now I can't go home [with the children], that's the hardest thing. I'm terrified of losing my life here. When I was married I could go home when I wanted.'

Madeleine found that some of her support network broke up after separation. 'Divorce can be viral and some woman are nervous of being around a new single mum.' This may be true for all separations. For an immigrant, with no access to your family, you are more dependent on your support network. If that has gone, you have limited people to lean on in a time of need. Madeleine overcame this by seeking out new friends while doing all she could to keep the friends she had. 'Through that I have created great and lasting friendships with women.' One of these friends organised a surprise thirty-fifth birthday which is now an annual gathering tradition. 'Everyone loves it because it's the only time we all get together again. My birthday is less of the occasion and more the excuse, but it's perfect.'

Getting on with life

Work

After her lengthy divorce, Madeleine found that getting a job and getting involved in the local community helped. 'That's what helped me to feel I belong, and that's what I needed. It opened doors and expanded horizons.'

Lena: 'Get out and communicate with people. I wish I'd joined the preschool group earlier. It opened a whole new world. With small children it is good to mix with others.'

Where to live

When separating, the temptation to return to your homeland permanently or long term may be there, but returning may not be a straightforward solution, as Sylvia could see. 'If I left New Zealand now, where would I go, what would I do? I would have to create a whole new life again. Where would I stay without latching onto my siblings and their friends? I would have to start all over. I may as well stay here and keep the friends and the job. When you separate, you have to recreate a life. I thought it better to stay here. I've lived in these two countries the same amount of time, so it would be just as difficult. I was beyond going back.'

Believe in yourself

Katy: 'It was good that she [my mother] didn't come because I had to stand on my own two feet. My sister reminded me that I could do it. I had already moved all the way over here. "Back yourself on this one sis!" I don't want to, but I have to.'

Madeleine has read a lot on divorce, and her feeling is: 'As a woman, I think it is extremely important to really find out who you are and forgive yourself for not being everything to everyone. It's just not possible. It's important to treat yourself with respect, and if respect is not given to you by your husband, partner or children, then you have to make a stand and not put up with it. I have found more strength with female friends, who although may not have gone through divorce, really love you and support you.'

After separation, Amber felt differently about being an immigrant. 'It used to be that I was here for him, now I know I'm here for me. It is why I am so happy now and stronger as I did go through it on my own. Here I am starting a whole new life in a whole new country on the opposite end of the day.'

Key points

1   Separation is likely to create or enhance a feeling of, 'What am I doing here?'

2   The reaction of wanting to return to your homeland to be nurtured is common.

3   You may avoid contacting your family in case you increase their worry, as you feel they can't do much for you.

4   Your family and friends in your homeland *will* be worrying about you and caring for you.

5   To return to your homeland may not be the best choice. You may not be able to return.

»

»

6   Your support network in your adopted country may change when you separate.

7   Looking for different support networks in work and your community can offer a new sense of belonging.

8   Whether you stay in your adopted country or go to your homeland, there will be changes in your life after separation.

9   Recreating your life in your homeland may be more work than staying in your adopted country.

Strategies

- Communicate with your family and friends in your homeland. Knowing they are thinking of you can help.

- Rely on trusted friends or find new friends. Get out into the community. Accept help or seek support on separation.

- Consider when you could go back to your homeland, even for a short visit.

- Be realistic before you change your life again. *Is* the grass greener in your homeland?

- Believe in yourself. You have come this far, you can probably get through this and be stronger.

18 Shall we join you?

 ## When friends or family are thinking of emigrating

Hooray!

Learning that members of your family, or close friends, are contemplating emigration to your adopted country can create great excitement.

The women I interviewed had valuable advice to share with those thinking of emigrating.

Vanessa: 'Go for it! It is a big thing to do. Think seriously about it, but if you want to do it, then why not give it a go? If you don't do it, you may always regret it. Even if you do it and it doesn't work out, so what? Go back. You may have lost money, but you can lose money in all sorts of ways.

'Something like this will give you more experience. It will enrich you. Once we decided to emigrate, we started doing all sorts of other things. It was a stimulus opening other avenues. Bear in mind that whatever you read about and research, you will not know how it is living here. Even if you come here on holiday, you may not know how it is to live until you are here.

'Open your mind, it may open up to being different, I think it is better to challenge yourself. Someone said you are getting out of your comfort zone, which is beneficial. It is totally outside your comfort zone, which can be a positive thing, but it is still uncomfortable. Even if the experience doesn't work for you, you are still enriched by it. It's all positive.'

Elizabeth, with fewer words, was just as positive: 'It is the best decision ever.'

But wait, caution

If you only sing the praises of your adopted country, ignoring the unfavourable aspects, your family and friends may think you have a perfect life in a perfect place. Attracted by this perceived perfection, and perhaps frustrated with some aspects of their own lives, they may consider emigrating. What do you do? Be enthusiastic and positive, like Elizabeth and Vanessa above, or introduce some of the realities?

Vanessa: '[Tell them not to] think it is perfect, or the place where everything will be perfect. It is just the backdrop to life. It is just the scenery ... I constantly say, have I done the right thing? I wish I was still here or there. Sometimes it's good; sometimes I feel, definitely. Depends where you're at. Give yourself time, appreciate it is a big thing to do and there is quite a settling-in process ... Acknowledging the desire to go back for visits is very important.'

Olivia: 'It is not a place to escape. Moving to another country is not going to fix your problems.'

Nina warns that the emotional aspects are distressing in the first year: 'How you think is up to you. Look on the brighter side and I'm sure it will not be as bad.'

Pain is inevitable, suffering is optional.
- Unknown

 # Research

Olivia suggests emigrants should plan before they come. 'Interview for jobs; get a feel for the place before you get here. It may seem like a big adventure, but if you can research first, it will take away some of the stress and anxiety. If you have been here before, that will take out significant stress.'

She wouldn't mention the emotional side – the sense of loss – to potential emigrants, but instead would ask, 'What are the things which make you happy? Is this the place for you?'

Although Olivia was delighted when her parents expressed an interest in joining her, she was also concerned, because she knew her gain would mean her nephews and nieces would lose a set of grandparents.

Madeleine: 'When marrying a foreign person and immigrating, for life, to his country, take a little time to experience it before you make the leap, because a leap it is, and it is not easy. I know, from my perspective, I thought on a very spiritual level, and calculated level, I would make it. Making it meant having a successful marriage and life, but I didn't know what that really meant to me. I was giving up my life to a man and a country I didn't know.'

Think about what you'll miss

Katy would advise prospective immigrants to think hard about what they will be giving up. She has been in her adopted country for more than twenty years and although she has a good life, says: 'I miss Mum so very much. I didn't know that I would feel like I do. It is an empty disorientated aching feeling. I thought I was this traveller person, that I would be fine. But it knocked me for six. This is just life thousands of miles away, not an adventure.'

Similarly, Sylvia would advise people to thoroughly assess the pros and cons of emigration, bearing in mind that the process can be difficult, and being away can be hard: 'You miss your everyday life in your homeland. You have to start again. [People from the UK] will miss the weather, the drizzle, even though you think you won't. You will be surprised at some of the things you will miss. They are often very subtle. You hear or smell things and you think, that reminds me of England.'

I heard a Swiss immigrant say that he missed the Swiss-style buildings when he emigrated. I sometimes reminisce about buildings in England – the fishermen's cottages in Cornwall, the terraced houses of the industrial revolution or *Coronation St* fame, the Georgian houses of Bath and the Tudor pubs with low beams and uneven floors. I even miss the council houses built in the sixties and seventies – collections of solid three-bedroom houses, identical apart from the differing paint colour of each front door. These different building styles characterise the history and people of the area. I miss the sense of belonging to England, with its centuries of history.

New Zealanders may miss their distinctive buildings: the white weatherboard villas with detailed fretwork, the railway workers' cottages, the old beach houses, the solid state houses on a quarter-acre section (plot), complete with chicken-wire fence and citrus trees.

You don't know what you've got till it's gone.

Anon

Budgeting for visits 'home'

On the practical side, you may want to advise those thinking of emigrating about how best they can keep links with their family, for example through the Internet (see Chapter 5) and through visits to their homeland. When my sister suggested that she was interested in emigrating to New Zealand, I felt I had won a prize. Once I'd calmed down, my first piece of advice was, 'Allocate money for a visit back every few years. Make sure you include this in your budget.' (See Chapter 8.)

Remember, the immigration process is lengthy

'How much do I want this?'

When I was trying to gain permanent New Zealand residency, I had to spend up to seven hours, every six months, queuing from five o'clock in the morning until midday, in order to keep my work visa current. While I waited in the queues, in tired magnolia-coloured offices, I pondered on whether I really wanted to stay in New Zealand. During one such wait, I noticed how the expressions of the three staff processing applications – a Sikh, a Maori and a young woman with red hair – didn't change at all. I may be in a different country, but dealing with government staff was disappointingly similar to my experiences in England.

When it was my turn, I strode to the desk, my grin hiding a curdling anxiety-hope mix. The smile made no difference to whether or not the redhead or her colleagues stamped my passport. When my passport was stamped, I wanted to kiss the surly staff. (Perhaps that's why they sit behind toughened glass.)

I had my work visa extended four times, and two years later my passport was stamped with permanent residency.

My experience illustrates that the immigration process takes a long time and a lot of effort. While it's important that those thinking of immigrating appreciate this, on a positive note, knowing the hassles that lie ahead can help people decide whether or not they are serious about emigrating.

When Vincent and Jill decided to emigrate to join Vincent's brother Tony and his wife, Tony did everything he could to ease the process for them. Vincent and Jill returned to their homeland after three years, and I wondered whether

Tony had made the migration procedure too easy for them. If somebody wants to emigrate, encouragement and support may be enough. They need to be convinced in themselves that they are doing what is right for them; getting through the long process will help them be certain.

They also should be aware of some of the emotional challenges they may have to face. Let them read this book.

Key points

1   Immigration is and should be a long process.

2   Having family with you in your adopted country will decrease your sense of loss.

3   Family or friends who join you may be at a different stage of being an immigrant, and may want to live life differently to you.

4   Big decisions generate excitement and open new doors.

5   The grass is not always greener on the other side of the fence.

Strategies

•   Ask those considering immigrating to identify what makes them happy. How will migrating match up with this?

•   How do they think migrating will affect them?

•   You should not be making the decision for those considering migrating, but you can help them make an informed choice. Encourage them to do plenty of research and thoroughly consider the realities before making a decision.

•   Let prospective immigrants go through the process in their own time.

•   If they end up coming, help them, welcome them, support them and enjoy them.

19 funerals and your faith

*I didn't attend the funeral, but I sent a nice
letter saying I approved of it.*
- Mark Twain (1835-1910)

 ## What if you should die?

Have you ever pondered on your funeral? I have. Not so much on where the funeral would be or what it would entail, but rather, as an immigrant, on who would turn up and where they would place my ashes. These questions have made me reflect on my feelings of connection with England and New Zealand. Over time, my thoughts have changed.

As a new immigrant, my vision of my funeral was an almost-empty church with a few friends in the front pew, their handbags beside them to make the pew look more full. This sad speculation reminded me that my family and most of my friends were too far away.

Decades later, I'm happy to presume there would be more than two front pews occupied, especially if the service were held at our small church. I have sufficient friends to think that, even if none of my family from England could be at the service, there could be enough people to prevent an awkwardly empty church.

Somewhere beyond this review of whether I am loved or liked enough to chalk up the numbers at my funeral, is a contemplation of my life in New Zealand. How fulfilling is my life here? I like to have engaging relationships, so how have I connected with people around me? Are they important to me, and am I important to them? If considering your funeral allows you to reflect on how you feel about your life, doing so could be a worthwhile speculative, if egocentric moment.

David once asked me where I would like my ashes placed. I used to feel they could be divided between Opoutere, a New Zealand beach I fell in love with in, and Forty Hall, a large park with hundreds of ancient oak and yew trees that I used to play among as a child. Dividing my ashes was a touching idea that nicely represented my connection with both countries. However, having been an immigrant for a couple of decades, this no longer seems so necessary. I am quite happy to have my ashes put wherever those left behind find comforting.

While I'm on the subject of those left behind, you should consider what would happen to your children or dependents, especially if they were left with no one to care for them. Vanessa and George re-wrote their wills soon after they immigrated. They wanted to make sure there was someone in their adopted country who would look after their children.

Yvonne and Mark have adapted their wills as their children have grown. 'Our goal is for the family to stay in our adopted country if we die. We have spoken to our children about this, and when the eldest was eighteen, we asked if he would be prepared to be the guardian, so the children could stay together and life could be somewhat normal.'

Elizabeth has considered options. 'Last year, I did [think of my death/ funeral] because I nearly died. If I died, I hope that Jim would stay here with the children. If we both died they would have to go back to England. I can't expect any of my friends to take on my children.'

Anita and her sister have discussed what would happen in the event of their deaths: 'My sister and I are on each other's list as we feel we would love our children as our own.'

 # faith

My faith has given me many things. As an immigrant, faith has given me a sense of belonging. When I had been in New Zealand for a year or so, I moved to a different area of the city. I had noticed a Catholic church, and felt drawn to go to Mass there. I had had a Catholic upbringing, but being in my mid-twenties had whittled my attendance down to CEO: Christmas and Easter only. At the Mass, I warmed to the strong sense of belonging. I was familiar with the service and its rituals, the smell of candles and the pattern of standing, kneeling and sitting. I enjoy the pattern and there may be some truth in David's description of it as an 'aerobics session'. At least the movement keeps everyone alert. In the service I could join in the prayers with the people around me. I started going to Mass more often. The familiarity of the church was invigorating, and was a relief from the unfamiliar territory surrounding and shaping the rest of my daily life.

Going to church allowed me to do something on my own from my pre-immigrant days. I had been lucky to have David show me the city he grew up in. My own local lad, parking for outdoor concerts with minimal walking, introducing me to the delights of DKD's cafe, which, in 1987 not only had one of the first cappuccino machines in Auckland, but also made the best chocolate cake. However, sometimes the 'welcome to my world' felt unbalanced. I had been in his world for more than a year. Focusing on something familiar from my past was reassuring.

This may have worked just as well if I had re-joined a singing group or started playing a sport again. Going to Mass was the activity that helped. There I could feel familiar, reflect on my life and its actions and get to know a new group of like-minded people.

My faith gave me a feeling of being at home. I cherished the caring and acceptance, the familiar spiritual and ceremonial side of my faith. In talking to my God, I have often asked for help to get through the emotional challenges of immigration. Prayer has helped me. God is a great listener. My faith has given me not only a feeling of belonging, but strength, and a sense of community.

If you have faith, I recommend nurturing it, especially if you can find a faith that feels like home. If not, consider going to a place of faith. They are usually welcoming and can be a good place to be meet people.

Key points

1 Considering your funeral may help you to reflect on your life or sum up how you feel about your life as an immigrant. The process may reveal your sense of connection with your adopted country and the people around you.

2 Returning to an activity that you did before you were an immigrant can help you with a sense of belonging in your adopted country.

3 Nurturing a faith can help you feel less alone.

Strategies

- If you imagine your funeral and are not happy with the vision, change what you need to.

- Revise or rethink your will. Consider guardianship of your children.

- Recognise any changes in your views when you contemplate your funeral. They may be a good indicator of how settled you are feeling.

- Try out familiar and unfamiliar places of faith to see if they feel right.

- Ask your God for help when you are troubled.

20 You have a part to play

Immigrants can feel like foreigners in two places they call home. They feel cut off from their homeland, and don't quite fit in their adopted country. However, even a foreigner has an impact on people's lives. They have a part to play.

In your adopted country

As an immigrant you introduce your adopted country to a different way of thinking. When you visit your homeland, there are unique opportunities to contribute to the people there. When you have visitors you give them a chance to holiday with you and have an insight into life in a different country.

The first friend I made in New Zealand once challenged me when I was struggling with living in an in-law world. Married people usually have in-law-challenges, but if the only family gatherings you have are in-law ones, the challenges can feel overwhelming. As an immigrant you feel a foreigner anyway; with the in-laws there are differences too. The combination of the two made me feel an outsider, only being able to observe and follow their ways, not feeling comfortable enough to contribute. My friend reminded me, 'You have a part to play in this. Perhaps you are here to expose them to a new way of thinking, acting or believing. If they were never exposed to you then they would not have been introduced to an alternative view on life.'

Her reminder was a turning point for me, because I realised how I had been seeing myself. I was different, therefore my input was not valid. Once I realised I could have valid and constructive input, I felt less of an outsider. I felt more valued, as an individual, as part of my in-law family and my adopted country. From then on, I made an effort to contribute more in discussions and activities.

 # In your homeland

The next time I felt I had a part to play as an immigrant was when my father was dying. During the two weeks before he died, my eight siblings, their spouses and children and I were in and out of the hospital, spending time with our father and devoted mother who constantly stayed at his side. My siblings and their partners had to look after their children and their work. My children and David were still in New Zealand. While I was in England, I had only myself to look after, so I was the right person to take care of my mother during this time.

I shifted from mothering my three preschoolers in my adopted country to mothering my mother in my homeland. What an honour. For those two weeks, I was able to provide home-cooked meals for my mother three times a day and be on call for her. I was able to provide flexible meals at the family home catering for whoever decided to stay over. I felt a freedom to be dedicated to my family and contribute in a significant way. At this tough time, I was there for them. I was there too, arms linked with my mother, as we followed my father's coffin down the same aisle I had walked down on my wedding day, but that time, my arms were linked with my father's.

On to happier events … my sister has pointed out to me that when I go to London, the family gets together. When immigrants visit their homeland, there is a sense of occasion. As this sister said, 'Hey don't kid yourself that we do this all the time. We only get together on special occasions. You are often the catalyst. Sometimes I haven't seen one of the others since you were last here.'

As an immigrant you may be seen as the ideal person to talk to about big issues. Being geographically distant, the amount you can actually do about the issue is limited to the time you are there (see Chapter 9).

Anne finds big issues are often discussed when she is back in California. As her presence is temporary, she can suggest or instigate events that may not happen if she lived there. 'I had been on speaking terms with my dad, and my sister hadn't, so we made a way for my dad to meet my sister, with Andrew and me being there too, to smooth the water.'

Another similar incident occurred during a visit. Anne didn't have a car, so had to rely on others for transport. 'When Dad was dropping me off at Mum's, it was dark, so Mum came out. She hugged him and said something like, "I missed you." They started texting, usually about me. They continued to text. It was [also] through me that he started to see my younger sister. It was a cool thing that it was an offshoot from my visit.'

Sometimes, taking even the small opportunities is rewarding. When Sylvia's father died, Sylvia, in an opposite time zone, was able to share tea and chats with her mother at three o'clock in the morning.

When Sylvia's mother had cancer, her retired siblings cared for her at home. 'I felt I needed to do my bit, so in the September holidays, I went home and looked after her for two weeks, and during the Christmas holidays I went back and looked after her again. She died in those holidays. It was really important to know that I played my role.'

A family gathering is also a splendid occasion when it takes place in your adopted country. When Sylvia's daughter got married, all of Sylvia's siblings came out to New Zealand for the wedding. 'We hired a yacht. We had a marvellous time … They all said they were coming back. The occasion had been made possible because they'd all come out for the wedding.'

Key points

1   You have a role to play.
2   There will be significant occasions in your homeland where you are the best person for the job, because you are not always there.
3   You may be perceived as a safe confidante.

Strategies

- Recognise the impact you have on your family and friends from your homeland.
- Be aware of the influence you can have on the people around you in your adopted country.
- When you can, embrace opportunities to help your family in your homeland.

21 The immigrant life cycle

There could be said to be five stages of an immigrant's life cycle. They may not always occur in this order, and certain features may overlap, but they can be roughly categorised as:

1   **The new immigrant**: Working life/career adaptations; trying to fit in.
2   **The intermediate immigrant**: Having a young family, missing your reference points.
3   **The established immigrant**: The sandwich years – how can you care for your overseas parents?
4   **The empty nester**: Are your children more inclined to migrate overseas? Retirement. Are trips to your homeland still affordable?
5   **The grandparent**: Coping with overseas grandchildren.

The new immigrant

You are discovering how systems in your adopted country work; your career may be disadvantaged because you have no experience in your adopted country (see Chapter 15). There will be culture shock, but this will decrease as you become more familiar with the various aspects of your new country. If you take a trip 'home', there may be questions and comparisons.

The intermediate immigrant

Having a young family is never easy, but as an immigrant there is the extra challenge brought by the absence of your homeland family and friends. This was the stage at which I first significantly missed my family. I could not show off my children's milestones; I didn't know whether my children would ever properly know their grandparents, their cousins and my culture (see Chapter 13).

The established immigrant

The sandwich years are those where both your children and your parents need care. Being involved in caring for your parents means travel and being far away from your home for significant lengths of time. Frustrations develop if you can't get to your parents.

This was a tough time for Sylvia – her teenagers needed her and her parents needed her. At the same time she was going through a divorce. She described being torn between the needs of the two as 'very difficult.'

When my mother collapsed in Marks and Spencer from a suspected heart attack, I immediately went on alert. I know all my siblings did too. My alert involved being ready for a twenty-eight-hour plane journey. Fortunately, the collapse wasn't from a heart attack and she was discharged from hospital after two days. During that time, not only was I on alert, but I just wanted to go there and see that she was okay.

 The empty nester

Empty nesters' children have left home at least once; most have learnt to accept and work with this new stage of their life. Those who have been an immigrant for twenty, thirty or more years have become used to an immigrant life.

Jessica said, 'I have lost so much of my cultural identity. I have come far enough now that I think, well, that's how it is.'

Sylvia has lived in her adopted country for longer than her homeland. Now that she is less busy with her own children, she enjoys having more time to connect with her siblings.

Yvonne finds her feelings towards going back to her homeland have changed as the family situation has changed: 'The fact that my family in Northern Ireland doesn't need any help is a relief.' She feels that her children need her to stay in her adopted country, and that this outweighs both the needs of her family in Northern Ireland, and her own needs.

Retirement

I have the time to go to my homeland, but do I have the money?

Hanneke found that her latest trip to The Netherlands, where she was well into her retirement, was probably the best of her life. This time they organised a trip to suit themselves, rather than the people they were visiting. 'We chose a house where we stayed too far away from people to visit all the time. It was a holiday.' She said she was not so sensitive about the reaction of people when she didn't visit them as much as they expected. At this stage she was more accepting of the decisions she made and their consequences.

The grandparent

When your children are grown up, you may have to face the possibility of them becoming migrants. As an immigrant you have shown your children that it is possible to be brought up in one country and live in another. During their life, you may have encouraged their connection with your homeland. To migrate may feel normal for them, and the migration may not be to your homeland. Hanneke's four immigrant friends all have the majority of their grandchildren overseas.

I hope I have introduced my children to many of the features of being an immigrant. Perhaps they will read this book and be able to make a more informed choice than I did.

 Other aspects to consider

What happens when your parents die? How will you keep in contact with siblings? Sometimes, after their parents' deaths, siblings develop a stronger bond than they had when their parents were alive.

What happens when your generation becomes aged? How many funerals will you miss or attend in your homeland? I don't know the answers. With regards to my own situation – I will probably make my decisions when the time comes with the resources and information I have, just as I have done for the rest of my life as an immigrant.

Whichever stage of the immigrant life cycle you have reached, there will be some advantages of being in your adopted country. Enjoy them. I don't imagine I would go back permanently, as the idea of setting up life again is too overwhelming. I will probably stay where I am and take up all the opportunities for an enjoyable and fulfilling life.

Key points

1   In your life as an immigrant, there will be times when the emotional challenges are harder on you.
2   Accept the consequences of the choices you have made in life.
3   our children may explore the world too – just as their parent(s) did.

Strategies

•   Remember, you made the right decision at the right time with the information you had.

»

»

- Do not forget your retirement. How are you going to fund your trips to your homeland?
- Relationships with your siblings may become stronger when you are 'orphans'.
- Your children may want to become immigrants too. Give them this book.

Afterword

In the intervening time between interviewing the immigrants and finishing this book, our local bar-tailed godwits migrated to Alaska and back four times, I have been to England and back twice, and my mother has travelled the same distance in reverse order. Life has gone on and our experiences have continued to shape us.

Charlotte and Mitchell are now parents. Having their son, Tom, has made Charlotte feel more at home. She eats breakfast with him in the garden and watches him spend hours in the sandpit or playing outside. She has made friends with Tom's friends' mothers. When Tom was small, Charlotte's mother came out for the first time, accompanied by Charlotte's aunt. She says it helps that '… now they know where and how we live.' Charlotte has been back to England with Tom, and although she loved the familiarity, she '… was keen to get back to Tom's routine and his buddies.' She is feeling far more settled now than when I interviewed her. 'Someone said give it eighteen months, but I know I took a lot longer. I still miss people, but with Tom, this feels the right place to be.'

Rebecca has become a citizen. 'It was almost like getting married, really making a commitment. We were invited to wear our traditional dress. I was a bit short of a Pearly Queen dress so I wore black. There were women looking beautiful in their saris and men in suits. We all sang the national anthem and tried not to spill ketchup on our smart clothes as we ate the sausage rolls. I did say to Brent, "Can we go home now?" Joking. I do still feel I have a foot in each camp, but I couldn't take this [my adopted country] away from my children. This is their home. I took them back to England for five weeks. They didn't understand that you couldn't run around on your own at Heathrow Airport, let alone in bare feet. We went to the castles, the museums. I loved the history, but I realised that my children were learning different things. You are not English because your mother is English, you are English because you were brought up there.'

Rebecca also commented that she is more settled now. 'I have friends I can have proper conversations with. They know me more. It's less superficial. I don't have to operate on that high level of politeness … I have become more involved in the children's primary school. It was intense at first, but now there is a sense of belonging and I no longer worry about making social faux pas.'

Although she misses friends and family, she is now able to recognise that being an immigrant is not the sole reason for her sadness. 'I used to think when I was having a bad day it would be better if I wasn't here, but I used to have bad days in England. A bad day is just a bad day.'

Katy has reunited with her husband and they are living in her homeland for 'a long while'. She is glad to be with her family, but with one of her children in her adopted country she realises there are still immigration challenges. 'My children are a product of me. They have two worlds, two homes. They have to adjust, decide and choose where they want to be.'

Monica rushed back to England when her father died suddenly. She spent a few weeks there with her mother and sister before she returned to her adopted country. On the day she returned, she rang me and suggested I include a section on how husbands can make your return more welcoming, '… for example, tidying the house or at least doing the dishes.' Dismissing the impulse to go back to her homeland, she said she was considering leaving her still-packed suitcase outside, tidying the house and making a banner that said, 'Welcome Home'. Then she would wait outside until her husband came home and would re-enact her arrival. 'At least then,' she said, 'he would know what I would like.'

Amber has bought a house and is engaged.

During one of my trips back, I was able to go to a reunion with my friends from secondary school. We had all turned 50. We had a wonderful week together, and I felt I fitted in as if I had hardly been away. Thirty-five years after school days our conversations had glided from the teenage excitement of sexual exploration, to enjoying sex with the threat of pregnancy beyond us. My school friends hadn't migrated, but they had each had personal challenges which they had worked through and were still working through. Migrants or not, we were still beautiful women, able to laugh and share life.

I have missed another sibling's wedding and some funerals. I have listened to other immigrants go through similar scenarios. I have become more understanding of my own reactions when I go home for a visit, and am more equipped to deal with them. The leaving is still distressing. My last pre-leaving tension was as bad as ever. My sisters and their husbands were walking along a narrow country lane with rambling roses spilling onto the pathway. A brother in-law who was walking alongside me broke the silence and asked me what time I was flying out. I burst into tears. 'What did I say?' he said. 'What did you say?' my sister shouted to her husband. It was nothing he had said, and there was nothing they could say to make me feel better. I knew I was again leaving the people I loved and the people I loved being with. The parting from them is always painful. In a way it's the way it should be. It is because I love them. Any scars on my heart are worth it.

Since writing this I have become involved with a number of online communities that help migrants. This type of information and support wasn't accessible twenty years ago. I have researched immigration, and have spoken and written about migrants. Some aspects of immigration can be distressing and challenging, but there are ways to lessen the burden. It is difficult for non-immigrants to understand your feelings. They have not walked in your shoes, but they can help you, if you explain the help you need.

I have become older and more ready to accept what *is* rather than what *might be*. As immigrants we have sad moments and scars. We also have adventurous, settled and happy times. We have times of discovery and learning. We have a global outlook on life. We have an exposure to different histories, cultures and climates. We have opportunities that we hadn't even contemplated.

Emotional challenges as an immigrant can be worked through, but working through them may mean a letting go of some of your past and looking at what is in front of you. The missing is a sign of the loving. Embrace the loving, accept the missing and find what you can to have a great life in the country you are living in.

Find out more on the emotional challenges of immigration by visiting www.migrantemotions.com and signing up for the newsletter.

Acknowledgements

Hooray for the interviewees! Not only have they let me share their stories, they have also shared their wisdom, and offered an understanding ear during my time as an immigrant.

To my family and friends in England for welcoming me when I have turned up – for putting your lives on hold to see me, for organising events, for tolerating my jet lag and emotional unease, and for all your trips to New Zealand.

To my family in New Zealand, whose inclusion and support gave me a family here, and to my New Zealand friends, who embraced my differences in Kiwi-relaxed style. You patiently asked how the book was going, and gave me the encouragement I needed to carry on.

To David and our fabulous children Christopher, Emily, Amanda and Ingrid. We may be more of a quirky bunch than a Brady bunch, but our differences keep us interesting. Thank you for supporting me to 'get the book done', and for making room for both cultures in your lives.

Thank you to those in the writing world. Editing from Sue Copsey, John Langdon, James George and Linda Grigg; design from Marie Low, and encouragement from Jocelyn Watkin.

Thank you to all those in the non-writing world who with peer reviews helped me keep the book developing. Your time, opinions and encouragement kept me believing it was all worthwhile.

An excellent book for anyone considering migrating – new migrants and even experienced ones. Having moved countries several times I hadn't realised how much I'd had to learn slowly and through experience – this book will help you take the short cut!
Kim Chamberlain, Author of over 10 books on personal development, Speaker ATM, APS

This book is a must-read for immigrants and those considering immigration.

Ellie Baker weaves the story of her own experience as an immigrant with those of similar women. She reflects deeply on the feelings and experiences an immigrant will encounter throughout different life stages in a new country.

Her book validates the impressions and reactions of those living in a new country and prepares the new immigrant for the life that lies ahead.

She writes clearly, with empathy for those who have made the journey and for those left behind. This is a brave book that refuses to accept 'no-go-areas.'
It is packed with psychological depth and practical strategies.
Henriette Politano, BA, Dip.Couns, Reg. Psychotherapist (PBANZ), MNZAC, MITAA, IARPP

I do believe it is a much-needed book; I sure could have used it in my first year in New Zealand. Despite having a wonderful husband and loving New Zealand, I felt depressed and I didn't quite understand why. Your book would have helped me normalise my feelings, pointing me to the reasons why and to the possible solutions.
Emmy Spijker, from The Netherlands

As an immigrant myself, reading the testimonies of the contributors to this book was like looking into a mirror of my own experiences. Ellie Baker has written a sincere and well-written manual that can help anyone about to emigrate from their homeland, and anyone suffering from the pangs of homesickness. Through the richness of immigrants' experiences, it points out the challenges and struggles of the migratory process, but at the same time, the rewards of being able to 'survive' away from home.
Maria Angel, BA, MSc, MRes, Doctoral Candidate, Anthropology Department, University College London

Printed in Great Britain
by Amazon

82609259R00108

Free Bonus from C ---y
(Available for a Limited time)

Hi History Lovers!

Now you have a chance to join our exclusive history list so you can get your first history ebook for free as well as discounts and a potential to get more history books for free!

Simply visit the link below to join.

Or, Scan the QR code!

captivatinghistory.com/ebook

Also, make sure to follow us on Facebook, X, and YouTube by searching for Captivating History.

Table of Contents

Ancient Greece

Discovering Lost Stories from Greek History

Introduction

Ancient Greece has long captured the imagination of many, be it historians, scholars, or casual readers. Its history is brimming with tales and legends that speak of great conflicts like the Battle of Thermopylae, stunning architectural wonders like the Parthenon and the many open-air theaters, and a pantheon of mighty gods and heroes who continue to inspire modern fiction. From Leonidas's bravery against the Persians to Homer's beautiful musings, ancient Greece often feels like the birthplace of everything we value—philosophy, democracy, drama, and even the Olympics. However, despite its fame, there is a side to this celebrated ancient civilization that remains hidden or rather overlooked that, when uncovered, could surprise even the most avid history buffs.

Sure, many may be very familiar with Herodotus and his extensive documentation of the Persians; few may be aware of Pytheas, the Greek merchant and explorer who dared to sail beyond the known world. The Greeks were experts in trade, war, and colonization, but they never ventured far beyond their familiar map. Pytheas was among the earliest to have set his sights on something far more ambitious. His voyage led him to the edges of the known world, allowing him to witness various natural phenomena the Greeks initially thought to be nothing more than just stuff of legends. Yet, his story is often overshadowed by the more famous exploits of generals and kings.

Images of the Spartans, clad in their bronze armor and marching with spears, often appear in our minds whenever we think of ancient Greece. Some may have even heard of the city-state's law of discarding infants they deemed unworthy off Mount Taygetus. This grim narrative endured for centuries, but is it even true? The Spartans were certainly merciless, but their history and daily life were far more nuanced—and perhaps even more intriguing. For a city-state famous for its military discipline, the realities of life and death reveal a society that was both brutal and deeply misunderstood.

Apart from their wondrous architecture, the Greeks also had a peculiar obsession with tragedy. Interestingly, this obsession was not only limited to their plays but also to their lives in general. Ancient Greece gave birth to a myriad of figures with the greatest minds, yet so many of them often met ironic or downright bizarre ends. The Stoic philosopher Chrysippus contributed many of his ideas to the ancient civilization, particularly in the realm of physics and ethics. His ironic death, however, soon became a topic of discussion, overshadowing his contributions. An Olympic athlete once won a wrestling match despite dying in the match. These peculiar episodes prove that even death wasn't free from the dramatic flair that shaped so much of their culture.

It is sufficient to say that ancient Greece was more than just feats of gods, monuments, wars, and conquests. The history of civilization is a patchwork of ideas, innovations, and contradictions. This book's purpose is not to revisit the well-trodden paths of Greek history. Instead, it offers a window for those curious enough to take a peek into the overlooked corners, of the stories that remind us that, even in antiquity, humanity was wonderfully complex.

Chapter 1 – The Strange Case of the Athenian Plague

It was 480 BCE, and Xerxes I had been defeated at Salamis, his great ships rammed to pieces by the Greek triremes commanded by Themistocles. This was the day that the Greeks had been waiting for. After years of seeing their lands overrun by the Persians, this victory allowed them to regain the upper hand. Many Greeks were confident that they would never be forced to bow down to the Persians anymore—except for the Athenians.

Athens was worried that it would only be a matter of time before the Persians regrouped and attempted another invasion. So, Athens spearheaded the formation of the Delian League, which comprised key member states such as Chios, Lesbos, Rhodes, Delos, Samos, Naxos, and Thasos. This coalition of Greek city-states was united under a banner of collective defense. The league's aim was to maintain a force formidable enough to meet any Persian resurgence. Member states often contribute ships and immeasurable funds in the name of this goal. These riches were stored in a treasury located in Delos, a sacred island where the league's meetings were held.

However, as the years passed by, it became clear that the Persians were not capable of launching more invasions into Greek territory. The Delian League began to evolve into something altogether different. As tribute from member states flowed into the league's treasury, Athens began to utilize it, turning the riches into a tool for the city's own prestige. Even the treasury was moved from Delos to Athens. This presented a clear message to the member states. Athens was not just a self-proclaimed leader of the alliance; it was, in fact, a hegemon.

Athens entered its golden age because of the funds of the Delian League. Pericles, the city's charismatic leader and statesman, went on an ambitious program of public works to uplift Athens' status. Dozens of monuments were erected, and multiple other construction projects were commissioned. From the Parthenon to the famous Long Walls and the Erechtheion dedicated to both Athena and Poseidon to the sprawling Agora, Athens soon rose as the region's most glorious center of art, philosophy, and, of course, democracy.

However, it is safe to say that this flowering of Athenian culture came at a cost. To the other Greek city-states, Athens' transformation into an empire was not seen as an inspiration. Rather, it alarmed them. Sparta, in particular, was concerned about Athens' growing naval and economic influence; it feared a challenge to its own supremacy in Greece. Sparta was also a staunch supporter of the oligarchy, which differed from Athens' advocacy of democracy. Because of this, as well as a few other factors, a civil war brewed on the horizon where Greeks would fight against Greeks.

What began as nothing more than a skirmish over Corcyra and Potidaea eventually escalated into a full-scale conflict known as the Second Peloponnesian War (also referred to simply as the Peloponnesian War). The war erupted across the Aegean in 431 BCE and was fought between the Delian League, led by Athens, and the Peloponnesian League, which was commanded by Sparta.

The Beginning of Terror

The second year of the war began with the sound of Spartan boots trampling through the plains of Attica. Fertile fields that had once been abundant with olive trees and wheat were torched. The blue skies turned gray as the smoke rose. However, the Spartans, under the command of King Archidamus, were not planning on simply breaching Athens' walls. They knew very well that the Athenians were exceptional architects and that their fortifications were pretty much impenetrable. The mighty Spartans sought another way. They decided to force the city into submission through starvation.

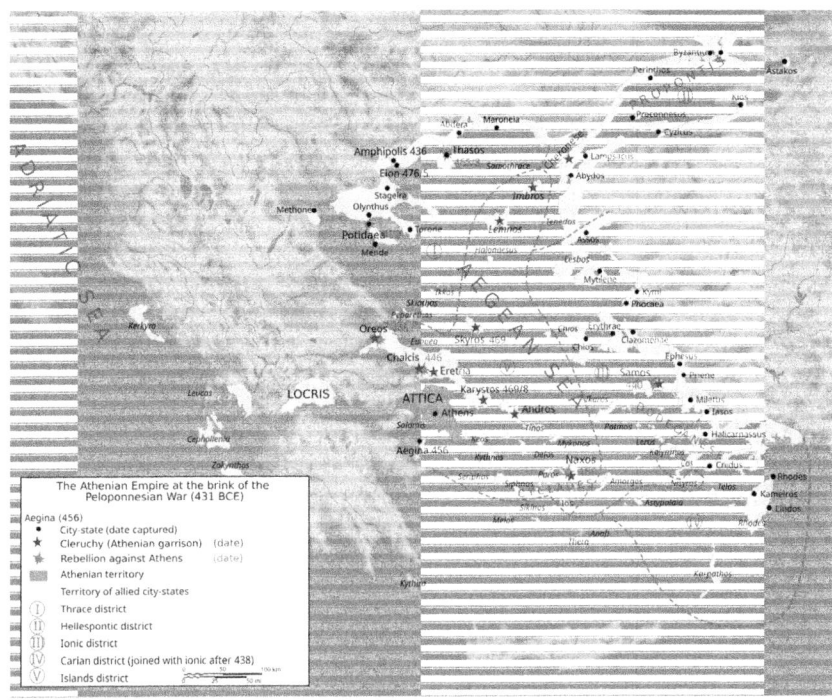

The Athenian Empire by the time the Peloponnesian War erupted.[1]

Pericles had anticipated this move. He ordered the rural populace to abandon their farms and make their way behind the walls of Athens. The Long Walls provided safety. Since the walls stretched to the port of Piraeus four miles away, Athens was able to maintain its naval lifeline. However, the influx of refugees from the countryside strained the city's capacity. This eventually gave way to something far worse than war.

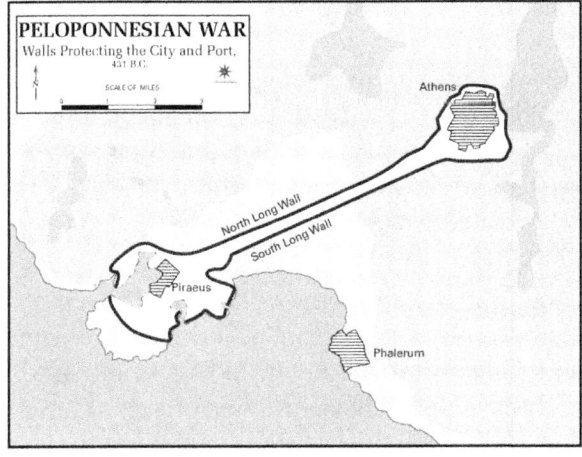

Ancient Athens protected by its Long Walls.[2]

Among the citizens of Athens was a man who was part of the military. Just weeks prior, he had been fighting alongside his comrades. He was used to wounds and scars from the battlefield, but a sudden throng of pain made him worried for his life. At first, he felt a searing pain in his head. It was as though his entire skull was set aflame. His throat then grew extremely parched as fever suddenly terrorized his body. His stomach constantly churned, often emptying itself in violent convulsions. When his body could not take it anymore, the man collapsed.

He was not the only one to have contracted this unknown disease. Almost everyone around him showed the same symptoms: raging fevers, inflamed eyes, diarrhea, ulcerated throats, and extreme thirst. Many succumbed to the disease within days. Despite the man's suffering, he survived. Perhaps as a warning or a guide should the mysterious disease break out again in the future, the man decided to record the nightmare that struck Athens. His name was Thucydides, and in his book *History of the Peloponnesian War*, he described everything in meticulous detail, from the early symptoms of the sickness to the signs of death and even the state of Athens and its populace amidst the plague.

It was believed that the plague arrived via sailors and merchants at the bustling port of Piraeus. The sickness itself, however, was thought to have originated beyond the Greek world. Thucydides claimed that it came from Ethiopia and had made its way to Egypt and Libya before it began ravaging the Athenians.

Thucydides wrote that symptoms typically began in the head. Those who contracted the disease would feel as if their heads were on fire. Their eyes would turn red and inflamed as fever began to make its appearance. The first internal symptoms were equally harrowing: throats turned raw and bloody, tongues swelled, and breaths turned rancid. This, however, was only the beginning of the suffering. From here on, the illness would work its way down. Sneezing was common, and people's throats would become so hoarse that their voices were reduced to rasping gasps. The sickness would then attack the chest. Victims would let out hacking coughs that racked their entire bodies, often leaving them desperately gasping for air.

The heart was not spared from the terror of the disease. Once the sickness seized control of the organ, it induced agonizing convulsions that lasted hours. The victim's body would expel bile in different colors and shades, such as green, yellow, and even black. Those who lasted to this point had to endure episodes of empty retching.

The plague also changed the skin of its victims. Pustules and ulcers would typically emerge, their fiery red color contrasting with the patient's flushed complexion. Their bodies usually did not feel hot to the touch, but the internal burning was indescribable. Oftentimes, those who contracted the disease could not even bear wearing even the thinnest of linen garments; they were so desperate for the cool relief of air or water that they would tear up their clothes or be naked. Ancient records claimed that many hurled themselves into wells or plunged into cold baths in the hopes they could escape from the burning ravaging their body.

The disease also terrorized their instincts. Thirst became an insatiable torment, driving the infected to swing between extremes. Some drank only sparingly, while others gorged themselves on water. Sleep became an unfamiliar term; the patients knew they needed it, but the continuous agony kept them wide awake. Their bodies craved rest, yet their minds would not allow them to sleep; they were trapped in a relentless cycle of exhaustion and despair. The internal burning would eventually reach its boiling point on the seventh or ninth day. From here on, the patients would be free from their suffering as they stepped into a whole different realm: the land of the dead.

As for those lucky enough to survive all of this, the plague delivered a final test—or rather, a final devastating blow. Victims would feel the disease shifting its focus to the belly. Ulcers erupted inside, followed by unforgiving diarrhea. Thucydides noted that this was the worst stage since it drained even the strongest of survivors of their remaining strength. Death came to some, but instead of a sudden strike, it came creeping in slowly.

As more Athenians contracted the disease, many tried to make sense of the origin of the plague. However, fear bred speculation. Whispers soon turned into wild accusations. Since they could not completely fathom why or how such a calamity could strike their great city, many Athenians believed that the Spartans were the ones who caused it. Rumors spread across the dying city that the Spartans spread the disease by poisoning the wells of Piraeus. They thought the plague was an act of war. This suspicion undoubtedly deepened the already bitter relationship between the two city-states.

An illustration of Athens during the plague.[3]

The Spartans continued their campaigns after learning what had happened to Athens. However, they were cautious enough to avoid direct confrontation with the city. The Peloponnesian War, now in its second year, did not stop with the plague. But for the Athenians at that time, the Spartan army was no longer the immediate enemy—the invisible disease was.

For days, Athens witnessed the increasing death of its population. Even the city's physicians, who were highly regarded for their expertise, were left speechless. They found themselves powerless, as their knowledge and remedies proved to be futile. Ironically, their dedication to studying more about their patients and the plague often led to their own demise. The more frequently they interacted with the infected, the more likely they were to contract the plague and succumb to its horrifying symptoms. With no treatment in sight, the Athenians became hopeless.

As the epidemic worsened, fewer and fewer were willing to approach the sick and tend to their condition. This resulted in hundreds dying in isolation, abandoned entirely by their families, friends, and neighbors. The city's air was thick with the stench of decay as bodies were left to rot in the streets and alleyways. The huge number of dead made it impossible for the Athenians to conduct proper burials. Thucydides himself provided a grim picture of Athens during this time, stating that corpses were piled atop one another in public spaces. These bodies were then thrown into mass graves with little to no ceremony. This account is supported by modern archaeology. Excavations near the Kerameikos cemetery revealed a mass grave that contained nearly a thousand skeletons dating between 430 and 426 BCE.

What remains of the Kerameikos cemetery today.'

Perhaps because there was no more land to bury the dead, those tasked with removing the bodies often added them to funeral pyres that were still burning from previous cremations. Once done, they would quickly step back, afraid that the plague would latch onto them next. Thucydides described that even animals refrained from going near the contaminated remains.

Those fortunate enough to have survived the plague were able to let out a small sigh of relief. Not only were they free from the agonizing fever, headache, and diarrhea, but the survivors also seemed to have developed immunity. Thucydides said that these survivors became the caretakers for the sick. Some believed that the gods had given them a second chance, while others simply fostered a deep empathy for the suffering of others.

It is safe to say that the Athenians were deeply religious. Religion was embedded in their culture for as long as they could remember. Yet, as the plague continued to terrorize the city, the Athenians' faith in their gods began to crumble. They began to doubt their religious beliefs. Since the disease struck without exception, sparing neither the devoted nor the impious, many questioned the purpose of their prayers and sacrifices. The same question lingered in their minds as they battled the sickness. If the gods would not protect their devoted subjects, then what was the point in worshiping them?

The temples of Athens experienced a great change. Once filled with various food or objects of offerings and the scent of burning incense, these temples turned into sites of great suffering. Refugees from the countryside, who had been brought into the city to avoid the Spartan invasion, sought shelter wherever they could, including temples. So, the very places where the Athenians had once communed with the heavens became choked with the stench of decay and the echoing howls of the sick.

While they were religious, the Athenians were also highly superstitious, like most Greeks of their time. Some believed that the plague was not an act of war ignited by the Spartans but a divine punishment. There was an oracle who predicted that Apollo himself—the god of prophecy, healing, and diseases—would side with Sparta if the Athenians chose to fight them with all their might. Because of this, many thought that the divine favored their enemies and that the plague was a manifestation of Apollo's wrath.

Of course, not everyone in the city was willing to accept such explanations. Thucydides, for one, approached this claim with skepticism. In contrast to his other contemporaries, Thucydides dismissed the idea that the divine had any hand in unleashing the plague. Instead, he chose to hold strong to the medical theories of his day, particularly those stemming from the school of Hippocrates (a group of ancient Greek physicians and scholars). Led by Hippocrates, the Greek physician who laid the foundation for modern medicine, the school highlighted that diseases arose from natural causes rather than divine intervention. The Hippocratic school also emphasized the balance of bodily humors (blood, phlegm, yellow bile, and black bile). Imbalances in these humors, rather than supernatural causes, were believed to cause illness.

Thucydides preferred to approach the plague with a rational and almost clinical eye. He strove to document its symptoms and progressions through careful observation. He even noted the strange absence of carrion-eating birds and animals in the city when the plague was at its height. He expected these creatures to feast on the unburied corpses scattered throughout the streets of Athens. Yet, he did not see any. This led Thucydides to deduce that they either died after consuming the infected bodies or, driven by instinct, avoided getting near them entirely.

The Athenian Plague in the Eyes of Modern Medicine Practitioners

Despite Thucydides's vivid description of the plague, the Athenian Plague remains both a subject of fascination and debate among historians and medical researchers. Even today, the precise nature of the disease remains unknown, even though scholars have spent centuries trying to uncover its cause. At first, researchers deduced that the illness was an outbreak of the bubonic plague, which was famously known to be the culprit that devastated many populations across Europe and Asia in the medieval age. Yet, after a closer analysis of Thucydides's writings and more research conducted on the outbreak's patterns, new theories emerged.

One of the earliest alternative suggestions made by modern researchers was typhus, a type of bacterial infection typically transmitted by lice. This disease features symptoms that align to some extent with Thucydides's account, such as high fevers, chills, and a characteristic rash. Typus can also spread rapidly, especially in overcrowded and unsanitary locations. This theory, however, is not accepted by everyone. Some doubt this hypothesis due to the absence of certain symptoms, such as the distinctive "rose spots" associated with typhus.

Some scholars and researchers have also drawn similarities between the Athenian Plague and smallpox. Also known for a high fever, smallpox causes pustular rashes and severe internal symptoms, all of which were once experienced by the unfortunate Athenians. However, the rashes from smallpox typically leave survivors with almost permanent scars—a detail missing from Thucydides's account. Measles could also be a contender. This viral disease has a high contagion rate and usually includes symptoms like fever, cough, conjunctivitis, and widespread rash. The only challenge to this theory is the absence of the internal ailments that Thucydides noted in his writings. Severe diarrhea, intense thirst, and bile evacuations are not associated with measles, making it an imperfect fit.

In recent years, scholars have come up with yet another suggestion: viral hemorrhagic fevers such as Ebola or a related pathogen. Thucydides's description of the plague surprisingly bears striking similarities to the symptoms of Ebola, from high fever to severe diarrhea, constant vomiting, and internal bleeding. What made researchers even more confident is that according to Thucydides's notes, the Athenian Plague might have been traced to Africa, specifically Ethiopia, before it spread through Egypt, Libya, and eventually Athens. This geographic origin aligns with the historical prevalence of viral hemorrhagic fevers in sub-Saharan Africa.

The recent outbreaks of Ebola in Africa have shown how the disease can ravage populations in densely packed areas. When the plague struck Athens, the city and its surrounding regions were home to around 250,000 to 300,000 people. The densely packed urban centre itself was home to 140,000 residents, many of whom had fled from the countryside due to the war. Thucydides also noted the absence of scavenger animals during the outbreak, which aligns with observations of modern Ebola outbreaks where animals often stay away from infected bodies and carcasses. There is no definitive evidence that could firmly link the Athenian Plague to Ebola. Without access to ancient DNA or more definitive archaeological evidence, we can only guess. However, the similarities are striking and compelling enough to make it one of the most plausible theories.

What Became of Athens Following the Plague

It is sufficient to say that the Athenian Plague was catastrophic. It left a mark on the city's history. The plague killed around 25 percent of its population, amounting to somewhere between 75,000 and 100,000 people. Other than the staggering death toll, the disease also deeply affected the Athenians' social and moral life. Chaos and despair replaced order and unity, two of the city's greatest virtues.

The plague lasted for three years, likely ending because of the eventual development of herd immunity among survivors and the natural waning of the outbreak over time. However, Thucydides wrote that it took Athens fifteen years to recover its population.

Pericles himself fell victim to the plague. As a figure who had guided Athens through its golden age, his passing was a turning point for the city. Just a year before his passing, Pericles delivered the Funeral Oration. Delivered during the funeral of the fallen soldiers of the Peloponnesian War, the famed speech was intended to inspire both hope and unity among the Athenians during the war. According to Thucydides, in his speech, Pericles praised the valor of Athenian democracy and emphasized the strength of its people. He talked about the ideals of freedom and civic duty while instilling positivity. Yet, even as he spoke, the plague loomed on the horizon, mocking his very optimism.

Pericles's funeral oration.[5]

The political stability in Athens crumbled as the city saw the death of its leader. The Athenians never again saw a leader who could match Pericles's intellect, charisma, and exceptional ability to navigate the complexities of war and internal governance. Athenian politics turned into factionalism, where rival leaders vied for control. Athens became increasingly divided as a result.

Before the sickness arrived and took away Athens' glory, the city was known for its powerful military. Athens had shown its naval might during the First Peloponnesian War (460-445 BCE). The city's fierce fleet of triremes was known throughout the Aegean, and its influence spread across the Mediterranean.

Of course, the city's military strength was not only focused on its navy. Athens was also known for its disciplined hoplites. This unit of heavily armed infantrymen was composed of citizen soldiers. They usually marched into battles wearing linen armor (linothorax) or muscle cuirass, greaves, and the striking Corinthian or Phrygian helmet. Typically armed with a round shield, an eight-foot-long spear, and a two-foot double-edged sword for close combat, the hoplites were instrumental in forming the phalanx formation. This tightly packed formation consisted of rows of soldiers standing shoulder to shoulder. Once in position, the hoplites would then hold their shields so that they overlapped one another. This served as protection for incoming projectiles. They also pointed their spear outward. This formation was especially effective against enemy cavalry and less organized infantry.

Unfortunately for Athens, the plague disrupted its military might. By the time the Second Peloponnesian War erupted in 431 BCE, the city still had its well-trained hoplites and navy. But the moment the plague made its appearance, it ravaged Athens' military power, just as it did the civilian population.

With the disease claiming the lives of many seasoned veterans and newly trained soldiers, it was impossible for the military to maintain its discipline. With fewer able-bodied men to defend the great city, Athens became more reliant on mercenaries and its allies. Mercenaries fought for pay rather than loyalty to Athens, while allies could shift their stance, especially when Athens was in the midst of chaos.

The naval crews, who were once the backbone of Athenian power, also fell victim to the disease. The triremes that had once patrolled the Aegean were left idle at the harbors. Since Athens also relied heavily on the navy to avoid direct land battles with Sparta (the Greek city-state was traditionally dominant on land), the city had no choice but to witness it crumble.

Athens was unable to mount decisive offensives following the plague, which allowed Sparta to gain the upper hand. In 404 BCE, about twenty-seven years following the start of the Second Peloponnesian War, Athens surrendered to Sparta, marking the end of its golden age. The Spartans imposed harsh terms on Athens. They diminished the city's fleet, reducing it to only a few ships, and the Long Walls were torn down. The Athenian Empire was dissolved, and an oligarchic regime was installed. Known as the Thirty Tyrants, the regime was established to govern Athens and the former members of the Delian League.

However, this was not the complete end of Athens. A democratic uprising took place in 403 BCE, which successfully overthrew the Thirty Tyrants. From here on, Athens was able to regain its independence, though the city never succeeded in returning to its former glory.

The Greek world, on the other hand, entered a tumultuous period, with Sparta briefly asserting hegemony over the others. This would change when the Greeks saw the rise of Thebes and, later, Macedon under Philip II and Alexander the Great.

Chapter 2 – The Alexander Conspiracy Theory

Alexander the Great knew no boundaries when it came to war and conquest. As he surveyed the battlefield, he noticed that his army was acting differently. Weary from years of unrelenting campaigns, they were about to face yet another formidable foe—the massive forces of King Porus. When the Battle of Hydaspes commenced in 326 BCE, it immediately became known as one of the fiercest encounters the Macedonians had ever faced. The Macedonian phalanx had to survive not only volleys of arrows and slashes of enemy swords, but it also had to hold its ground against the Indian king's war elephants.

Victory eventually belonged to Alexander and his mighty army, yet it came at a tremendous cost. They faced huge casualties, and combined with fatigue that came after years of endless combat, the soldiers began to fracture. Their morale and fighting spirit were not what they had been at the start of the campaign. The campaign had finally reached its end, not because of external forces but because of issues from within.

Despite winning at Hydaspes, Alexander's men mutinied. Longing for their home, the soldiers refused to march any farther into the Indian subcontinent. Alexander gave a speech to his soldiers, persuading them to continue, but he eventually changed his mind. Claiming that the omens were unfavorable for further advancement into India, the conqueror announced that the campaign was done and that their next stop was home.

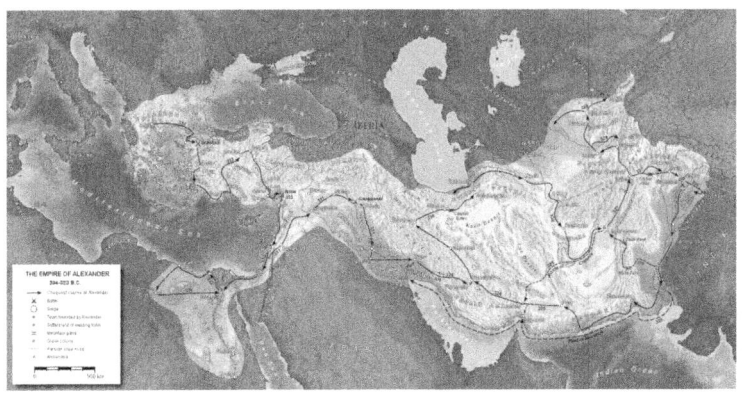

Map detailing Alexander the Great's empire.[6]

However, the march back home was no walk in the park. Alexander's troops had to endure skirmishes, treacherous terrain, deadly sickness, and the punishing weather. They finally reached Babylon in 323 BCE, where the city welcomed its king with celebrations. Some viewed the mighty conqueror as a living god or a man who brought glory to the Macedonian Empire. Others saw him as an unpredictable conqueror whose ambition knew no bounds. Alexander's time in Babylon was full of grand celebrations and more planning for future conquests. But beneath the surface, Alexander was actually a man burdened by loss.

The previous year, Alexander had lost his closest companion and confidant, Hephaestion. Raised together in Macedon and sharing an education under Aristotle, the two were nearly inseparable. Hephaestion was not just a general in Alexander's army; he was also the other half of his soul. There were even whispers that the two were entangled in a romantic relationship. Hephaestion was Alexander's adviser and his mirror; he was the only person who truly saw the complexities of the man who sought to conquer the world.

Alexander and Hephaestion (dressed in red cloak) at the Battle of the Hydaspes.[7]

When Hephaestion died, possibly from typhoid or another illness he contracted during their campaigns, Alexander was plunged into a deep depression. His grief was indescribable. He saw to it that Hephaestion was honored with extravagant funerary rites and declared that his friend would be worshiped as a hero. There was also a shrine dedicated to Hephaestion in Babylon. Alexander even went as far as to petition the oracle at Siwa to deify Hephaestion.

Alexander was said to have withdrawn from his court and those surrounding him. He refused to eat for days. Ancient sources recorded that the mighty conqueror was so consumed by sorrow that he would lie on Hephaestion's bed, often weeping inconsolably. At this point, those around him were sure that Hephaestion's death had left a void inside the conqueror that no amount of glory or conquest could ever fill. As the months passed, Alexander began to feel his health deteriorating.

The Fall of the Great Conqueror

In the spring of 323 BCE, Alexander hosted a grand banquet. It was a celebration held for his admiral, Nearchus, who had successfully explored the Indian Ocean and returned with tales of its marvels and riches. The feast was unsurprisingly extravagant; it was hosted by the conqueror of the known world. There was music and wine as Alexander's closest generals and loyal companions mingled. However, this night of revelry would soon turn into a tragedy.

Although accounts vary, many ancient sources suggest that Alexander drank excessively that night. The Greek historian Plutarch, for one, wrote that Alexander even joined a drinking contest where he consumed enormous amounts of unmixed wine. The consequences of this were severe. Alexander woke up the next day with sharp abdominal pains that continued to worsen as the hours passed. It was said that the stabbing pain was so intense that the conqueror, who had survived through the harshest of wars, howled in agony. His attendants could only watch helplessly as he clutched his stomach, screaming for the pain to subside.

Days later, his condition had become even worse. A fever soon took hold of him, absorbing whatever strength Alexander had left. Eventually, the Macedonian king became bedridden, unable to rise, let alone oversee his vast empire. His attendants, physicians, and generals took turns crowding him over the days. They were desperate to ease his suffering, yet their efforts were all in vain.

His inability to speak in his final days left many puzzled. However, it is possible that it stemmed from an old injury that he sustained during the siege of Cyropolis years earlier. During the siege, Alexander was struck in the neck by an enemy projectile. Although not fatal at the time, the effect was perhaps delayed; it could have left lingering damage that compromised his ability to speak under extreme stress or illness. Nevertheless, as the fever ravaged his body, his vocal cords gave up.

Alexander was acquainted with paranoia in the days before his death. The conqueror had always been a man who believed in omens and divine signs. Plutarch described an omen that foretold the misfortune that was about to befall the Macedonian king. He told stories of a flock of ravens circling over the palace in Babylon before falling dead at Alexander's feet. Another story involved Alexander's prized lion, who was inexplicably kicked to death by a mule, a creature often associated with sterility and bad luck.

There was also another prophecy that talked about Alexander's impending doom, though Alexander likely never realized this until his death. Known as the prophecy of Calanus, it involved an Indian sage who accompanied Alexander's campaign in India. According to ancient records, Calanus chose to voluntarily self-immolate (an act of setting oneself on fire) upon discovering that he was ill. The sage claimed that he would prefer to die with dignity rather than be a nuisance. However, before he departed, Calanus was said to have cryptically told Alexander, "We shall meet in Babylon." His words were dismissed at the time. However, as Alexander's health worsened following his return to Babylon, the prophecy took on a chilling significance.

Alexander was more or less a living corpse by the ninth day of his illness. He could no longer move. The once mighty conqueror only lay in his bed, barely conscious, while surrounded by his grieving generals and loyal companions. His fever reached its peak on the tenth day. Alexander finally breathed his last. It was believed that his generals remained by his side, perhaps waiting for a sign of recovery. It never happened.

Interestingly, ancient sources wrote that Alexander's body did not decay for six days following his passing. Plutarch, ever superstitious, and other historians suggest this was strong evidence of his divine lineage.

The Poisoning of Alexander

It is not surprising that the idea of divine retribution captivated several ancient writers. Although Alexander was a man of superstition, he could not refrain from doing actions that were considered an affront to the heavens. His claim of divine ancestry, his deification, and his disregard for sacred customs, including the burning of the palace at Persepolis and adopting Persian practices, were thought by some to be acts of arrogance that invited divine retribution. While this concept of divine wrath gave a rather poetic explanation to the mighty conqueror's mysterious death, other scholars and historians suggest a more earthly culprit: poison.

Poisoning was one of the most effective methods of eliminating powerful rivals in the ancient world. Since it often left little trace, this subtle weapon often became the choice of those seeking to seize power in the court. As for Alexander, his sudden illness and death happened during a time when his empire was fraught with tension, both political and familial. One suspect that might have played a role in his death was Antipater, one of Alexander's former allies.

Antipater once served as regent of Macedon when Alexander was away campaigning in Asia. With the king's absence, it was up to Antipater to oversee Macedon. He was a trusted figure at first, but his relationship with Alexander began to take a negative turn in the later years of the campaign. Alexander, despite clashing with the Persians day and night during his campaign, surprisingly grew fond of their culture. When he began adopting Persian customs, the conqueror made an enemy out of Antipater, whose loyalty to the Macedonian aristocracy was unmatched. These two became increasingly estranged.

Tensions soon reached a boiling point when Antipater's son, Cassander, visited the Macedonian king's court in Babylon, acting as a representative of his father. Cassander was said to have expressed dissatisfaction over Alexander's adoption of the Persian practice of *proskynesis* (the act of bowing or prostrating oneself before the king). Enraged, Alexander grabbed Cassander by his hair and slammed him against the wall. This humiliation undoubtedly broadened the rift between the king and his Macedonian elites, particularly Cassander and Antipater.

Some claim that Antipater, having seen the conqueror growing erratic as the days went by, began to see Alexander's death as the only way to secure his influence. His reputation was smeared in 324 BCE when

Alexander dismissed him as regent, passing the position to Craterus, another one of Alexander's most trusted generals and companions. Through another one of his sons, Iollas, who served as Alexander's cupbearer, Antipater poisoned the Macedonian king while he was at the grand banquet held for Nearchus.

However, the exact poison used (if he was indeed killed by poison) remains a subject of speculation. Some suggest it contained hemlock since it was a well-known and readily available poison in the ancient world; this was the very same poison drunk by the famous Greek philosopher Socrates. Although hemlock can cause paralysis and respiratory failure, its effects are usually immediate. It took Alexander ten days to die, so hemlock seems unlikely. Others have suggested that the poison was made from ergot, a toxic fungus that grows on cereals. This poison causes high fevers, vomiting, and death in severe cases. However, while ergotism might explain some symptoms, such as fever, it does not account for Alexander's sharp abdominal pain or the gradual loss of motor functions.

Strychnine, a rare but potent poison, is another possibility. Since it could have been easily masked in wine, it would have been very difficult for Alexander or his attendant to detect it. However, its effects are completely different from what the king experienced. Instead of causing a high fever, the poison typically leads to convulsions. The white hellebore might be a better candidate. While the plant was known among the Greeks for both its medicinal and toxic properties, those who consumed it in large quantities could experience severe abdominal pain, vomiting, diarrhea, and fever—all of which matched the symptoms of Alexander before he passed away. Hellebore poisoning also aligns with the timeline of his decline, as it often leads to a protracted and painful death. White hellebore does not cause a loss of speech or motor functions, but scholars answered this mystery by suggesting that these symptoms were exacerbated by his previous injuries, particularly the neck wound sustained during the Siege of Cyropolis.

Plausible Diseases That Killed the Conqueror

Although speculation of foul play surrounds Alexander's death, it is plausible that the Macedonian king did not depart the world as a result of political intrigue. Alexander lived a life full of relentless military campaigns, which often rewarded him with immense physical and emotional stress. All those years of marching through hostile environments might have eventually weakened his immune system. The Indian campaign that he launched during the last few years of his life had pushed not only his army to its limits but also his own body. Coupled with the loss of Hephaestion, which added another layer of emotional strain, it could be possible that the conqueror succumbed to death because of an illness.

Scholars and historians have pointed to several diseases as likely candidates for Alexander's death. One of them is the West Nile virus. If this virus really was the culprit, then Plutarch's account about birds dying in Babylon around the time Alexander's death was near—a story that has long been interpreted as a dramatic embellishment—might actually reflect a real event. Birds are known to be the carriers of the West Nile virus. Their deaths could indicate the presence of the disease in Babylon at the time. The virus is typically transmitted to humans through mosquito bites. Babylon was surrounded by marshlands and abundant mosquitoes. Thus, we could assume that Alexander might have been infected by the virus during his stay in the city.

The only problem with this hypothesis is that many aspects of Alexander's symptoms did not align with the virus. While fever is a common sign of the West Nile virus, the virus can also cause delirium or confusion. No historical accounts ever suggest that the Macedonian king experienced such symptoms. Paralysis and coma are rather rare symptoms, even in fatal West Nile virus cases.

Another possible candidate is malaria, which was endemic to Mesopotamia. Since the Euphrates River flowed through Babylon, it could be plausible that the city was a prime breeding ground for malaria-carrying mosquitoes. Alexander could have contracted the disease when he was in the city or perhaps even earlier in his campaign, with the infection growing fatal later on. Alexander started off with a fever, which fits one of the symptoms of malaria. If the disease gets severe, malaria can also cause neurological complications, which would explain Alexander's gradual loss of motor functions and his eventual coma before his death. However, malaria never causes sharp abdominal pains.

The ancient world was also familiar with typhoid fever, another fatal disease that often ravaged the lives of many. Since this disease is spread through contaminated food and water, typhoid became a constant threat, especially in densely populated cities like Babylon. Alexander's severe fever, abdominal pain, and eventual loss of key bodily functions align with the symptoms of a typhoid infection. Alexander's neurological decline could have been the result of encephalitis (inflammation of the brain), which is one of the complications of typhoid.

This theory is accepted by many since typhoid is known to have the ability to cause intestinal perforation, which would explain the sudden onset of sharp abdominal pain that Alexander suffered from. A ruptured bowel would have caused immense pain and rapidly worsened his condition, eventually leading to his demise. The only challenge to this theory is that a perforated bowel usually happens in later stages of a typhoid infection; Alexander experienced this much earlier.

Alexander as a Prisoner of His Own Body

There is another theory surrounding his death, which is far more unsettling than the rest. Some scholars suggest that the mighty conqueror did not actually die when those around him pronounced him dead. Instead, he was afflicted with a rare and severe neurological disorder known to us today as Guillain-Barré syndrome (GBS). If this theory holds any truth at all, the implications are rather chilling. Alexander the Great might have been alive the entire time but trapped in his own body. He could do nothing as the world mourned him and made preparations for his burial.

GBS is a condition in which the body's immune system mistakenly attacks the nervous system, causing progressive neurological damage. One would feel extreme weakness taking over their body or tingling in the limbs that eventually escalates to severe paralysis. As the disease goes on, GBS will typically impair breathing, speech, and even movement. In the end, the patient will be rendered almost completely immobile. Although they cannot move a muscle or even let out the faintest whisper to communicate their plight, those suffering from GBS are actually fully conscious and aware. GBS can also develop after certain infections, including typhoid fever and acute necrotizing pancreatitis, both of which have been suggested as possible causes of Alexander's illness.

This theory also explains a certain detail recorded in ancient accounts. According to these sources, Alexander's body did not decompose for several days after his death. While some believed this was because of his almost divine status, scholars suggest this was because Alexander was never dead to begin with. In the ancient world, death was not determined by checking for a pulse or brain activity; instead, it was determined by the cessation of breathing. If Alexander had GBS, the condition would have caused near-total paralysis, including a slowing of his breathing to the point where it became imperceptible to those around him. The paralysis would have reduced his body's need for oxygen. This would have made his minimal breathing appear even less noticeable. Alexander might have appeared lifeless to those at his "deathbed." They could not see the conqueror's chest rising and falling, but in reality, he was still breathing, albeit very slowly. His heart never stopped beating, and his organs were still functioning, preventing any sort of body decomposition.

This theory reveals a deeply disturbing possibility. Alexander the Great, the mighty ruler who conquered the known world, was helpless in his final moments. He was aware that his coffin was being made. He heard his attendants and loyal companions weeping for his fate, yet the once unstoppable, almost divine conqueror could not even open his eyes or give the smallest signal as physicians prematurely declared him dead. He might have been a prisoner of his own failing body, treated as a corpse while his mind remained intact. The king, whose voice had commanded thousands of armies and whose actions had shaped the course of history, could do nothing in the end except wait for his eventual death, perhaps days after he was declared dead.

Chapter 3 – The Legendary Battle of Marathon

Under the reign of King Darius I, the Persian Empire rose to become one of the most powerful forces to ever exist in the ancient world. Its territories stretched from the edges of India to the shores of the Aegean, with each region guarded by a fierce army that was once feared by many. Yet, the Persians were rarely free from challenges, especially on the western fringes of their empire. By the late 5th century BCE, the spark of defiance was clearly in the air, leading to a conflict that would soon alter the course of history: the Ionian Revolt.

The Ionian Greeks inhabited the areas along the western coast of Anatolia. Ever since Cyrus the Great's successful conquest of the Kingdom of Lydia (sometime in 547 BCE), the Ionians were put under Persian rule. The Ionians were allowed a degree of autonomy, but they were also forced to pay tribute to the Persians. Tensions began to simmer beneath the surface. Eventually, these tensions began to reach a boiling point. Desiring independence, the Ionians, led by the city of Miletus, rose in rebellion against the Persians in 499 BCE. One of their earliest acts of defiance included the burning of the Persian regional capital at Sardis, which undoubtedly enraged Darius I.

However, the Ionians knew that in order to fully go against the mighty Persians, they needed a stronger force. So, they sought aid from mainland Greece. Without hesitation, Athens and Eretria responded to their call. The two city-states sent ships and troops to support the Ionians, further drawing the ire of the Persian king.

Unfortunately, the revolt ended in failure by 494 BCE. The Persians decisively defeated the rebels at the Battle of Lade. As a result, Miletus, the heart of the revolt, was destroyed. Its once-thriving harbor became nothing more than a thing of the past. Its people were forced to face their nightmare as they were taken into slavery. However, the consequences of the revolt were not limited to the lands of Ionia. Darius was furious at the Greeks' interference, particularly the Athenians and the Eretrians, and wanted to punish them. According to Herodotus, Darius's anger toward the Athenians was so great that he ordered one of his servants to say "Master, remember the Athenians," three times before his dinner every day.

This anger resulted in the first Persian invasion of Greece. Apart from being an act of punishment for both Athens and Eretria, Darius was also determined to expand Persian dominance over the entire Greek mainland, sending a clear message to those who dared to challenge him. Without wasting too much time, Darius sent a preliminary expedition in 492 BCE, which sought to secure the northern regions of Greece and establish a foothold for a larger campaign. Led by Mardonius, the expedition achieved some success before misfortune struck. Perhaps sent by Poseidon himself, storms arrived near Mount Athos, ravaging the Persian fleet.

Never known to back down that easily, Darius launched another campaign two years later. This time around, the campaign was spearheaded by Datis and Artaphernes. The Persian fleet sailed across the Aegean, hoping they could avoid the wrath of the Greek god of the sea. As if luck was on their side, the Persians were able to capture a few islands and establish garrisons along the way. Eretria fell swiftly to the Persian advance. Not planning on showing mercy, especially with its involvement in aiding Ionia, the Persians sacked the city. Temples were burned, and the population was enslaved.

With Eretria subjugated, the Persians turned to their main target: Athens. The Persians marched toward the city, displaying both the empire's vast resources and organizational might. The army commanded by Datis and Artaphernes was said to have numbered about twenty-five thousand infantry, supported by seasoned cavalry and another fleet of hundreds of ships. In contrast, the Athenians only had roughly ten thousand hoplites to spare, each armed with spears and shields.

The sheer size of the Persian army, combined with its reputation for annihilating its enemies, made the coming confrontation seem like a hopeless endeavor to the Athenians. However, the Athenians were not dissuaded. Like the Ionians, the Athenians knew that they needed not just strategy but also reinforcements to defeat such a colossal army. And so, the Athenian generals turned to their most powerful ally, Sparta. The Spartans were, after all, formidable soldiers, and with their support, Athens could have a chance at tipping the scales in their favor.

Since the two Greek city-states were over 130 miles apart, the Athenian military had to dispatch a *hemerodromos*, a type of courier, to deliver their request for aid to the Spartans. They chose a man named Philippides for this task. He was thought to have been the best among the *hemerodromoi* (plural for *hemerodromos*). Not only did he have experience traversing the rugged terrain of ancient Greece, but Philippides also had unmatched stamina and endurance, allowing him to cover hundreds of miles in a matter of days.

Philippides's task was rather straightforward: run to Sparta, deliver the message, and return to Athens with their answer. However, the journey was grueling. He had to run through rocky trails and make his way through sun-scorched plains and dense forests. Fatigue undoubtedly weighed heavily on his body as the miles wore on. Yet, Philippides knew that Athens' fate rested on his shoulders. And so, he pushed forward. Suddenly, a faint voice came out of the dense forest, calling out his name. Philippides halted, but his heart continued to race.

The *hemerodromos* was left speechless when he realized that the voice came from the god Pan, who stood before him. Pan, with his goat-like legs and horns, was the Greek god of the wilderness, shepherds, and hunters. Unlike the Olympian gods who ruled from Mount Olympus, Pan called the wilderness his domain since he was, more or less, the embodiment of the untamed forces of nature. His presence was also believed by the Greeks to have the ability to instill terror; the term "panic" was derived from the god's name.

"The Athenians once worshiped me as they do the Olympians," Pan said to Philippides. "But tell me, Philippides, why did they stop when I have aided them in the past?"

After finding the courage to finally speak, Philippides responded to the god. Knowing that the Athenians needed all the help they could muster—both mortal and divine—he reassured Pan that the Athenians would soon honor the god with shrines and temples again. He then expressed his hope for the god to aid Athens should the time come.

"Very well," Pan responded. "You may go now. I will lend my hand to the Athenians as I have before."

This legendary encounter was recorded by the ancient historian Herodotus. Although Herodotus is widely known today as the "Father of History," his accounts often blended fact with myth and oral tradition. This was a common practice among many writers of his time.

Philippides then continued his journey, eventually reaching Sparta. Without wasting a second, the *hemerodromos* made his way to the Spartan officials and delivered Athens' plea. He explained the imminent threat that loomed over Greece and Athens' dire need for Spartan warriors to join them at Marathon. Although the Spartans agreed to lend their spears, there was a problem. The battle was about to begin at the same time as the Carneia festival, a sacred period during which Spartan law prohibited military action until the full moon. Sparta was also in the midst of internal unrest. There was news of a potential revolt brewing among the Messenians. So, despite being willing to fight the Persians alongside the Athenians, the Spartans could not send their army at that moment. They did, however, promise to march after the festival's conclusion. The Spartans ended up arriving a day after the battle took place.

A 17ᵗʰ-century drawing of Pan, currently held at the National Gallery of Art, Washington, DC.[8]

Although disappointed with the answer, Philippides hurried back to Athens so that he could deliver Sparta's response to the officials. Once safe behind the walls of the city, Philippides recounted his experiences to the Athenian generals. He told them all about Sparta's decision and his encounter with the god Pan. The Athenians believed every one of his words. In their eyes, his encounter with the god was a sign of divine favor. The Athenians worked to honor the god. Shrines and temples were constructed in Pan's name, and rituals were performed to worship him.

The Battle Commenced

The Persians reached the plains of Marathon in early September 490 BCE. To them, the location of the battlefield was strategic. The flat land was spread between the mountains and the sea. The Persians could use it to their advantage by deploying their fierce cavalry to overwhelm their enemies. For days following their arrival, the Persians raided nearby villages. Datis and Artaphernes spent day and night preparing their forces and waited patiently for the Athenians to respond.

Meanwhile, in Athens, the population braced itself for the clash. The Athenian army, which numbered only ten thousand, was put under the command of generals Callimachus and Miltiades, both of whom were extremely experienced in the art of war. Despite the fact that they were greatly outnumbered by the Persians, the Athenians were able to remain hopeful due to their knowledge of the terrain—and perhaps the divine favor of the gods.

After ensuring everything was prepared, the Athenian army began marching to Marathon. Miltiades played a key role in the battle, not only because he was a seasoned general but also because he had once served under the Persians themselves. He even accompanied the Persian army during Darius I's campaign against the Scythians in 513 BCE. All those years fighting with the enemy allowed him to understand the Persians' strengths and weaknesses. Miltiades devised a bold strategy to counter the Persians' numerical advantage. Relying on the discipline and superior training of the famous Greek phalanx, the Athenians focused on strengthening their flanks.

An illustration of the Greek hoplites marching in phalanx formation.[9]

This deliberately thinned the center of their formation, but it was a calculated risk. Miltiades anticipated that the Persians, confident in their numerical superiority, would exploit the weakened center and push forward aggressively. By drawing the Persian forces into the center, the Athenians could envelop them with their stronger flanks. The disciplined Greek hoplites on the wings would hold firm and then pivot inward, creating a pincer movement to trap the Persians in a double envelopment. This maneuver would make use of the Greeks' strength in close combat, as the well-trained hoplites could easily overwhelm the lighter Persian infantry. The plan was bold and ambitious. If it was executed correctly, Athens could live to see another day.

The battle began at dawn, with the Athenian hoplites charging down the slopes. Clad in bronze armor and armed with spears and shields, they attacked the Persians as if there would be no tomorrow. After all, the Athenians had to win the battle, or Athens might crumble entirely since the city had no more soldiers to spare should the Persians decide to attack the city itself. The Persians did not hold back; they launched volleys of arrows as the Athenians advanced. This, however, failed to disrupt the Athenians' momentum since the Greek hoplites were covered in heavy armor.

The Athenian troops charging into the Battle of Marathon.[10]

Legend has it that the god Pan was present the entire time. The god observed the battle from a cave near the field. Perhaps true to his promise to Philippides earlier, Pan was believed to have eventually intervened in the battle, lending his divine assistance to the Athenians. But at the beginning, he lay low, waiting for the right moment to strike fear into the hearts of the ambitious invaders.

The battle raged for hours, and for a moment, the Athenian center started to falter under the relentless assault of the Persians. With their superior numbers, the Persians pressed hard, hoping they could break the Greek lines entirely. The Greeks, refusing to back down, were holding their ground when they suddenly noticed a figure emerging on the battlefield out of nowhere. According to ancient records by Herodotus and Pausanias, this mysterious figure was Echetlaeus (Hero of the Plowshare).

Pausanias claimed that Echetlaeus had an archaic and otherworldly demeanor. Instead of wearing heavy armor and a helmet similar to the hoplites, his clothes were rather simple and rustic. He looked like a farmer but had the frame of a bodybuilder. The mysterious warrior also wielded an *echetlon* or a plowshare, which he swung around with a precision that bordered on the supernatural. Each strike was precise; Pausanias recorded that Echetlaeus cut down the Persians without difficulty as he swiftly moved through the chaotic battlefield.

Herodotus added a haunting detail to the tale. On the battlefield was an Athenian soldier who went by the name Epizelus. He fought bravely on the front lines, but something extraordinary occurred that changed his fate. Herodotus claimed that Epizelus suddenly turned blind even though he had never been struck by a weapon. The last thing he saw was a mysterious muscular man—neither an Athenian nor a Persian soldier—with a beard so long that it covered his entire shield. It was believed that the cause of his sudden blindness was the result of divine energy that came from Echetlaeus striking down a Persian soldier next to him.

Seeing that the gods were on their side on the battlefield, the Athenians pushed on and executed Miltiades's brilliant strategy. While the center steadied and held its ground, the stronger wings of the Athenian formation enveloped the Persian sides. This was the moment when the Athenians successfully broke through the enemy's ranks, driving them into disarray. The Persian soldiers, now hemmed in on all sides, began to fear that they might not leave the battlefield alive.

As if there was some kind of cue, the god of wilderness, Pan, was believed to have taken the chance to intervene. He sent waves of panic through the Persian ranks. Some even claim that the god himself appeared before the Persians, his wild eyes and goat-like legs and horns instilling fear into the hearts of the invaders to the point where they broke formation and scrambled toward their ships in desperation. It was a chaotic scene, with the panicked Persians trampling one another, desperate to leave the battlefield.

And so, victory belonged to the Athenians. While the Athenians only lost 192 soldiers, the Persians left behind a far more staggering number of casualties. Herodotus, who was prone to exaggeration, recorded that the Persians lost about 6,400 men in total.

Upon seeing the Persian forces retreat, the Athenians thought it would be good to spread the news of their victory to the rest of the city-states. Philippides was summoned once more and tasked with delivering the message to Athens. Exhilarated by the triumph, Philippides immediately set off on yet another grueling journey. He ran for nearly twenty-six miles from Marathon to Athens. Upon reaching the city-state, Philippides was said to have burst into the assembly and proclaimed "Χαίρετε, νικῶμεν" (*Chairete, nikomen*—"Hail, we win!") before collapsing to the ground and dying of exhaustion.

A depiction of a runner, possibly Philippides, arriving in Athens to announce the victory at Marathon.[11]

Celebrations were in order for the great victory, yet the Athenian soldiers could not help but think about the mysterious figure who had appeared on the battlefield to assist them in turning the tide against the mighty Persians. Despite their efforts to look for Echetlaeus, the Athenians failed to find him; it was as if he had vanished into thin air. Perplexed, the Athenians turned to the Oracle of Delphi. As the most sacred authoritative source of divine wisdom in Greece, the oracle must have some answers about the mysterious figure. However, when asked about Echetlaeus's identity and whereabouts, the oracle simply replied that it was the will of the gods that the Athenians honor him as a hero. The Athenians did not question any further. Eager to fulfill the gods' will, they erected marble monuments to commemorate the mysterious warrior. His depiction can be seen today in the Stoa Poikile (Painted Portico) in Athens, where his image was carved alongside other heroes of Marathon.

Although the Athenians were satisfied with the oracle's answer, the mystery surrounding Echetlaeus captivated many others, especially historians and mythologists. Research and theories have emerged to uncover the truth behind who the muscular hero who fought at Marathon really was. His name offered the first clues. Derived from the Greek word *echetlon*, which means "plowshare," the name Echetlaeus literally translates to "he of the plowshare." This association with a farming tool led many to believe that Echetlaeus symbolized the agrarian roots of Greek society; he represented the strength of the common people who toiled the land and defended their homeland.

Of course, many also came to the conclusion that Echetlaeus was not a mortal warrior. Some ancient accounts suggest that he was a divine being sent by none other than Pan, who had given his word to Philippides that he would help the Athenians. Although Pan was known for his unpredictable nature and power to cause panic in his enemies, some suggest that the god might have taken a physical form on the battlefield to fulfill his promise.

A depiction of Echetlaeus fighting with his plow carved onto an Etruscan funerary urn.[12]

Others associated Echetlaeus with the goddess Demeter and Persephone, both of whom were considered central figures in Greek mythology. While Demeter was the goddess of agriculture and the harvest—fitting the appearance of Echetlaeus, who looked like a farmer—Persephone was the queen of the underworld. In this interpretation, the mysterious warrior was seen as a manifestation of their divine influence, a protector of the land and its people in a battle fought on the soil they deeply respected. Some even suggested that the plowshare symbolized Demeter's dominion over the earth and the idea of renewal after destruction.

Unfortunately, despite these theories, the true nature of Echetlaeus remains a mystery. We will likely never be sure whether he was just a farmer inspired to fight and defend his homeland, a strong hero whose deeds were mythologized, or even a divine emissary sent by the gods, but we can safely say that Echetlaeus represents the enduring Greek belief in the intertwining of the mortal and the divine.

As for the Persians, the Battle of Marathon was not their last clash with the Greeks. A decade later, in 480 BCE, the Persians, under Darius's son, Xerxes I, would embark on a larger campaign in Greece. These episodes of war brought forth another set of new heroes and legendary battles, including the popular stand of Leonidas and his three hundred Spartans at Thermopylae, as well as Themistocles's outstanding naval strategy at Salamis.

Chapter 4 – Spartan Myths, Misconceptions, and Untold Stories

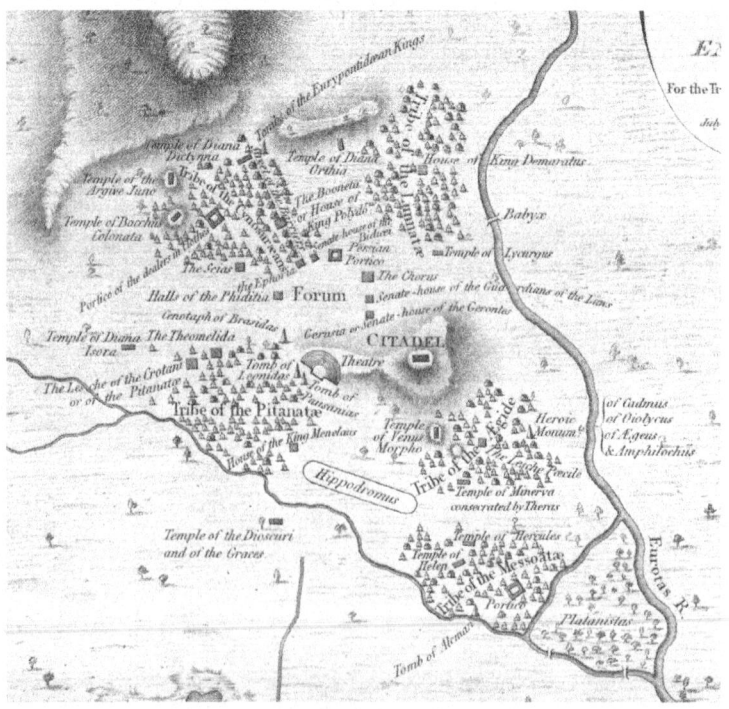

An old map of classical Sparta.[18]

The silence of dusk was shattered with the sudden cry of a newborn. Born into a modest Spartan family, the child was cradled by his dear mother, who held him close to her chest. The baby soon calmed down. He cooed softly, eventually drifting into a deep sleep. The mother smiled but only for a moment, as she could not ignore the tension that had been hanging heavy in the room. Sparta had a law where every child must be judged for their worthiness to live.

The father carefully took the boy into his arms. Nodding to his wife as if to tell her everything would be fine, he walked out of their humble home and set out toward the Lesche. Other than being a public gathering place typically used by elders, citizens, and philosophers for discussions, storytelling, and making civic or political decisions, the Lesche was also where Spartan elders would gather to determine the fate of newborns.

The father was hesitant as he made his way through the village, his heart beating even faster the moment he laid eyes on Mount Taygetus looming in the distance. According to ancient tales, the mountain's peak, also known as Taleton, was a place of reverence. It was dedicated to Zeus and the god of the sun, Helios. The peak was once a place of sacred rituals, where horses were sacrificed in the name of the gods. However, for many Spartans, the mountain was significant for another reason; it was believed to be a site where unworthy infants were left to die at a chasm down below.

When the father arrived at the Lesche, he immediately saw the elders. The Spartans lived by the belief that the city's survival depended on the physical and moral excellence of its people. Thus, it was of the utmost importance for the elders to examine the baby thoroughly. They checked for signs of sickness, deformity, and frailty. The father could only watch as the elders did this. The father could not help but think of his neighbor's unfortunate child. Just a week earlier, the elders had deemed the child unworthy. His neighbor was ordered to discard his newborn at the chasm of Mount Taygetus.

The father was brought back to reality when one of the elders called his name. They announced that his son was indeed strong and healthy, showing potential that he could one day serve the city.

"You must raise him well," one of the elders said.

The father, forever thankful to the gods, could finally let out a huge sigh of relief. He took his son into his arms, eager to return home and deliver the good news to his dear wife.

However, one question remains. Did the Spartans really practice this? Or was it nothing more than a myth told by ancient sources or enemies of the city-state to exaggerate Sparta's image as a cold and calculating society?

Archaeologists have uncovered forty-six human remains at the foot of Mount Taygetus. But interestingly, none of them belonged to infants. All of the bones that were discovered, which were dated to the 6th and 5th centuries BCE, actually belonged to individuals over the age of eighteen. This physical evidence contradicts the stories of how the Spartans left their unworthy babies in the chasm. Scholars suggest that instead of infants, the Spartans might have thrown criminals and prisoners off the mountain as a form of punishment. After all, Sparta was known to have dealt with criminals harshly, so the use of the mountain for such a purpose fits more closely with what is known about their justice system.

An 18th-century painting depicting a scene where infants were being judged by the Spartan elders.[14]

While the story is most likely a myth that stems from the cultural perception of Sparta as a militaristic state—they valued physical perfection above all else—infant exposure was not unfamiliar in the ancient world. In certain Greek city-states, it was practiced, albeit only occasionally. Although it was by no means the norm, the Greeks resorted to this in response to severe deformities or extreme poverty. Athens, for one, allowed fathers to leave their unwanted infants, especially illegitimate or severely deformed children, in public spaces. Some sources claim that these infants were first put into jars or a clay pot before being left on the roadway. Babies who were lucky enough would be saved by passersby, while the rest would have to face their demise slowly.

Mount Taygetus as seen from Sparta.[15]

This practice of exposing a child to the elements or outright killing a child was not only limited to Greece; it also happened in other parts of the ancient world. At times, it was done as part of a religious practice or for population control. The Carthaginians, for instance, were said—or rather accused since there is no concrete evidence to prove it—to have sacrificed children in the name of their gods. Ancient China and India also participated in infanticide, though it was usually done for females. In ancient China, these unfortunate female babies were typically drowned, suffocated, or starved to death. There were also cases where they were placed in baskets and hung on trees, where they would die from the elements or starve to death.

However, despite the existence of these practices, the idea that Sparta systematically discarded infants who they deemed unworthy seems to be an exaggeration of Spartan culture. This claim might have been crafted by their enemies to paint a harsh picture of the Spartans.

The Krypteia

Meanwhile, far in the Spartan countryside, an episode of murder would take place. It began with a laborer who was perhaps walking home after a long day's work. It was obvious that the weight of exhaustion slowed his steps as he trudged along the dirt path between the fields. Suddenly, he caught a sight of something ominous. Squinting into the shadows, the laborer could see a figure slumped against a gnarled olive tree. He looked at the figure for a few seconds, yet there were no signs of any movement. With his heart pounding, the laborer crept closer, letting his curiosity take over him.

It was a lifeless body. The laborer had seen the dead man before. He was one of the helots (the enslaved class) and was known to be a leader among the Messenian rebels. Beneath the body was a pool of blood, and as the laborer's eyes moved up, he noticed that the poor helot had his throat slashed. The laborer quickly took a step back. He knew very well that this was the work of the Krypteia. Not wanting to meddle in their affairs, the laborer made haste to his home, hoping he could erase the image of the dead helot from his mind.

The Krypteia worked silently in the shadows, yet everyone in Sparta knew of them. They did not target random civilians or laborers—only helots. This was the subjugated class who toiled on the fields and fed the Spartan war machine. Without them to work on the fields, the Spartan society would crumble. But why were the helots treated as if they were criminals? In the eyes of the Spartans, the helots were a threat to the fragile balance that kept Sparta intact.

The Spartans had a hierarchy. At the top were the Spartiates, the full male citizens who had gone through the military training known as the agoge. Next in the hierarchy were the Perioeci. These were the free men who lived in neighboring cities and villages under the governance of Sparta. They lived their lives working as craftsmen and traders and produced various other goods. They handled much of the economic activity that the Spartiates themselves avoided. The Perioeci, however, only had political rights in their own cities. They did not hold any in the state of Sparta itself; these rights were reserved exclusively for the Spartiates. At the bottom of the pyramid were the helots. These people, who often hailed from Messenia and Laconia, had been conquered by Sparta.

Of course, these people had not always been slaves. Before they had been captured, they were free. They could work their lands without fear and live a normal life. It all changed when Sparta came during the Messenian Wars. After conquering the region, the Spartans, as typical as it may sound, reduced them to servitude. They bound them to the land as agricultural laborers. These people were forced to grow crops for their Spartan overlords. Some say that the Messenians and Laconians were once proud people. So, it was not a surprise that resentment simmered over time. When Sparta was struggling during a massive earthquake in 464 BCE, the helots took this as an opportunity to strike. Unfortunately, the Spartans proved to be mightier; the uprising was unsuccessful.

The Spartans decided to make their cruelty to the helots even clearer. Plutarch described a scene where the Spartans forced the helots to drink excessive amounts of wine until they were drunk. They were then paraded during public messes, known as syssitia—an event where Spartiates would gather every day to share meals in communal dining halls. This was said to serve as examples of the disgraceful effects of excessive drinking and drunkenness. The helots were also often forced to sing and dance in degrading ways during banquets and other public events.

The Roman historian Livy provided a more daunting account of Spartan oppression. According to his writings, helots who were accused of desertion were usually subjected to public whippings. However, their punishment did not end there. After the whippings, they were immediately put to death. There was also an episode where two thousand helots mysteriously disappeared. Some believe that they were victims of a mass killing.

In order to instill fear in the helots, the Spartans established the Krypteia. Although its exact origins are debated, some historians suggest that the Krypteia's roots trace back to the Dorian invasion of the Peloponnesian Peninsula. It was initially created as a guerrilla force tasked with suppressing resistance among conquered peoples before evolving into a more formalized institution. Other scholars claim that Krypteia's origins did not stretch that far back. Instead, they suggest that it was developed in the 6th century BCE when Sparta was heavily focused on consolidating its power.

While its origin is still unclear, we can be sure that the Krypteia drew its members from the agoge. This infamous Spartan education and training system was designed to transform Spartan boys into warriors capable of upholding the city-state's military supremacy. Training was compulsory for all male Spartiates, beginning when boys reached the age of seven. They were removed from their families and lived communally with each other. These boys had to go through years of relentless physical and mental challenges. They were expected to come out of the program exceptionally disciplined, obedient, and, of course, masters of martial skill—both with weapons and in unarmed combat. Spartan men typically graduated from the agoge at the age of thirty; this was also when they were allowed to marry and start a family.

Candidates for the Krypteia were chosen from this highly disciplined pool of young men. It is safe to assume that the selection criteria were stringent. Only those who showed signs of exceptional leadership, combat prowess, and a knack for stealth were selected. Once their names were listed to join the Krypteia, these young men would undergo additional training. Although details of this stage of training remain shrouded in secrecy, it likely involved advanced training in survival, espionage, and assassinations, which were all necessary for their future missions.

The Krypteia's main goal seemed straightforward: its members had to identify and eliminate potential helot leaders or agitators before they could fuel a rebellion. Oftentimes, the Krypteia worked under the cover of darkness; this was when they infiltrated helot communities. Usually working alone or in small groups, the Krypteia members were armed lightly. They carried only a dagger and minimal supplies that were enough for them to survive. Secrecy was their utmost priority. The Krypteia members had to conceal their true identities. Precision was also important when it came to assassinations; the Krypteia had to ensure that they eliminated their targets without leaving any traceable evidence.

Despite operating in secret, the Krypteia succeeded in creating an atmosphere of constant fear among the helots. With the removal of so many helot leaders, successful rebellions were considered almost impossible. Perhaps consumed by fear of getting slaughtered by the Krypteia, some helots refrained from even listening to early plans of revolt. Instead of facing the Spartan secret service's wrath, they chose to obey their masters.

The Krypteia also played a role during wartime, with its members often engaged in espionage and reconnaissance. They focused on gathering intelligence that proved invaluable to Spartan military campaigns. Scholars suggest that the Krypteia likely played a key role in the Greco-Persian Wars. During this chaotic period of war, the members of the Krypteia were the ones responsible for conducting covert operations, which eventually contributed to the Spartan victory at the Battle of Plataea in 479 BCE. The same could also be said during the Peloponnesian War, where the Krypteia, again, were instrumental in counter-espionage operations against Athens.

Of course, everything had its ending. The Krypteia saw its influence gradually wane when Sparta faced a series of catastrophic defeats and political issues. However, it was the Battle of Leuctra in 371 BCE that marked the turning point. When the Thebans decisively defeated the mighty Spartans, the Messenian helots were liberated. This was undoubtedly bad news for Sparta since the people had long relied on helot labor to sustain both its economy and lifestyle.

With the loss of Messenia and its agricultural wealth, Sparta was plunged into an episode of economic and social crisis. Due to years of warfare and strict citizenship requirements, the population of the Spartiate class dwindled to only a thousand adult males. Sparta could no longer sustain its warrior culture. These major changes eventually rendered the Krypteia irrelevant.

The Battle of Tegyra

When speaking of Sparta, one could not help but think of its military prowess. The Spartans forged their reputation by emerging victorious in countless battles, even those where the Spartans were greatly outnumbered. The famous Leonidas, for one, went down in history as one of the greatest Spartan kings. With only three hundred Spartans to spare, he successfully held off a massive Persian force, though victory in the famed Battle of Thermopylae eventually belonged to the Persians. Despite this reputation as an invincible force, there was a moment when this myth was broken. This time around, it was not the Persians but the Thebans who proved that Spartan steel could definitely be bent and broken despite their strong numbers.

Thebes had a rather complicated history with Sparta. It was once a key member of the Boeotian League, which was formed in 550 BCE. However, when Thebes fell under Spartan control in 382 BCE, many Theban leaders fled to Athens. Unwilling to bow down to the Spartans, they bided their time, waiting for the golden opportunity to reclaim their city. That moment came in 378 BCE under the command of Pelopidas. A daring leader, Pelopidas led 300 exiled Thebans back to their homeland and launched a nighttime assault on the Spartan garrison of 1,500 soldiers. Following this, Thebes was free from Spartan claws once more.

The Spartan kings, Agesilaus II and Cleombrotus, were quick to acknowledge the danger posed by Thebes. They launched several campaigns to retake the city and reestablish Spartan control over Boeotia. This, however, failed, leading to other Boeotian cities like Tanagra, Haliartus, Lebadea, and Coronea to make a bold move—they expelled their own Spartan garrisons. By 375 BCE, these cities had announced their allegiance to Thebes. The Boeotian League was reborn. Seeking to secure their influence and power, the Thebans—now led by Pelopidas and his close ally Epaminondas—set their sights on Orchomenus, the last Boeotian city under Spartan influence.

When word reached Pelopidas that a large Spartan garrison had left Orchomenus for a battle in Locris, he immediately planned his strategy. Since the city was left undefended, Pelopidas rode to the city. Ancient sources wrote that he took with him three hundred members of the Sacred Band. As an elite Theban infantry unit, the Sacred Band was popular for its extreme bravery and cohesion. The unit was composed of 150 pairs of soldiers, each bound by ties of friendship and love. This made them fiercely loyal and almost unbeatable in battle.

Upon nearing Orchomenus, Pelopidas learned that the city was far from defenseless; additional Spartan reinforcements had arrived to protect the city. The Thebans lacked siege weapons at the time, and coupled with insufficient manpower to take an entire city by force, Pelopidas ordered a retreat. Perhaps hoping to avoid direct contact with the Spartans, Pelopidas led his men north of Lake Copais.

However, in a twist of fate, Pelopidas received a messenger who carried bad news. The Spartan army knew the Thebans were just miles away from them and were marching straight toward them. Knowing that retreat was no longer viable, Pelopidas chose to fight.

Since both sides were caught off guard by the encounter, it is safe to assume that they had little time to plan. The Spartans were led by the polemarchs (commanders) Gorgoleon and Theopompus. They numbered between 1,200 and 1,800 troops compared to the Thebans, who only had 500 men at most. The Spartans were confident. Not only were they well trained and had experience from countless battles, but they also greatly outnumbered their enemy. However, Pelopidas had the strength of the Sacred Band.

The armies clashed. Details of the encounter are scarce, but some accounts described that the Theban cavalry managed to harass the Spartan flanks long enough until the Sacred Band was in position to strike. With precision and speed, the elite Theban infantry attacked the Spartan right flank, eventually killing the polemarchs. The Spartans were now on the battlefield without their commanders. It did not take long for them to falter, giving way for Pelopidas and the Thebans to gain the upper hand.

In another version of the battle, records narrate that instead of attacking the Spartan flanks, Pelopidas had his forces focus on the Spartan center. Using tactics almost similar to those employed by the Theban general Pagondas at the Battle of Delium (424 BCE), the Sacred Band successfully drove a wedge through the Spartan ranks. This broke their formation, thus leaving the flanks completely vulnerable for the Theban cavalry to wreak havoc on the Spartans.

Regardless of the exact strategy, the outcome of the battle was the same. The Spartans, despite their numerical superiority, were defeated by the Thebans. Those who survived managed to flee the battlefield and regroup with the garrison at Orchomenus. Nevertheless, the Thebans succeeded in proving to the world that the Spartans were far from invincible. This victory at Tegyra was only the beginning. Thebes would continue to challenge Spartan dominance, eventually reshaping the balance of power in the ancient Greek world.

Gylippus of Sparta

It was 415 BCE, and Athens had just launched one of its most ambitious campaigns: the Sicilian expedition. The Athenians had suffered the plague, and the Peloponnesian War was not going well for them. They believed that by securing Syracuse, a city of immense resources, Athens could once again tip the balance of the ongoing chaos in their favor.

The invasion of Sicily was spearheaded by a few Athenian generals, including Nicias, Alcibiades, and Lamachus. The campaign itself was beset by obstacles in the beginning, such as disagreements between the generals and logistical problems, but with a fleet of over 130 triremes and thousands of soldiers, Athens achieved some success in the early stage of the expedition. However, Syracuse was not ready to back down that easily. The people mounted a fierce resistance against the Athenians. Nevertheless, perhaps believing in their superior naval power and resources, the Athenians pressed on, hoping that they would eventually defeat the Sicilian defenders and claim the city for themselves.

Finally realizing the gravity of their situation, Syracuse requested help from its allies, especially Sparta. The Spartans were well aware of the strategic importance of Sicily. If Athens succeeded, the city-state would have no difficulties securing a foothold in the western Mediterranean, which would threaten Sparta even more.

In the meantime, Athenian General Alcibiades had been recalled to Athens. Upon learning that he was charged with sacrilege—the controversial general was said to have mutilated and mocked the sacred statues of the Eleusinian Mysteries—Alcibiades made the decision to defect to Athens' enemy, Sparta. He then advised the Spartans on how to stop the Athenian campaign in Sicily, which was by appointing a certain general named Gylippus.

Gylippus was not an ordinary Spartan. His family had a rather bad reputation—his father had been exiled for accepting bribes—but Gylippus managed to create a name of his own through years of military experience. When the seasoned general was appointed as the leader of Syracuse's defense, Sparta was a step closer to ensuring Athens suffered a massive defeat.

With only a small contingent of troops, Gylippus's arrival almost immediately boosted the morale of the Syracusans who had been trapped in the city. The Spartan commander's first priority was simple: break the Athenian siege of Syracuse. Gylippus began working right away. Upon surveying the battlefield, the seasoned general found the Athenians' key weakness: their reliance on maintaining control over their siege works. Without wasting more time, Gylippus launched his troops—composed of infantry and cavalry—to harass the Athenian forces. The plan was to disrupt the Athenians' efforts to complete their encirclement of the city. Gylippus also paid attention to Syracuse's fortifications. He oversaw the construction of counter-walls that could render the Athenian siege lines ineffective.

Gylippus soon witnessed the Athenians falter. The Athenian forces did not lose just one but two of their leaders. Alcibiades had defected shortly after the expedition began, and Lamachus died during one of the skirmishes that took place outside the city walls. Morale was depleting. Disease soon wreaked havoc throughout the Athenian camp, further diminishing their numbers. With their supplies running terribly low and reinforcements arriving late, the Athenians began to lose hope.

Gylippus made use of every one of the Athenians' weaknesses. After successfully coordinating with Spartan allies and Corinthian forces, they agreed to send reinforcements and ships to improve Syracuse's defense. With these additional resources in hand, Gylippus made the decision to fight the Athenian navy. Under his command, the Syracusan fleet engaged the Athenian fleet in the Great Harbor of Syracuse. Athens suffered terribly during this series of brutal naval battles. The Athenian fleet had once been known as one of the ancient world's greatest naval powers; what remained of the Athenian fleet was only splintered hulls and desperate crews.

Nicias attempted to withdraw his forces, but Gylippus was not planning to show mercy. Knowing that victory was near, he ordered multiple blockades on the escape routes, both by land and sea. The Athenians, realizing there was no way out, launched one final assault. It ended in catastrophe. Those who attempted to flee overland were hunted down and captured by Gylippus's men. As for Nicias and his commander, Demosthenes, they were both taken prisoner. Gylippus was said to have sought ways to spare the Athenian commanders, but he was overruled. Nicias and Demosthenes were executed.

The Athenians had set sail for Sicily with tens of thousands of soldiers and crews. Yet, only a handful of them managed to return home. Those who had been captured were either killed or enslaved. Gylippus returned to Sparta a hero. However, his later life contrasted with his military achievements.

Shortly after the end of the Peloponnesian War, Gylippus was accused of embezzlement. Sparta had received funds from Persia throughout the war—the empire sided with Sparta so that Athens would fall—and these resources were entrusted to Gylippus. According to ancient records, Gylippus was said to have tampered with the money bags. He secretly took some of the funds and resealed the bags, making them appear as if nothing had been taken.

Unfortunately for Gylippus, his tricks were discovered. He was forced to go into exile, a fate mirroring that of his father's.

Chapter 5 – The Story of Neaira

Women in ancient Greece, especially in Athens, lived a life that was largely confined to the home. They were restricted from meddling in public affairs. Their daily lives basically revolved around managing the household and caring for their children. While men could carve their life achievements by participating in politics, war, and philosophy, Greek women, for the most part, had little independence or opportunity to leave their names in history. Public roles for women were very rare, and most of them were limited to religious duties, such as serving as priestesses.

It is safe to say that, even compared to Rome, Greece was more restrictive when it came to women's visibility in history. Yes, women were also treated unequally in Roman society, but history remembers women like Livia Drusilla and Agrippina the Younger, both of whom have been recognized as two of the most influential figures in the imperial court. In Greece, however, only men could debate and make decisions in the Agora; women could not even comment on state affairs, let alone participate in them.

Helen of Troy, Medea, and Penelope are some of the names that likely come to mind whenever we think of female figures from ancient Greece, yet these are (more than likely) mythological figures. Some may recall the name Aspasia of Miletus, but many often remember her largely due to her association with her husband, Pericles, rather than for her own intellect or influence. More often than not, her reputation in ancient sources was rather controversial; it was common for the wife or partner of ancient leaders to be subject to criticism.

As for Neaira, her story is almost like a whisper. Few have heard of her name. However, it is this silence that makes her story so unique. We know parts of Neaira's life primarily because of a speech made by Apollodorus of Acharnae, an Athenian politician. However, his accounts of her were far from positive. In his speech, which was preserved in the Demosthenic corpus—a collection of speeches used in law courts, political debates, or other public forums—Apollodorus talked about her early life as a courtesan and her struggles. Yet, they were talked about not to offer a glimpse into her life but to tarnish her reputation and convince the jury to side with him.

Neaira's story began in the ancient city of Corinth. Although it once thrived as a bustling hub of commerce and culture, Corinth was infamous for its indulgence and vice. In contrast to Athens, where the lives of women were restricted, Corinth offered some freedom to women, especially those who chose to be courtesans. Although courtesans were often exploited for their beauty and charm, some chose this path so that they could at least gain some kind of public visibility and influence rather than being forever confined to domestic life and excluded from all public affairs.

As for Neaira, however, she did not choose to be a courtesan. We know nothing about her childhood and family except the fact that she was sold into slavery at a very young age. Her journey as a courtesan started when she was bought by a woman named Nikarete. It was said that Nikarete was once a slave, but after gaining her freedom, she began to shape her influence and wealth by becoming a madam. She could often be seen at the Corinth slave market, where she would buy young girls to be trained as *hetaerae*, the celebrated courtesans who mingled with the elite. Unlike common prostitutes who were confined to brothels, *hetaerae* enjoyed a level of social mobility and independence. *Hetaerae* accompanied the men who paid for them to symposia (drinking parties common in ancient Greece) and games. Neaira once accompanied a young aristocrat named Simus of Thessaly to the Great Panathenaea (a Greek festival) of 378 in Athens.

Many claimed Nikarete to have had a good pair of eyes. She could see the potential of young girls just by looking at them. The madam was also adept at creating the illusion of respectability. She bought the girls from the slave market, but she would often claim that she adopted them. Nikarete often referred to the girls as her daughters. This way, she could increase their value and attract influential customers. It was more likely for wealthy patrons to pay a premium price for the company of young women they viewed as "untarnished" and "refined" rather than a simple slave from the market who had been sold for only a few drachmae.

Neaira became one of the madam's most prized daughters. She was groomed well. Other than training in the art of engaging conversation, she was also taught music and dance. Combined with her beauty and charm, Neaira quickly became one of Nikarete's most sought-after protégés alongside two others, Metaneira and Anteia. Apollodorus himself claimed that Neaira was highly sought after by wealthy men to the point where they were all willing to pay outrageous amounts of money for her company.

A Greek *hetaira* attending to her client.[16]

But still, Neaira's life was far from secure. Her life was under the control of Nikarete, and all of her movements were dictated by the demands of her patrons. Every drachma that she earned from her work did not flow into her own coffers but straight into Nikarete's pockets. However, things were about to change when Nikarete decided that she had had enough of profiting from Neaira's beauty and charm. Nikarete decided to sell Neaira. This was commonly practiced by Corinthian madams, especially when the *hetaera* had passed their prime years. However, instead of landing in the slave market yet again, Neaira was instead sold to two men who were once frequent patrons. Known as Timanoridas and Eukrates, the two had grown extremely fond of her and did not think twice about taking her off Nikarete's hands. They bought Neaira for 3,000 drachmae (equivalent to somewhere between $25,000 and $175,000 in today's time), which was undoubtedly an extraordinary amount for purchasing a person.

Of course, Timanoridas and Eukrates eventually planned on building their own family. They had met their soulmates and wished to marry them. They knew that keeping Neaira as a companion could only bring problems. However, the two were so fond of her that they did not have the heart to cast her aside. So, they chose a middle path. Timanoridas and Eukrates offered her freedom but on one condition. Neaira had to buy her way out of servitude. Despite appearing better than outright abandonment, Neaira was thrown into a moment of desperation. She could see freedom in front of her, but she had to pay for it using money she did not have.

Not known for giving up, Neaira chose to turn to her former patrons. Leveraging on their lingering affections for her and perhaps a pinch of their generosity, Neaira sought funds from them. One of the men she contacted was a wealthy Athenian named Phrynion. Along with several others who had once been enamored with her, they each contributed a portion of their wealth until Neaira could finally meet the price demanded by Timanoridas and Eukrates. And so, with enough money, Neaira was finally free after years of servitude.

Perhaps eager to turn a new chapter, Neaira chose to leave Corinth for Athens. However, she did not go to the city alone. Neaira went with Phrynion, one of the men who helped buy her freedom. At first, Phrynion appeared like a benefactor, but as she spent week after week with him, Neaira began to see his darker side. It is easy to assume that Phrynion did not see Neaira as a partner but rather as a possession.

Apollodorus described a harrowing incident that befell her. Phrynion had been invited to attend a grand feast hosted by the Athenian general Chabrias. He accepted the invitation and brought Neaira with him. Since the general was celebrating his recent victory at the Pythian Games, the feast was very opulent. Influential men were mingling, and wine flowed endlessly into their goblets. Neaira, having spent most of her early years as a *hetaera*, was well accustomed to such events, so she mingled with the guests as she always had. At one point, Neaira, who was also intoxicated from all that wine, fell asleep. This was when the night took a darker turn. While unconscious, she was assaulted by both guests of the feast and a few slaves. Phrynion was present when this all happened, yet he did nothing.

This was only one of the many mistreatments and humiliations that Neaira had to go through under Phrynion's roof. It was clear that the man saw her as nothing more than a trophy to flaunt. He cared very little for her dignity and well-being. So, around 372 BCE (possibly only a year after she arrived in Athens), Neaira decided enough was enough. She packed everything she could carry—her clothing, jewelry, and a few other items that belonged to Phrynion—and left Athens. She was also said to have brought along two maids.

Neaira's next chapter of her life brought her to Megara. While the city looked like it could finally offer her peace and a sense of autonomy, Neaira could not help but think of the risk she faced for leaving Phrynion. As a woman without any influential familial ties, Neaira was exposed to challenges that could drag her into the confines of slavery once more. But at least in Megara, there was a distance between her and the abuses of Phrynion.

Here, Neaira found herself working in an industry with which she was familiar. She became a *hetaera* once more to sustain herself. However, times were harsh since Greece was deeply embroiled in war. Neaira began to think of Athens again. Although the city-state was also involved in the war, Athens remained better off economically compared to Megara. However, returning to the city meant there was a possibility she would face Phrynion once again. Despite the man not having legal claim over her as her master—technically, Neaira had purchased her own freedom—Phrynion could easily accuse her of so many things, such as stealing, and those around him would believe every word he said. In the Greek world, once accused, even if baseless, one's life would be ruined. Neaira knew that in order to set foot in Athens again, she had to find protection.

Perhaps the Olympian gods heard her plea. Protection eventually reached her in the form of Stephanos. Hailing from Athens, Stephanos had come to Megara and stayed with Neaira for a time. It was unknown what the two discussed, but Stephanos was said to have laid out a solution to Neaira's problem. Neaira could return to Athens with Stephanos and live in his household. She was not obligated to accept this option. She was, after all, free and no longer confined to any masters or madams. Neaira could choose to remain in Megara, but her decision to follow Stephanos suggests that she believed in him. She probably saw a better future in Athens. Whether it was security or companionship, Neaira soon set off to Athens and shared a roof with Stephanos.

As she had foreseen, Phrynion soon discovered she had returned to the city. He was headstrong about taking her back into his household. Stephanos, however, was not planning on letting him do so easily. He resisted and argued that Neaira had never been his property but was instead a free woman. Enraged, Phrynion was said to have planned on challenging this claim in court. He was determined that he could prove Neaira had no right to claim independence. What followed is obscure, yet Apollodorus told us that an agreement was eventually reached through arbitration. It was decided that Neaira was indeed her own mistress or kyria (Greek: κυρία). However, the arbitrators did compel her to split her time between Stephanos and Phrynion. So, despite being acknowledged as a free woman, Neaira was somehow neither free nor entirely bound. Her own desires were never considered in the arrangement. Neaira obeyed the arrangement, though at some point, Phyrnion's name went off the record. The reasons behind this remain unknown, but it is possible that he simply died.

We will likely never be entirely sure about the details of her life following this. However, we do know that Neaira was forced to face yet another obstacle when she entered her fifties. Neaira was brought to trial. This was when Apollodorus delivered his speech. It is also worth noting that Apollodorus knew Stephanos from a couple of incidents that took place years earlier. In 348 BCE, for instance, Stephanos had publicly accused Apollodorus of sponsoring an illegal policy. As a result, Apollodorus was ordered to pay a hefty fine. As if this did not already tarnish his reputation, Apollodorus was also said to have been accused by Stephanos again in 346 BCE. This time, Stephanos claimed he had murdered an enslaved woman. Unlike his previous accusation, this one was dismissed due to conflicting testimonies. We will never know whether the accusation was true, but it is safe to assume that Apollodorus saw Stephanos as a massive thorn in his side.

Sometime between 343 and 340 BCE, Apollodorus decided to point the finger back at Stephanos and, of course, Neaira. Since it was known that Stephanos and Neaira lived together, Apollodorus accused them of having married illegally. Under Athenian law, this was a serious offense. Marriages between Athenian citizens and foreigners were strictly prohibited. This law, enacted sometime in 450 BCE, sought to preserve the exclusivity of the citizen body and protect its citizenship. It was also enacted so that the Athenians could protect their access to political rights and inheritance.

Interestingly, Neaira was said to have arrived in court with two men and a woman. They were believed to have been her children, and they all lived with Stephanos in Athens. The uncertainty of whether they were the product of her union with Stephanos or not became the foundation of Apollodorus's case.

An 18th-century painting depicting a different *hetaira* (possibly Phryne) on trial.[17]

However, the claim that the children were in fact Neaira's raises doubts among many. Neaira began her profession as a *hetaera* under Nikarete ever since she was a young girl. It was highly unlikely that Nikarete would keep her if pregnancy ever occurred. Such a condition could have definitely jeopardized her marketability and physical appearance, diminishing her value as a courtesan. Even if she had become pregnant, it would be more realistic for her to abandon her child through the practice of exposure. She was, after all, penniless since every coin paid for her service went straight to Nikarete. Some might suggest that they were her children with Phrynion, but it is hard to imagine that Stephanos would have willingly supported children who brought them no benefit.

Apollodorus drew upon the arrangement that Stephanos and Neaira had agreed on when they were in Megara years prior. Apollodorus claimed that through this pact, Neaira managed to persuade Stephanos to raise her children as Athenian citizens. In return, Neaira would remain with Stephanos under the same roof. This arrangement set in motion their illegal marriage. Apollodorus had nothing to support this claim other than his words. He was not even present when Stephanos and Neaira met in Megara, so how could he know what their arrangements were? Many questioned the credibility of his account.

Since there was no evidence that the two were ever married—there was no such thing as written contracts or official ceremonies when it came to marriage in Athens—Apollodorus could only claim it by highlighting how Stephanos treated the children. In ancient Greece, it was common for sons from legal marriages to be introduced to their father's *phratry* (kinship group). They were then registered as citizens when they became adults. Daughters, on the other hand, were typically married to citizen husbands. Apollodorus claimed that Stephanos had done all of the above for the children. Phano, the only daughter, was even married twice, with dowries provided each time. To Apollodorus, this was clear evidence that Stephanos and Neaira had indeed entered into an illegal marriage.

However, it is weird that no one ever raised objections in the decades after Neaira's return to Athens. If the children were the offspring of Neaira, why did no one in Stephanos's phratry ever question it? This led some to conclude that the children were, in fact, not Neaira's but rather Stephanos's children from his previous marriage with an Athenian woman. Even Apollodorus was ready to acknowledge this possibility and drop the case—if Stephanos could prove it. It was said that Apollodorus proposed torturing two of Neaira's slaves, the ones she brought from Phrynion's household. He was certain that the slaves would tell the truth. Stephanos, however, refused to do so. Whether it was an act of compassion since the slaves had been through so much with Neaira, an action to protect the truth, or perhaps just a choice to avoid them giving out false information—most people would say anything if they were desperate—we can never be certain.

This was not the only claim Apollodorus made to support his case. Another sensational allegation made by the Athenian politician was that Neaira never stopped working as a *hetaera*. Apollodorus claimed that Stephanos worked together with her. While Neaira's main task was to lure men, Stephanos would orchestrate schemes to extort her clients. As per usual, these were nothing more than baseless accusations; no witnesses were ever presented to support this.

Again, Apollodorus turned his attention to the daughter, Phano. He condemned Phano's participation in major religious rites in Athens. In his eyes, Phano was Neaira's daughter, so her status as a non-citizen of Athens restricted her from taking part in such activities. This was considered sacrilegious under Athenian law. Apollodorus's strategy was simple: he hoped to inflame the jury's outrage by narrating how this family flagrantly violated societal norms. Yet, the question remains. If Phano had never been a citizen, why had the religious authorities remained quiet all that time? This silence, much like the lack of objections to the children's citizenship, raises doubts about Apollodorus's version of events.

Unfortunately, without Stephano's defense speech, we can never uncover the full picture of his and Neaira's lives. It is indeed frustrating that we will likely never know the trial's resolution. It is plausible that, due to Apollodorus's lack of concrete evidence, Neaira was allowed to return to her life, with this trial being the last obstacle she had to endure. However, it is also hard to dismiss the possibility of Apollodorus succeeding in swaying the jury, especially if he played on their prejudice and fears.

Chapter 6 – The Daunting Fall of Influential Greek Figures

Aside from its architectural wonders, epic battles, and myths that made it into books and movies, ancient Greece also had a long list of big personalities. From war generals to philosophers, thinkers, poets, and kings, they all left their mark on history in the most unforgettable ways. However, despite their brilliance and ambition, not all of them were bestowed with the glorious ending they might have imagined. Some of them met their demise rather ironically, adding an unexpected twist to their legends and stories. Take the Ionian mathematician Pythagoras, for instance. His life was all about numbers, philosophy, and harmony. But his death? That is a whole different story.

The Death of the Great Pythagoras

By the 5th century BCE, Pythagoras was considered the most influential philosopher in Croton, a Greek city in southern Italy. He and his followers, referred to as the Pythagoreans, were best known for their esoteric teachings that blended mathematics, music, and spirituality. Interestingly, the Pythagoreans operated almost like a secret society. However, their secretive practices and growing influence over local politics eventually alienated the wider populace. According to ancient sources, this was where the chaos began. A violent uprising erupted in 510 BCE when the citizens of Croton targeted Pythagoras and his followers. The angry mob was said to have cornered them in a temple. What happened afterward, however, remains debated, as ancient records were often written with a blend of both facts and myths.

Pythagoras teaching a class of women.[18]

One version talked about how the Croton citizens burned the meeting place of the Pythagorean schools. While some claimed Pythagoras was absent during the time—he was said to have been on the island Delos—others narrate a scene where he and his small group of followers narrowly escaped the blaze. They fled to the city of Locris, where they pleaded for sanctuary. Unfortunately, their request was denied, so they made their way to Metapontum. Here, Pythagoras and his followers found refuge in the Temple of the Muses. Starvation struck the Pythagoreans, but rather than desecrating the sacred site for food, they chose to die.

Another version of the story, recorded by the philosopher Porphyry, claimed that Pythagoras died by his own hand. Failing to find an escape route as the flames consumed their meeting place, the Pythagoreans chose to lie down on the ground, forming a safe path for their master to escape. Pythagoras managed to escape to safety, but as he turned around to see the bodies of his followers, the mathematician was immediately overwhelmed by grief. Unable to bear the loss, Pythagoras took his own life.

However, the most popular tale of his death revolved around fava beans. This story suggests that Pythagoras managed to escape from the burning of his meeting place. The angry mob was not planning on letting him live, though, so they pursued him relentlessly. Pythagoras ran but halted when he came upon a field of fava beans. Long believed that these beans held the souls of the dead, Pythagoras refused to continue his escape, afraid that he would trample upon the poor beans. When the angry mob caught up with him, they did not think twice about killing the philosopher.

A 16ᵗʰ-century drawing of Pythagoras turning his face away from the fava beans.[19]

To this date, his demise remains unsolved; no one has been able to uncover the real cause of his death. Regardless, it is safe to assume that he did not die peacefully. Some said it was an ironic end for the man who sought to unveil the universe's secret harmony.

Alcibiades, an Athenian Commander Hailed Both as a Hero and a Traitor

Alcibiades could sense that his end was near. He had taken refuge in a modest home in the heart of Phrygia (located in west-central Anatolia). Alcibiades was once the darling of Athens. A charismatic general gifted with both looks and brilliance, he had led the city-state to victory in many conflicts. But now he was a man in exile, hunted and despised.

Alcibiades (left) and his mentor, Socrates.[20]

What seemed to be a normal day in 404 BCE quickly took a turn for the worse with the arrival of assassins near his house. These assassins were thought to have been sent by Pharnabazus, the Persian satrap of Phrygia. Pharnabazus initially welcomed Alcibiades when he arrived to seek protection in Phrygia. However, things changed when he was pressured by Lysander, a Spartan admiral who feared that Alcibiades would regain influence in the fragile balance of power in Greece. Lysander persuaded the Persian satrap into thinking that Alcibiades was nothing more than a liability. So, the assassins were sent, tasked to return only when Alcibiades's body had touched the ground.

The assassins set Alcibiades's quarters ablaze, yet the Athenian managed to escape the fire. Armed with only a dagger—or a sword according to some sources—and his cloak wrapped around his arm, acting as a shield, Alcibiades rushed toward his attackers. The assassins were caught off guard by his sudden emergence from the fire and fled at first before standing their ground upon finding a safe distance. They then unleashed a flurry of arrows, which pierced the Athenian's torso. Alcibiades's corpse was left on the very spot he fell until his mistress, Timandra, found him and buried his remains.

Alcibiades's life was not always filled with obstacles; he had not always been an outcast. He had actually been a respected military leader and statesman. Born into a wealthy and influential family in Athens, it was not a surprise that he had been groomed for greatness from a young age. Yet, his insatiable ambition and tendency to place self-interest above loyalty became his undoing. Thucydides claimed that he was over ambitious when he proposed the ill-fated Sicilian expedition, which he proved to be right about since the campaign ended in a catastrophic defeat. However, before the expedition reached its end, Alcibiades had already switched sides. Fleeing Athens after being charged with sacrilege, the Athenian commander offered his services to Sparta.

Alcibiades assassinated by Persian soldiers.[21]

Alcibiades enjoyed his time in Sparta at first. He advised the Spartans on strategies to counter Athens; he was said to have been credited with so much honor that some Spartan soldiers grew discontent. When rumors of his affair with the Spartan king's wife began to surface, Alcibiades was forced to flee once more.

This time around, he defected to the Persians, serving as the adviser to the satrap Tissaphernes. At the same time, he was also negotiating his return to Athens. He promised the city-state that he could secure Persian support for Athens. His political maneuvering eventually impressed the Athenian oligarchs who controlled the fleet at Samos. They recalled him in 411 BCE, hoping that his aid could help them turn the tide of war. Indeed, once back in his homeland, Alcibiades led a series of successful campaigns, thus restoring his reputation. However, his success would not linger for long. Later on, the rival Athenians turned against him, and he was exiled yet again.

Alcibiades then made his way to Thrace. Once more, he tried to help his fellow Athenians by warning them about an incoming Spartan attack. Yet, his words were ignored, and the Athenians were decimated. By this time, he knew Thrace was no longer safe for him. This was when he took refuge in Phrygia, which, little did he know, would be the last location he would ever set his eyes on.

Themistocles

The Battle of Salamis had just begun, and Themistocles stood on the prow of his trireme, commanding his men to strike at the enemy. The narrow straits had purposely been chosen by the hero for their strategic advantage. He knew the Persians would find it difficult to steer the ships. Making use of both speed and their knowledge of the region, the Greeks soon outmaneuvered the Persian vessels. They rammed the Persian fleet and sank the ships. Others were boarded by the Greeks. In the end, the Greeks succeeded in sinking over four hundred of the Persian ships while losing only forty of their own.

An illustration of Greek triremes at the Battle of Salamis.[22]

Following the battle, Xerxes postponed his campaigns into Greece, giving the city-states more time to unite. Themistocles returned to Athens as the savior of Greece.

Unlike Alcibiades, who had been born into an already influential family, Themistocles was raised by a rather modest family. Themistocles's political savvy and knack for appealing to the common people allowed him to climb the challenging political ladder in Athens, which was typically dominated by aristocrats. Even as a young politician, Themistocles felt the growing threat that the Persians posed to his homeland, so he wasted no time in proposing the strengthening of Athens' navy. Upon hearing news of the newly discovered silver mines at Laurium, Themistocles persuaded the city to use a portion of its wealth to invest in a stronger fleet of triremes, which ultimately played a decisive role in the Greek victory at Salamis.

However, not everyone was fond of the great general. Some said it was also Themistocles's growing arrogance and penchant for self-promotion that caused him to be alienated by several leaders of Athens. He was eventually accused of corruption; he was believed to have accepted bribes from

An illustration of Themistocles.[23]

63

Greek allies, extorting funds under the guise of Athenian protection, and manipulated the Oracle of Delphi to sway political decisions in his favor. After losing more support, Themistocles was ostracized (a practice in Athens where citizens were given a chance to vote an individual into exile).

Forced to flee Athens, Themistocles sought refuge among those he had once defeated: the Persians. The Persian king, Artaxerxes I, surprisingly welcomed the Greek hero with open arms, perhaps knowing the value of Themistocles's experience. The Persian king held him in such high regard that Themistocles was given the governorship over Magnesia. Things, however, changed when Artaxerxes put him in a precarious position. The Persian king allegedly ordered the Greek hero to lead a Persian campaign against his own people.

Themistocles did not have the heart to betray the land he had once called home. So, the Greek hero chose death over dishonor. According to the narratives from ancient sources, Themistocles staged a somber yet ritualistic sacrifice. He sacrificed a bull on an altar in the name of the gods. He then filled a cup with its blood and drank it to his death. This was viewed as his ultimate refusal to turn against his people, even those who had previously ostracized him.

While this account gave the hero a rather dramatic end, other historians claim that after years of enduring strain, Themistocles eventually died of natural causes. Whether it was sickness that robbed his life or foul play involving jealous Persian courtiers, Themistocles never got to redeem himself to the Athenians. While he was branded a traitor by the Athenians, the Spartans remembered his contributions at Salamis and viewed him as a hero.

Cleomenes I, the Spartan King Who Slashed Himself to Death

Cleomenes came to power in the 6th century BCE when the Greek world was in the midst of great instability. His reign left a mark on Sparta. He introduced several reforms and foreign policies that managed to elevate the city's influence. One of his greatest military achievements was the Battle of Sepeia, where the Spartans defeated their longtime rival, the Argives.

Off the battlefield, Cleomenes knew how to navigate the realms of diplomacy and politics. His decision to support Persian King Darius I secured Sparta's position in the larger geopolitical landscape. However, Cleomenes could also be unpredictable. He soon betrayed the Persian alliance, which undoubtedly contributed to the decline of Sparta's foreign relations. Cleomenes was also infamously known to have bribed the Oracle of Delphi so that she would influence decisions in his favor.

Yes, Cleomenes enjoyed many successes in his early years. But as time went on, cracks in his rule began to become apparent. His controversial policies and erratic behavior alienated many of his companions and peers. According to ancient records, the king gradually became mad. Rumors of his instability spread to the civilians. One day, as he walked along the streets of Sparta's agora, the king was said to have hit anyone he encountered with his staff. Each day, his behavior grew increasingly unpredictable, which eventually forced the Spartan ephors (a board of five magistrates in ancient Sparta in charge of the city-state's judicial, religious, legislative, and military decisions) to act.

Cleomenes was arrested in the name of protecting the king himself and, in extension, Sparta. While he was in custody, Cleomenes managed to persuade a helot guard to hand him a knife. With this small weapon, the king was said to have mutilated himself to death. The Spartans claimed he slashed not only his belly but also his shins and thighs. To many, this brutal act of suicide was thought to be the result of his madness, but historians claim otherwise. They suspect his madness was nothing more than a fabrication to discredit him posthumously.

There are modern theories that explain his death. Some argue that Cleomenes did not kill himself. Instead, he was a victim of political assassination orchestrated by his half-brother, Leonidas. Others, however, claimed that his gruesome death was a staged spectacle. Cleomenes had broken taboos before, especially when it was discovered that he had bribed the Oracle of Delphi. The Spartans might have staged his self-mutilation so that his death could serve as a cautionary tale against breaking Spartan customs and laws. Another theory is related to his deteriorating mental state. Contemporary sources describe him as erratic, with behaviors that suggest he might have suffered from alcoholism or a neurological disorder. If this theory holds any truth, it lends some credibility to the idea of suicide, though perhaps not in the grotesque form described by Spartan accounts.

Thales of Miletus, the Father of Philosophy Who Fell into a Well

Thales of Miletus was one of the Seven Sages of Greece (a title given to influential philosophers of archaic Greece). Also considered by many to be the father of philosophy, Thales dedicated his life to understanding the natural world through reason rather than mythology alone. He declared that water was the fundamental substance of all things; he claimed that water was the First Cause of all things and the basic substance of the universe, a view that was later discarded by philosophers.

Thales of Miletus listening to Urania, the Muse of Astronomy, revealing to him the secrets of the skies.[24]

According to Herodotus, Thales once accurately predicted a solar eclipse during a battle between the Lydians and the Medes around 585 BCE. When it happened, the sudden darkening of the sky was said to have abruptly stopped the battle. The Lydians and the Medes thought the occurrence was a sign from the divine to stop fighting. So, they sheathed their weapons and negotiated for peace instead.

However, despite being one of the ancient world's greatest minds, even Thales himself could not escape the hands of mortality. Plato mentioned a story of a Thracian servant girl who witnessed Thales falling into a well. However, instead of worrying about him, the girl laughed at the incident. She remarked that he was so focused on learning more about the sky that he failed to see what was in front of him. This might only serve as an allegory rather than a historical account; it was probably nothing more than an ancient warning about spending too much time philosophizing without caring about earthly matters.

It is highly likely that Thales met his demise sometime between 550 and 548 BCE. According to the biographer of the Greek philosophers, Diogenes Laërtius, Thales, who was around seventy-eight years old at the time, was attending the fifty-eighth Olympiad Games when he suddenly collapsed. Historians claimed the culprit behind his demise was a combination of old age and heatstroke.

Pyrrhus of Epirus: The Warrior King Who Died from a Roof Tile

Pyrrhus of Epirus was another one of ancient Greece's most accomplished kings and military leaders. As the second cousin of Alexander the Great, Pyrrhus was said to have modeled himself after his famous relative. He spent his life pursuing conquests across not only Greece but also Macedonia and Italy. Many agree that his campaigns against Rome forever immortalized his name in the records of history.

A statue of Pyrrhus in Ioannina, Greece.[25]

In 279 BCE, Pyrrhus emerged victorious against the Romans in the Battle of Asculum. However, the cost of achieving the victory was immense. While he successfully defeated the entire force of the Roman commander Publius Decius Mus, Pyrrhus's army suffered devastating losses to the point where he was unable to continue the broader war effectively. Ancient sources talked about his famous remark when he was congratulated for his victory: "If we are victorious in one more battle with the Romans, we shall be utterly ruined." The outcome of this battle also led to the term Pyrrhic victory. This term describes a triumph so devastating that it feels more like a defeat.

The death of Pyrrhus.[26]

In 272 BCE, Pyrrhus found himself involved in chaotic street fighting. Eager to seize the city of Argos, the king showcased his best military skills as he made his way through the narrow alleyways. Ancient accounts recalled a scene where an old lady who sat on a rooftop observed his fight with an Argive man. Many believed the lady to be the mother of the Argive soldier, and upon seeing his son almost defeated by the king, she quickly intervened. The old lady threw a piece of roof tile toward Pyrrhus, which knocked him off his horse. The mighty Greek king, with a part of his spine broken, could no longer move; his injury had left him paralyzed. While some said he died simply because of the impact, other ancient writers, such as Plutarch, claimed his death was assured when a Macedonian soldier named Zopyrus stumbled upon the unconscious king and beheaded him.

Aristomenes of Messene

Aristomenes of Messene is best known for his fierce resistance against Spartan domination during the Second Messenian War (c. 685–668 BCE). His status as a king of Messenia was further elevated when he achieved major early victories, including the one at "The Boar's Barrow" in the plain of Stenyclaurus. His success, however, did not last too long. When the Arcadian king, Aristocrates II, suddenly withdrew his forces, Aristomenes and his people were left with no choice but to face a catastrophic defeat at the battle of the Great Trench. They were forced to retreat. They managed to fortify themselves in the mountain stronghold of Eira, but the Spartans were relentless. They laid attacks on the Messenians there for eleven years.

Nevertheless, Aristomenes never planned on surrendering to the Spartans. Over the years, he led multiple raids. In one encounter, the king and fifty of his companions were captured by the Spartans. They were then thrown into the chasm on Mount Taygetus. Although his companions died, Aristomenes was said to have survived. Legend has it he was saved by an eagle who cushioned his fall. He then made his way to safety by following a fox, which appeared before him to guide his way.

However, there is another account that narrates his escape differently. In this version, Aristomenes was captured during a truce by Cretan auxiliaries of the Spartans. He was then freed because of the devotion of a Messenian girl, who later became his daughter-in-law.

Aristomenes saved by a Messenian girl.[27]

Even though Aristomenes managed to escape his fate, the hero was unable to turn the tide of the war. By 668 BCE, it was clear that the war had turned against the Messenians. According to the ancient geographer Pausanias, it all went to chaos for the Messenians when Eira was successfully breached by the Spartans. A heavy resistance ensued, which Aristomenes led. Yet, the Messenians were forced to evacuate. Leaving their homeland, they continued their journey and eventually found refuge with their Arcadian allies. Some said the former king of Messenia never stopped searching for ways to reclaim his domain. He was believed to have planned a journey to Sardis and Ecbatana, where he hoped to get aid from the Lydian and Median kings. Yet, fate had already caught up with him, and there was no escape this time around. Aristomenes died in Rhodes.

Chapter 7 – Ancient Greek Technology Revealed

It is common knowledge that the ancient Greeks were master builders. However, what's truly fascinating is how they managed to create structures that still amaze us today without the help of modern tools or machinery. There were no electric cranes, power tools, or even laser-guided measurements. Instead, they crafted their works using a combination of ingenuity, teamwork, and a deep understanding of mathematics and physics.

Cranes and pulleys, for instance, played an important role in the construction of many structures across ancient Greece. They were used to lift massive blocks of stone, allowing workers to assemble mighty columns and walls that could withstand some natural disasters and also the test of time. These ancient devices, albeit simple in design, were highly effective. The Parthenon is a great example, as it is well known for its grandeur. However, its true brilliance lies in the details. The temple, which dominated the Athenian Acropolis, once had subtle features that reveal the Greeks' extraordinary understanding of perception, artistry, and mathematics.

What remains of the wondrous Parthenon.[38]

Constructed in the 5th century BCE in honor of the goddess Athena, the temple's most fascinating aspect is its connection to the Fibonacci sequence. This mathematical pattern is often associated with natural harmony and beauty. This sequence, where each number is the sum of the two preceding ones (1, 1, 2, 3, 5, 8, etc.), appears frequently in nature, from the spirals of shells to the arrangement of leaves. This sequence can be seen in the Parthenon, especially in the dimensions of its columns and the number of steps on its base. The ratio of the Parthenon's length to its width is also close to the golden ratio, a proportion associated with the Fibonacci sequence.

This may suggest that the architects of the temple (Ictinus and Callicrates, who also worked under the supervision of the talented sculptor Phidias) incorporated this principle to achieve some sort of visual balance and proportionality, making the temple appear harmonious and naturally beautiful even if viewers are not consciously aware of it.

The Parthenon also had other fascinating details besides its mathematical precision. The columns, for instance, were never perfectly vertical. Instead, they were purposely constructed to lean slightly inward. If they extended upward, their axes would converge nearly a mile above the temple. This subtle tilt, combined with the curvature of the base and the tapering of the columns, gave way to an optical illusion; even if one focused their gaze on it from any angle, the structure appeared perfectly straight and balanced. Interestingly, even the spaces between the columns were not uniform. They were arranged with slight variations that enhanced the building's overall harmony.

Phidias showing his work on the Parthenon friezes to his friends.[29]

At the heart of the grand temple's artistic achievements is the work done by the master sculptor Phidias. Aside from the intricate carvings and friezes that beautifully adorn the Parthenon, Phidias was also responsible for creating the temple's crowning masterpiece: the colossal statue of Athena Parthenos. The statue was twelve meters tall and depicted the goddess of wisdom in gold and ivory. She could also be seen holding a smaller statue of Nike (the goddess of victory) in one hand and a shield in the other. The massive statue was then put atop a base that featured intricate reliefs that told the story of Pandora's birth.

Since myths and legends were deeply embedded in the Greek civilization, Phidias made sure to adorn other parts of the Parthenon with artistic carvings depicting scenes from various Greek myths and Athenian history. The east pediment, for instance, had carvings that narrated the birth of Athena herself from the head of Zeus. The west pediment told the story of the famous contest between Athena and

Poseidon, who once vied for the patronage of Athens. Meanwhile, the frieze that ran along the inner colonnade showed scenes of the Panathenaic procession, a grand festival honoring the goddess.

A small model of the Athena Parthenos.[30]

The Greeks are often celebrated for their construction of temples and theaters, but it is also hard to dismiss their mastery of water management. Since water is one of the most precious resources, the Greeks developed ingenious solutions to ensure its availability and utility. The aqueducts are the greatest example of this; this marvel of engineering is considered to be one of the earliest systems ever designed to transport water over long distances. The Greeks began constructing aqueducts as early as the 6th century BCE. Perhaps the most remarkable example of Greek aqueducts is the Tunnel of Eupalinos on the island of Samos. Over one thousand meters long, it was used to supply the city of Samos with water from the mountains.

To ensure smooth and steady water flow, the Greek aqueducts relied heavily on a combination of gravity and carefully engineered channels. The Greeks incorporated open channels, underground pipes, and clay pipelines in their aqueducts. This ensured the water was transported efficiently, supplying various other public structures in their cities, from public fountains to bathhouses to even private homes.

While it is true that Greeks pioneered many aspects of the aqueduct design, the Romans expanded on these concepts centuries later. Using the ideas born from the Greeks, the Romans went on to create massive aqueduct systems that became iconic symbols of their engineering prowess. Roman aqueducts like the Pont du Gard and the Aqua Appia were both built on Greek principles. The Romans used large-scale arches and elevated structures to transport water over vast distances.

It is also worth noting that Greek aqueducts were not only functional but also reflected a harmonious balance between practicality and aesthetics. These structures often blended in seamlessly with their natural surroundings, mirroring the Greeks' broader architectural philosophy by emphasizing utility without sacrificing beauty.

When it came to hydraulic engineering, the Greeks showcased their prowess by inventing the clepsydra, or water clock. Just as its name suggests, this device was designed to measure time. The Greeks did so by regulating the flow of water through the narrow opening into or out of a container. The early models of the clepsydra seem rather simple. The Greeks would simply use a container with a hole at the bottom. While this hole allowed water to flow out at a consistent rate, the markings on the inside indicated the passage of time. However, as the years passed by, models became more sophisticated, allowing the Greeks to measure time with greater accuracy.

Two outflow water clocks from the Museum of the Ancient Agora in Athens.[31]

The clepsydra was also used in courtrooms. The Greeks used this device to time speeches. This allowed them to be fair, giving each speaker an equal amount of time to deliver their statements. Aside from courtrooms, public meetings and assemblies also made use of the device to manage discussions efficiently. The clepsydra held scientific significance as well; it provided a reliable means of measuring time for experiments and astronomical observations.

Of course, the usage of this device was not limited only to the Greek world. The Romans and even early Islamic civilizations adopted the idea and improved its design to suit their needs.

The Antikythera Mechanism: An Ancient Computer

The Antikythera mechanism was once lost. It was not until the early 20th century that the device was finally discovered, left untouched in a shipwreck off the Greek island of Antikythera. Dating to around 150 to 100 BCE, the device is now considered a symbol of ancient Greece's engineering complexity.

The Antikythera mechanism was a compact bronze device encased in a wooden frame. It contained over thirty interlocking gears that allowed the device to perform precise calculations of celestial movements. On its front, the mechanism featured dials that scholars believe to have been used to track the sun, moon, and planets according to ancient Greek cosmology. There was another separate dial that displayed the different phases of the moon. On the back of the device, one could find two spiraling scales. One was used to track the Metonic cycle—a nineteen-year period of aligning the lunar and solar calendars—while the other showed the Saros cycle, which was used to predict eclipses.

A fragment of the Antikythera mechanism.[32]

It is safe to say that this level of precision required a great understanding of astronomy and mechanical engineering. Scholars praise the ancient Greeks for their ability to create gear teeth that were small and consistent enough for the mechanism to perform smoothly. Since the mechanism used a complex system of gears to perform precise calculations, the Antikythera mechanism is considered by many to be a prototype of modern analog computing devices. By turning a hand crank, the device could simulate the natural movements of celestial bodies. This made it a mechanical tool for understanding and tracking the patterns of the heavens, such as predicting eclipses and planetary positions. Its design is similar to later mechanical calculators, showing how physical parts can be used to solve real-world problems, much like early computers.

The Aeolipile (Hero's Engine)

The aeolipile, also known as the Hero's engine, was invented by the 1st-century CE engineer Hero of Alexandria. Regarded as the world's first steam engine, the aeolipile demonstrated the principles of steam propulsion centuries before such technologies would be widely utilized. Although the device itself appeared to be relatively simple, scholars agree that it was brilliantly effective. The aeolipile featured a hollow, spherical vessel mounted on a pivot. Protruding from its surface were two bent nozzles. When water was heated beneath the sphere, the steam that was produced would be channeled into the sphere through the hollow tubes. As the steam escaped through the nozzles, it created thrust, causing the sphere to spin rapidly. However, this device, despite going down in history as the world's earliest steam engine, was nothing more than a demonstration of physical principles.

The aeolipile was not the only invention that came from the brilliant mind of Hero. The engineer and mathematician also came up with other mechanical devices that were considered centuries ahead of their time. Blending his scientific curiosity with practical application, Hero invented a vending machine. However, instead of dispensing snacks and drinks like the vending machines we see today, Hero's invention was designed to dispense holy water in temples. Similar to modern vending machines, Hero's invention also required a coin. Once inserted, a lever would be activated to release a measured amount of water.

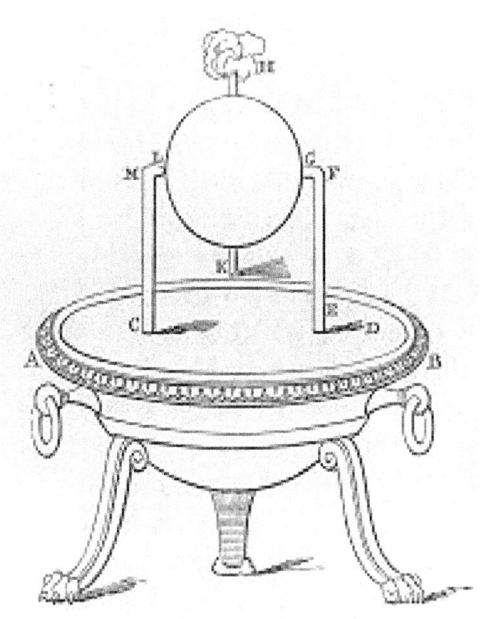

An illustration of Hero's aeolipile.[33]

Hero also devised a type of automatic door that was powered by heat and pressure. They were used at temples to "magically" open and close, giving visitors the impression of divine intervention. He also used air, water, and counterweights to create moving figures called automata. They were often used in theaters to further invoke a sense of magic and spectacle among the audience.

All of his inventions and creations were documented in works such as *Pneumatica* and *Automata*. These writings detail both the construction and principles behind his inventions. They also made sure that his ideas survived the test of time, becoming the precursor to many other modern devices and machines.

The Archimedes Screw

The innovative Archimedes screw was invented sometime in the 3rd century BCE. This device was beyond revolutionary back then, as it was used for lifting water in agricultural settings. This particular mechanism had a helical blade encased within a hollow cylinder tube. To use it, the Greeks would tilt the tube at an angle and rotate the screw manually, often using a handle. As the screw turned, water would be scooped up from a lower level. It was then carried upward along the spiral blade until it emerged at the top.

A water pump that uses the Archimedes screw mechanism.[34]

This invention was very helpful for irrigation and draining marshy areas. It allowed the ancient Greeks to better supply water to their fields or storage tanks. The Archimedes screw's ability to transport water against gravity made it extremely invaluable in regions with uneven terrain or seasonal flooding.

Although the Archimedes screw—sometimes referred to as the Archimedean screw—had a design that appeared rather simple at a single glance, but the device was agreed by many to be versatile. It required only minimal maintenance and had the ability to handle large volumes of water. Believe it or not, the Archimedes screw is still used today for tasks like wastewater treatment and flood management. Even some amusement park rides, especially those involving water, use this technology.

The Diolkos of Corinth

First constructed in the 6th century BCE, the Diolkos was a stone-paved trackway near the city of Corinth. Used as a route to transport ships overland across the Isthmus of Corinth, the Diolkos was popular back then as a shortcut. By using it, merchants and sailors could save time and avoid the long and treacherous journey around the Peloponnesian Peninsula.

The stone trackway was at least six kilometers long. It featured grooves cut into its surface, which was designed as a guide for wheeled carts that carried the ships. These carts, which were typically made of wood and reinforced with metal, were usually pulled by a group of workers or animals. The grooves along the way ensured stability during transport, while levers and rollers were used to assist in lifting and positioning the ships onto the carts.

What remains of the Diolkos today.[35]

The Diolkos also served a vital role in military logistics. With this trackway, the Greeks were able to deploy naval forces between the Aegean and Ionian Seas more efficiently. However, as time went by, the Diolkos eventually fell into disuse, largely due to the advent of more efficient transport methods.

The Odometer

Many may be familiar with the odometer, though these days, the device often comes in a digital form or a combination of both digital and mechanical. Thousands of years ago, however, the odometer was purely mechanical. The measuring instrument has transformed over the centuries, yet its function remains the same.

The origin of the odometer remains a mystery; no one can prove who invented it. Some suggest it was invented by Archimedes of Syracuse, who lived in the 3rd century BCE, while others attributed it to Hero of Alexandria, who lived over two centuries after Archimedes. Regardless of the inventor, we can be sure that the odometer was once used to measure the distance traveled by vehicles or carts. The odometer was typically mounted on carts or attached to chariots.

A reconstruction of the ancient odometer.[36]

The odometer was accurate and efficient. Its operation required no additional effort beyond the motion of the vehicle itself. In simple terms, the odometer worked through a series of gears connected to a wheel. As the wheel turned, it activated a mechanism. A pebble would be dropped into a container after a set number of rotations, each corresponding to a fixed distance. This allowed the ancient Greeks to calculate distances for various purposes, from road building to military planning. The odometer was also useful for mapmakers, allowing them to produce more precise maps by measuring distances between key locations.

Chapter 8 – The Cabeiri and Other Lesser-Known Mysteries

Ancient Greece was a land of gods and myths, but beneath the surface of its public religion lay a more enigmatic world—the mystery cults. These secretive groups offered something different from the grand sacrifices and festivals held in honor of the Olympian deities. For those initiated, the mysteries promised personal transformation, hidden knowledge, and often the hope of a better fate after death.

What distinguished these cults was their exclusivity and secrecy. Only initiates could engage in their rites, and they were sworn not to reveal what happened during the ceremonies. This cloak of mystery, along with the rites' promises of divine connection and cosmic comprehension, rendered them both appealing and elusive. Even now, much of our knowledge is based on fragments. We have to rely on archaeological remnants, inscriptions, and secondhand reports from those outside the cults.

Mystery cults touched on universal themes, including life and death, the soul's journey, renewal, and the search for divine favor. Their rituals were intricate and intensive, with purification rites, dramatic reenactments of tales, and symbolic gestures designed to bring participants closer to the divine. Though many of its secrets have been lost to time, what we do know reveals a world where faith was as much about transformation as it was about devotion—a world where the divine was encountered in ways that are as mysterious as they are fascinating.

The Cult of the Cabeiri

Hidden within the complicated web of the ancient Greek religion was the mysterious cult of the Cabeiri. This cult was said to have been dedicated to a group of minor deities whose devotion promised protection, spiritual development, and access to divine mysteries. Though much about the cult has been lost over time, its influence was profound, and its rituals were fundamental to religious life in certain parts of Greece, particularly on the island of Samothrace. The Cabeiri, or Kabeiroi, were frequently associated with chthonic powers linked to the earth and the underworld, as well as maritime protection. Because of this, the cult was particularly held in high regard by sailors and travelers. Their worship, centered on the Sanctuary of the Great Gods, was unique in Greek religion in that it welcomed initiates from all walks of life, from citizens to foreigners, from men to women, and even slaves, which was unusual in a society where most religious practices were closely linked to civic identity and exclusivity.

The cult of the Cabeiri's beginnings are as obscure as the gods themselves. According to some scholars, their devotion stretches back to the Pelasgians, a pre-Hellenic civilization that occupied areas of the Aegean and predated the Greeks. Others indicate Anatolian influences in their mythology and rites, drawing comparisons to religious practices in the eastern Mediterranean. The Cabeiri were assimilated into the larger Greek religious system during the classical and Hellenistic eras and gained more influence as they became protectors of sailors and sponsors of initiates who sought enlightenment or heavenly protection. Their Samothrace sanctuary eventually developed into a significant religious hub that drew followers from all around the Mediterranean.

Only those who had completed the initiation knew the rites of the cult's mysterious rituals. It is safe to assume that the initiation process was multi-staged. Scholars suggest it began with purification rituals aimed at cleansing both the body and soul. Initiates might have bathed in sacred waters, possibly in the nearby streams and springs of Samothrace, before entering the sacred precinct. The fact that ceremonies were often held at night gave the rituals a sense of mystery and solemnity. Animal sacrifices were presumably performed as well to honor the gods and establish a connection with the heavens.

The promise of divine protection, especially for those traveling across the violent seas, was said to have been central to the rites of the cult. To protect them on their travels, initiates were given sacred items—perhaps talismans—that had been imbued with the power of the Cabeiri. Evidence gathered from both literary references and archaeological remains points to the use of fire in the cult's many rituals. This implies a connection to transformation and purification. It is also likely that hymns and dances were performed to invoke the gods and create a communal sense of devotion among the members.

Archaeological finds at the Sanctuary of the Great Gods have revealed invaluable information on the Cabeiri cult. The site featured a certain construction known as the Anaktoron. Historians suggest this structure was once used as a center for initiation ceremonies. Rectangular in shape, the Anaktoron was where the cult's most sacred and hidden ceremonies were held. During such rituals, initiates might have received symbolic revelations or completed consecration rites. Another major structure, known as the Rotunda of Arsinoe, was nearby. This huge circular building was built during the Hellenistic period and was thought to have been used as a gathering place, possibly for communal worship or banquets.

The votive offerings unearthed at the site shed more light on the cult's practices and beliefs. One particularly intriguing discovery is a collection of bronze and terracotta artifacts that could have served as ceremonial tools or personal tokens handed to initiates. While the inscriptions carved into stone tablets provide insights into the rites and prayers performed in the sanctuary, their cryptic language maintains the cult's overall mystery.

The beliefs of the Cabeiri cult revolved around themes of protection, renewal, and the potential for spiritual awakening. Unlike other mystery cults that concentrated on the afterlife, the Cabeiri appear to have prioritized divine intervention and support in the present. Such promises were particularly tempting to sailors, whose jobs and lives were dependent on the whims of the sea. However, the cult's teachings were not restricted to maritime issues; they could have contained esoteric knowledge about the cosmos, human existence, and the interaction between the mortal and divine realms.

The Lesser Eleusinian Mysteries

The Eleusinian Mysteries were among the most prominent religious rites in ancient Greece, providing initiates with deep spiritual experiences based on the tale of Demeter and Persephone. The Greater Eleusinian Mysteries, celebrated every autumn in Eleusis, claimed to inspire a deeper understanding of life and death, spiritual rebirth, and the possibility of a glorious afterlife. Dramatic reenactments of Persephone's abduction by Hades and her subsequent reunion with Demeter were central to these rites, representing themes of death, rebirth, and nature's everlasting cycle.

However, before one could participate in the Greater Mysteries, one had to complete the Lesser Eleusinian Mysteries. The Lesser Mysteries, while smaller in scale and scope, were not a mere formality. These spring rites served as the first stage in a sacred path of purification and spiritual preparation, ensuring that initiates were fully prepared to participate in the autumn festivities.

The Lesser Mysteries took place in Agra, a suburb of Athens near the River Ilissos. These rites were performed every year in the month of Anthesterion (February-March). They served as an entry point for newcomers, introducing them to the Eleusinian tradition while also providing an opportunity to cleanse themselves of bodily and spiritual impurities. At this stage, initiates were led through a series of ceremonies aimed to prepare them for the higher spiritual truths of the Greater Mysteries.

Similar to other mysteries in ancient Greece, the Lesser Mysteries revolved around purifying rites. This particular mystery, however, included swimming in the Ilissos River. This symbolic act of cleansing indicated the removal of sins and the willingness to go on a transforming spiritual journey. As they embarked on their trip, initiates prayed and presented offerings to Demeter and Persephone in hopes of receiving their favor and guidance. The purifications were extremely personal, representing a symbolic rebirth and dedication to the mysteries' sacred path.

A relief depicting a scene of initiation to the Eleusinian Mysteries.[87]

Processions, sacrifices, and symbolic acts associated with the Demeter and Persephone myths were, of course, part of the celebrations. Participants might have carried sacred artifacts, or *hiera*, while they marched in procession. This symbolized Demeter's quest for her daughter. These procedures, albeit less elaborate than those of the Greater Mysteries, immersed initiates in the mythological narrative, giving them a sense of connection with the divine figures at the heart of the tradition.

Membership in the Lesser Mysteries was remarkably inclusive for its time. Unlike most Greek religious rituals, which were usually restricted to male citizens of a particular city-state, the Lesser Mysteries was available to anybody. Men, women, foreigners, and possibly even slaves could participate, provided they were willing to undergo purification and sincerely engage with the rituals. While the Lesser Mysteries were required for the Greater Mysteries, they were not just preliminary. For many, particularly those unable to return to Eleusis in the autumn, the Lesser Mysteries provided a meaningful spiritual experience in and of themselves, bringing purification, rejuvenation, and the hope of divine favor.

The Thesmophoria

The Thesmophoria was one of ancient Greece's most popular and intriguing festivals. It was held entirely by women in honor of Demeter and Persephone. Unlike other mystery cults, which were entrenched in secrecy and exclusivity, the Thesmophoria was a public event, though only married women were permitted to participate. Its rituals, however, were shrouded in mystery due to their extremely symbolic and esoteric character. The festival lasted many days and focused on fertility, agricultural rejuvenation, and the sacred connection between women and the earth.

The festival stemmed from the famous tale of Demeter and her daughter Persephone. According to the story, Hades's abduction of Persephone led Demeter to fall into a great depression. Her sorrow was so immense that the earth withered. This divine narrative served as the foundation for the Thesmophoria, as the festival was held to honor Demeter as the goddess of agriculture and Persephone as a symbol of the cycle of life and death. The name "Thesmophoria" comes from the Greek word *thesmoi*, which means "laws" or "customs." This reflects the ancient Greek belief that Demeter was the one who taught humanity the laws of agriculture and civilized life.

A painting depicting the Thesmophoria procession.[38]

The festival was celebrated in multiple Greek city-states. The exact details differed by region. Typically, the festival lasted for three days, with each having its own set of rites and significance. The first day, referred to as Anodos ("ascent"), commemorated the women's trip to a sacred site, typically a hill or sanctuary, where the festival was held. The journey involved carrying sacred objects and preparing the ground for the ceremonies to follow. The second day, Nesteia ("fasting"), was a day of sadness and introspection. Women fasted from meals and dressed modestly, symbolizing Demeter's sadness while searching for Persephone.

During this phase, most mysterious rites were performed. One particular ritual involved the retrieval of rotting pig carcasses that had been buried months earlier in sacred pits. These carcasses were placed on an altar and mixed with seeds. This was done to ensure a good harvest.

The final day, known as Kalligeneia ("beautiful birth"), was a celebration of fertility and rejuvenation. Here, an obvious mood change could be sensed. Solemnity turned to joy as women performed rituals to invoke Demeter's blessing on the land and their own families. Grains, animal-shaped cakes, and other agricultural products were offered to the goddess. The festival then concluded with feasting and dancing.

The Orphic Mysteries

The Orphic Mysteries was yet another one of ancient Greece's mystifying traditions. This particular Hellenistic mystery cult revolved around the legendary figure named Orpheus. Known in mythology as a poet, musician, and prophet, Orpheus was believed to have possessed the ability to charm every living thing in the world—mighty gods included—with his music. His story, however, was rather tragic. When his beloved wife, Eurydice, died from a snake bite, Orpheus set out on a journey into the underworld to retrieve her. Using his musical talent, Orpheus successfully charmed the underworld beings, including the ferryman Charon and the dog Cerberus. He was able to return to the land of the living with his wife in tow, yet upon failing to abide by Hades's condition, Orpheus lost his wife forever.

Orpheus charming various beasts with his music.[89]

Unlike other Greek mysteries, which focused on specific deities or cults, the Orphic Mysteries were more philosophical and personal. The religion focused more on the soul's journey and its relationship to the divine. Purity was an absolute priority, along with ascetic practices and a thorough comprehension of the universe's divine order. Orphism was founded on a distinct cosmogony that suggested the cosmos had been created by Chronos (Time) and the cosmic egg, a concept that differed from the more anthropomorphic stories of the Olympian gods. The figure of Dionysus Zagreus, Zeus's son who was torn apart by the Titans and then regenerated, was central to this religious system. This tale symbolized the cyclical nature of life, death, and rebirth.

Orphic rituals and practices were designed as a guide for initiates to achieve spiritual purity and the liberation of the soul from the cycle of rebirth. Initiates were expected to follow strict ethical and dietary codes. They had to indulge in vegetarianism since they believed eating meat perpetuated the cycle of violence and impurity. More often than not, rituals included purification ceremonies, chants, and prayers, as well as the study of Orphic hymns and sacred books, which were claimed to hold concealed knowledge about the universe and the afterlife.

Of course, the exact rituals, ceremonies, and practices were only revealed to members, but membership in the Orphic Mysteries was open to anyone, especially those willing to embrace its ascetic lifestyle and philosophical teachings. In contrast to other mystery religions that emphasized communal ceremonies, Orphism typically focused on personal devotion and inner transformation.

Orphic mosaics excavated from late Roman villas.[40]

Those who devoted themselves closely to the mystery were said to have been promised a great reward: freedom from the never-ending cycle of reincarnation and the eventual return to the divine. This belief was immortalized in small inscribed sheets of gold known as the Orphic gold tablets. Uncovered in various burial sites across the Greek world, these tablets were thought to be guides for the deceased, offering instructions on how to navigate the afterlife and achieve eternal bliss.

The Mysteries of the Great Gods

Sometimes referred to as the Samothracian Mysteries, this Hellenistic cult was considered among the most renowned religious rites in Greece, second only to the Eleusinian Mysteries. These rites, which took place on the island of Samothrace in the northern Aegean Sea, centered on a group of obscure deities known as the Great Gods. Unlike other mystery cults associated with individual Greek city-states, the Samothracian Mysteries welcomed all. Men, women, slaves, and foreigners were permitted to take part, making the cult unusually inclusive for their time.

Scholars cannot precisely pinpoint the exact origin of the Samothracian Mysteries. However, many suggest that the cult preceded the Greek colonization of the island. By the classical period, the cult was believed to have been fully integrated into Greek religious life. Its shrine soon became a popular pilgrimage destination, attracting people from beyond the Aegean. Although the Great Gods themselves were never fully recognized in Greek mythology, they were often associated with the underworld and their protective abilities. Even their identities and roles were intentionally concealed, as they were only known by the members of the cult.

First-time participants were known as *mystai*. They would typically begin their journey with purification rites that likely included bathing in the sacred streams or springs around the sanctuary. After preparing themselves for the divine experience, the *mystai* would then participate in processions. Since the processions were often held at night, torches would be lit along the way, further creating a sense of mystery and reverence. Hymns were performed, and prayers were recited to invoke the presence of the Great Gods. These rituals were accompanied by the rhythmic sounds of drums, which were beaten to heighten the participants' emotional and spiritual state.

Similar to the cult of the Cabeiri, sacred ceremonies were usually held in the Anaktoron. Here, initiates were said to have participated in rites that reenacted the stories of the Great Gods. While the specifics of these rites are obscure, ancient records indicate that they included symbolic acts of protection and rejuvenation. Some scholars also suggest that the rites involved the offering of sacred items known as *hiera*, which were given to initiates as part of their spiritual enlightenment.

The foundation of the Rotunda of Arsinoe.[41]

This was not the only holy site for ceremonies and rituals. The sanctuary also featured the Rotunda of Arsinoe. Known to many as the biggest circular building in the ancient Greek world, the site was thought to have been an important gathering spot for initiates. The open-air Theatral Circle was probably utilized for ceremonies that were more public or for meetings.

The Lernaean Mysteries

The Lernaean Mysteries were associated with the ancient site of Lerna in the Argolid region of Greece. Known by some as one of the most cryptic religious traditions of antiquity, Lerna was famous in mythology as the home of the Lernaean Hydra, a serpent-like beast killed by Heracles during one of his famed twelve labors. However, Lerna was also revered as a sacred sanctuary associated with chthonic deities and the underworld.

On the surface, this mystery religion appeared similar to the others. It was most likely centered on themes of death, renewal, and purification. The site of the cult featured a sacred spring known as the Alcyonian Lake, which many thought to be the very entrance to the underworld. Rituals at Lerna might have included symbolic descents into this dark realm to depict the initiates' confrontation with death and their eventual purification and rebirth, though no direct accounts of such rites have survived. Bathing or drawing water from the spring was likely important since the water was thought to have purifying and transformational effects.

Since the cult was closely associated with the underworld, rituals at Lerna appeared to have included sacrifices and offerings to the gods who called the realm their domain. Archaeological evidence indicates the presence of altars and pits, which were most likely used for libations and the burial of sacrificial remains. The rites might have been accompanied by hymns and prayers to the chthonic powers, invoking both their favor and protection.

Archaeologists have also discovered remnants of the House of the Tiles, a Mycenaean-era structure, as well as altars and other ritual sites. These discoveries point to the area's long-standing religious significance, which spanned multiple periods of Greek history.

While the exact details of the Lernaean Mysteries are limited, they appear to be consistent with broader Greek ideas about the cyclical nature of life and death. The emphasis on purification and renewal shows that the mysteries were designed to prepare initiates for both life's hardships and the voyage into the afterlife. The connection to the myth of the Hydra, with Heracles defeating an overwhelming monster, could have represented the soul's triumph over death or other spiritual challenges.

The Mysteries of Andania

The Mysteries of Andania also welcomed everyone, from men to women and even children. Since it was also dedicated to Demeter and Persephone, the cult shared similarities with the Eleusinian Mysteries, though it had its own local characteristics.

Rituals of this particular cult were commonly held in a small town in Messenia known as Andania, hence its name. Since these rituals were often dictated by local circumstances or specific significant events, they often took place at irregular intervals. Processions were an important feature of the rites, with participants wearing specific clothing and carrying religious artifacts. These processions likely recreated elements of the Demeter-Persephone myth, emphasizing the themes of loss, renewal, and divine favor. Sacrifices were likely common during the rituals, along with communal feasting and perhaps theatrical performances that dramatized the myths.

It is safe to say that the Mysteries of Andania were notable for their inclusiveness and detailed organization. The inscriptions uncovered at Andania provide further insights into the ceremonies' laws. These inscriptions specify the roles, tasks, and directions for all participants, including priests, priestesses, and ordinary initiates. Such painstaking planning indicates the mysteries' importance to the local community, as well as their dedication to maintaining the holiness of the rites.

Chapter 9 – Bizarre Deaths: Empedocles, Aeschylus, and More

The ancient Greeks were known to celebrate drama and tragedy. So, it should not come as a surprise that the deaths of their most influential figures were turned into stories that have an almost theatrical flair. Empedocles, for one, was known to be an extraordinary thinker by the Greeks, but the story of his death intrigued many. By the time he had risen to prominence, the world was still searching for answers to its deepest mysteries. While others pondered their existence, Empedocles was said to have had the ability to understand the world in ways no mere mortal ever had before.

He held strong to the belief that the entire universe was built from four essential elements: earth, air, fire, and water. He also suggested that these elements did not simply exist out of thin air. They were constantly shaped by two opposing forces—love, which brought them together, and strife, which tore them apart. These were forces that he believed to be the architects of everything we see, from the tiniest speck of dust to the countless stars in the galaxy. What made Empedocles even more unique was that he was not just another philosopher. He was also a poet. He often wove his theories into beautiful poetry. Empedocles had a way with words, so his works often feel almost divine, as if they had been whispered by the gods of Olympus themselves.

His story took a dark turn when Empedocles began to feel like something was missing in his life. He was far from content with being an influential thinker or poet. He believed that he was more than just a weak mortal. Some claimed Empedocles thought of himself as a god or a divine being who knew all the truths of the universe. To those skeptical about his capabilities, Empedocles wished to prove them wrong.

Legend has it that Empedocles, eager to prove that he was more than a mortal, made his way to Mount Etna. He stood at the edge of the fiery volcano, ignoring the smell of sulfur and the gurgling sounds of molten lava churning below. Dressed in his flowing robes, he turned to look at his followers who had come to see his actions from a safe distance.

With confidence, he claimed that he was no longer bound by mortal limits. He told his followers that he would not die from the lava below but simply be transported to the divine, the world where he had come from. He even proclaimed that they would not see his body once he leaped into the volcano, believing that he would merge with the divine forces of the universe. Some said this act was intended as a symbolic return to the elements—earth, air, fire, and water—that he believed made up all existence.

Empedocles leaping into Mount Etna.[42]

Empedocles looked into the lava below, glowing as if it were a portal to another world. Without hesitation, the philosopher jumped into the fiery depths. His followers were stunned, silence hanging heavy in the air. Their minds were reeling from what they had just witnessed. However, as if betraying his claims, the volcano erupted one of Empedocles's sandals. The sight of his sandal sitting at the edge of the crater answered his followers' question: Empedocles was, after all, a human bound by mortal limitations.

Aeschylus, the Tragedy Playwright Who Died Tragically

It was just another day for Aeschylus as he strolled under the blazing sun shining over the Sicilian countryside. He gazed at the sky, admiring the beauty of the world. The famed playwright often sought inspiration in nature, but that was not the main reason behind his decision to be outdoors that day. He was also trying to escape his death.

Aeschylus was one of the most celebrated playwrights of ancient Greece. As the "Father of Tragedy," he was no stranger to dramatic twists. His works, such as *The Persians*, *Seven Against Thebes*, and the *Oresteia* trilogy, were some of his most famous contributions that redefined Greek theater. He was credited with producing over eighty plays, but unfortunately, only seven survived the test of time in their complete form. Interestingly, Aeschylus was also the first dramatist to have ever presented his plays in a trilogy.

Like many other Greeks of his time, Aeschylus was a devout believer in the gods. Even his own life was thought to be touched by the divine. Before turning into a playwright, Aeschylus worked at a vineyard. He claimed Dionysus appeared in his sleep one day, urging him to pursue a career in the art of tragedy. He did so, and over time, Aeschylus earned widespread acclaim.

However, that was not the only time the divine had given him a sign. Legend has it that Aeschylus also heard of a certain prophecy that foretold his demise. He would one day be killed by a falling object. He thought that by staying outdoors, where the sky was the only thing above his head, he could trick fate. However, the sky was home to other beings, such as eagles.

One day, an eagle circled the sky with a tortoise clutched tightly in its talons. It was scanning the ground below, searching for a stone large enough to break a tortoise shell upon impact. Once it found its target, the eagle quickly released its grip, sending the tortoise hurtling toward what the bird thought to be a rock gleaming under the sunlight. Unfortunately for Aeschylus, the eagle had mistaken his bald head for a rock. With a sickening thud, the tortoise shell struck Aeschylus's skull.

The last moments of Aeschylus.[48]

The dramatist, who had dedicated decades of his life to producing Greek tragedies, met a tragedy of his own. The absurdity of his death quickly became a subject of legend. Nevertheless, his works continued to inspire many. The Athenians valued his works so much that they allowed his tragedies to be restaged in competitions. His talent and legacy were also inherited by his sons, Euphorion and Euæon, as well as his nephew named Philocles, who all became playwrights themselves.

Draco of Athens

Draco was born in a time when justice was anything but fair. He hailed from Athens, and back in the 7th century BCE, the Athenians had no consistent law system. Because of this, disputes often escalated into bloody feuds. Perhaps growing up witnessing the Athenians constantly fighting each other, Draco wanted to change the way laws worked in the city.

Draco of Athens.["]

It is unclear at what age Draco first stepped into the realm of law. Scholars have suggested that he was probably in his thirties when he finally obtained a standing in Athenian society. From then on, he was entrusted with the responsibility of codifying Athens' first ever written laws. This was indeed a groundbreaking effort to replace arbitrary decisions with a clear legal structure.

However, Draco's laws were known to be unbelievably harsh. Even those who were caught stealing petty items, such as a cabbage, could be sentenced to death. When asked why his solution to most offenses was the death sentence, Draco simply responded that he could not think of a higher punishment for the greater offenses. In his eyes, petty crimes already warranted the death penalty because of their harmful nature. There was no more severe consequence he could impose for more serious crimes. His laws were extremely strict and harsh to the point where his name eventually gave us the word "draconian," which is often used to describe overly harsh measures.

Although his laws are controversial, largely due to their severity, the Greeks saw them as revolutionary. Because of him, the Athenians could finally see order and consistency. Draco's laws became the foundation for future reforms that would later lead to democracy. Some might have feared his influence, but many others respected him for his dedication to justice.

Like many other great minds of the Greek world, Draco had to be remembered for his contributions. The Athenians decided to hold a grand gathering to honor him. Silence was immediately replaced with a round of applause when the Athenians saw Draco stepping forward to address them. At a single glance, he appeared modest—he wore only a simple cloak—but his presence commanded attention. However, the Athenians' love for him inadvertently killed him.

Perhaps eager to show their gratitude, the crowd began to throw their hats, cloaks, and other garments on the stage as a gesture of appreciation. As their enthusiasm grew, more and more items rained down until they formed a growing pile around him. Draco stood there, probably trying to calm the audience down. Unfortunately, the deluge of offerings continued, as the Athenians, completely consumed by their enthusiasm, ignored his words. The pile grew so large that Draco eventually collapsed underneath it. By the time the crowd realized what they had done, it was too late. Silence filled the air again. Their celebrated lawgiver had died, having been smothered by their own outpouring gratitude,

Chrysippus, the Stoic Philosopher Who Laughed to Death

Dying of laughter may sound ridiculous, but it is, in fact, a medical possibility, although it is a rare one. In extreme cases, excessive laughter can trigger a range of physiological responses. Asphyxiation might occur if the body fails to take in enough oxygen. Those who already have pre-existing heart conditions might become victims of cardiac arrest. This phenomenon is known today as fatal hilarity and had once befallen a certain Stoic philosopher of the 3rd century BCE named Chrysippus.

Chrysippus of Soli.[45]

According to ancient tradition, Chrysippus once stumbled upon a donkey eating a fig. He found the scene to be so amusing that he shouted, "Now, can someone give the donkey a drink of wine to wash it down!" His laughter escalated uncontrollably. He eventually collapsed to the ground, perhaps due to asphyxiation caused by his non-stop laughter, and died.

This was not the only account of his death. The ancient biographer of philosophers, Diogenes Laërtius, offered an alternative account where he claimed Chrysippus died during the 143rd Olympiad Games. He suggested that instead of excessive laughter, the philosopher met his fate as a result of drinking undiluted wine at a feast. However, without forensic evidence, we will never truly uncover the reason behind his death. Whether it was fatal hilarity or alcohol poisoning, Chrysippus succeeded in immortalizing his name. The philosopher was mostly known for his contributions in logic, the theory of knowledge, ethics, and physics rather than his end.

Heraclitus, the Greek Philosopher Who Spoke in Riddles

Heraclitus of Ephesus had a rather dim view of humanity to the point where he could often be found crying over it. Because of this, the pre-Socratic thinker was known by the Greeks as the "Weeping Philosopher." This was not his only epithet. Heraclitus was also said to have spoken in a cryptic manner, so many referred to him as the "Obscure," "the Riddler," and sometimes "the Dark One." He had some of the best insights and ideas, yet they were all typically expressed in dense aphorisms that challenged even the brightest minds of his time. Heraclitus was also the philosopher whose famous quote was "You cannot step into the same river twice."

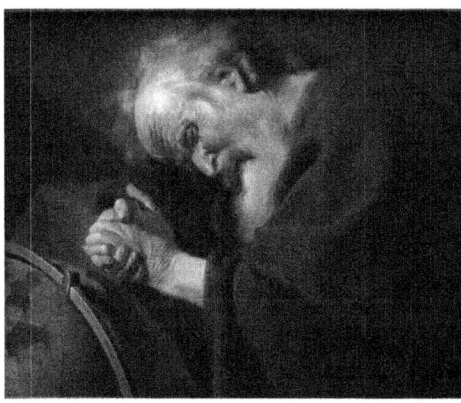

Heraclitus, the Weeping Philosopher.[46]

Heraclitus preferred a reclusive life. Perhaps tied to his view of humanity, he shunned public life and criticized common people and his fellow philosophers, claiming they failed to grasp deeper truths. His ideas influenced later thinkers, including Plato and the Stoics, but the episode where he met his demise is remembered by many.

Heraclitus eventually developed dropsy—today known as edema—as he neared the end of his days. This particular medical condition is characterized by severe swelling due to fluid retention. Possibly caused by either heart or kidney failure, it was undoubtedly a condition that was beyond the medical capabilities of his time. When Heraclitus noticed his condition was getting worse, he made haste to see the doctors. True to his style, the philosopher spoke metaphorically; he asked them whether they could make a drought after a storm. He probably was asking if the doctors could remove the excess fluid from his body. However, none of the doctors could understand him, which left Heraclitus frustrated.

He left the doctors and chose to take matters into his own hands. Believing that warmth was the answer, he devised a rather unconventional remedy. The philosopher covered himself with cow manure. He thought that with the manure's heat and drying properties, he could draw out the moisture that had been causing his medical condition. Unfortunately, this treatment failed, and the philosopher died while still being covered in a mixture of his own invention.

Other ancient records recalled Heraclitus lying still in the manure under the sun. However, the dung dried around him, transforming into a body cast. Unable to move, he could only watch as a pack of dogs came along to eat him.

Philitas of Cos, the Grammarian Who Starved to Death

Many might agree that Philitas of Cos's life revolved around words, but so did his death. Born sometime in the mid-4th century BCE, Philitas built his career as both a poet and a scholar. He was extremely obsessed with language, something that set him apart from other great minds of the Hellenistic world. His appointment as a tutor to the future Egyptian pharaoh, Ptolemy II Philadelphus, further catapulted him into literary stardom to the point where his influence was felt in the works of

A bronze statue of Philitas of Cos.[47]

poets like Callimachus and Propertius.

However, some found his expertise in language and obsession with the precise usage of words irritating. He would zealously correct errors in speech, no matter who the speaker was. Once he heard the wrong choice of words being used, Philitas never hesitated to argue and unravel why such a word was wrongly used—a behavior that even his admirers found exhausting. Imagine a man whom you do not know personally leaping into an exhaustive analysis upon overhearing a slip of the tongue and not stopping until the mistake was acknowledged.

His death revolved around his obsession with words and grammar. Ancient sources state that Philitas became so consumed by his scholarly pursuits that it slipped his mind to care for his own needs. He was too deep in his research, investigating a particularly erroneous use of words—Philitas was said to have been preparing an essay to expose the offending mistake—that the scholar forgot to eat. He accidentally starved himself to death, becoming the ultimate victim of his own insatiable pursuit of linguistic perfection.

Milo of Croton, the Wrestler Who Got Trapped in a Tree

When thinking of the strongest men in ancient Greece, many may immediately think of Heracles, the mythical hero whose strength allowed him to perform the famed twelve labors for King Eurystheus of Mycenae. A few may think of Milo of Croton. Like Heracles, Milo was not only popular for his might but also for his larger-than-life feats. He was a wrestler who immortalized his name in history by winning six Olympic titles and seven Pythian championships. He was also a skilled military leader. Milo once led the army of Croton (a Greek colony in southern Italy) to victory against their rivals from Sybaris.

The ancient Greeks claimed Milo possessed an almost superhuman strength. One legend told of his extreme training regimen that bordered on the mythical. He was said to have lifted an ox daily. He began lifting the animal when it was only a mere newborn and continued to do this each day until the ox grew into a full-sized beast. When the ox reached maturity, Milo was said to have been able to carry it with ease, showcasing his otherworldly strength and endurance.

The death of Milo of Croton.[48]

Yet, even Heracles could not escape death, let alone the mortal Milo. While the divine hero died because of a poison, Milo's demise ended because of the brutality of animals. According to traditional sources, Milo was walking alone through a forest. He came across a partially split tree with its trunk held open by wedges. Despite there being no one to watch him, the wrestler saw this as an opportunity to test his strength. With a deep breath, he inserted his rough hands into the gap and, with all his might, tried to tear the trunk apart. At first, it seemed as if he would pass his own test of strength. Unfortunately, the wedges soon fell out. The tree snapped shut, trapping one of his hands.

The mighty wrestler was now a captive of the tree and left vulnerable to Mother Nature. Wolves eventually arrived and devoured him.

Arrichion, an Athlete Announced Champion Despite Being Dead

The *pankratiast* was a type of warrior-athlete in ancient Greece. They typically fought using a blend of wrestling and boxing techniques to topple their opponents. The sport known as pankration was usually brutal; there was little room for mercy. The athletes were permitted to use anything to win the match, save for biting and gouging an opponent's eyes. While strength, skill, and endurance were all must-haves, the athletes also needed strategy and a little bit of trickery. Among the many celebrated *pankratiasts* in ancient Greece was Arrichion of Phigalia.

Ancient Greek pankratiasts fighting.[49]

Arrichion knew he had already cemented his reputation when he won two Olympic titles. So, when the fifty-fourth Olympiad was held in 564 BCE, he was confident that he could take on any opponent thrown at him. Proud of his strength and tenacity, he entered the arena, and as he expected, the crowd erupted with cheers the moment they laid eyes on him. The spectators knew Arrichion was no ordinary competitor. They expected the match to be a swift and easy win for the athlete.

However, much to their surprise, Arrichion soon found himself in a dire situation. He had been a tad too confident. His opponent turned out to be a determined challenger with powerful legs. The opponent wrapped around Arrichion's midsection and arms, trapping the proud athlete in a chokehold. Finding it difficult to breathe, the defending champion appeared as if he were only moments away from defeat. The crowd fell silent as they saw their hero slowly lose consciousness.

But Arrichion was always a step ahead. His unconsciousness was only an act so that his opponent would lower his guard. When his grip loosened, Arrichion made his move. Using every ounce of his remaining strength, the athlete made a sharp motion, twisting and snapping his opponent's ankle. The pain was agonizing, leading his opponent to immediately tap out and signal his defeat. The crowd celebrated with cheers and applause, but little did they know that Arrichion was already dead.

Many were puzzled, but it was later revealed that in his attempt to throw off his opponent immediately after the tap out, the intense pressure from the chokehold had inadvertently snapped Arrichion's neck. Regardless of his death, Olympic tradition held that the opponent's surrender meant victory. So, Arrichion was once again crowned champion, but this time around, only his corpse lay witness to it.

Chapter 10 – The Voyage of Pytheas

The Greeks had a general understanding of the known world, but they were only familiar with regions surrounding the Mediterranean and certain parts of the Near East. While they had heard stories of distant lands, which were typically shared by travelers and merchants, some tended to dismiss the details and descriptions, looking at them as nothing more than just fables and tales. Goods like amber, tin, and silk were commonly traded in Greek markets, but few Greeks were curious about the origins of these items. This was largely due to the Greeks often relying on intermediaries, such as the Phoenicians and the Egyptians, to bring the wonders of faraway places to them.

However, Pytheas had always been curious about the world beyond the Mediterranean. His hunger for knowledge and his desire to explore the world were not solely driven by the chance to expand trade or discover new markets. Pytheas had heard stories of a phenomenon that only occurred in the lands far to the north. In these unknown parts of the world—at least unknown to the ancient Greeks—the sun never set. While today, this phenomenon is considered normal (we now refer to it as the midnight sun), to the ancient Greeks, who lived in a temperate zone with predictable day and night cycles, the thought of not seeing the sun set below the horizon for days was bizarre. Many questions probably lingered in Pytheas's mind. Was it truly possible for such a land to thrive? If so, how were the lives of the people there when nighttime never came?

A statue of Pytheas at Palais de la Bourse in Marseille.[50]

It is safe to assume that Pytheas was not a man who would be content just by listening to secondhand stories and theories. The only way for him to uncover the truth about these lands was to set out on an adventure and experience the wonders of the unknown world himself. Pytheas recorded his extraordinary voyage in his book titled *Ta peri tou Okeanou* (*Things About the Ocean*), but unfortunately for us, the book has been lost to the sands of time. Some said it was once kept in the famous Library of Alexandria, and when the structure was destroyed, so was the book. Only a few fragments of his stories and descriptions of the journey were saved. They were preserved by ancient writers such as Timaeus, Pliny the Elder, Diodorus Siculus, Strabo, and Polybius. Although these secondhand accounts give us a glimpse into Pytheas's voyage, it is important to note that the writings are also full of biases and interpretations of the writers.

According to these secondhand accounts, Pytheas was thought to be a Greek merchant hailing from Massalia (now modern-day Marseille). The city was situated along the southern coast of Gaul, and its strategic location allowed it to thrive as a major hub in the Mediterranean. So, it makes sense for historians to suggest that Pytheas might have grown up surrounded by sailors and traders before becoming a merchant himself.

Even the exact details of his ship remain a mystery. However, since Pytheas could have been a merchant, scholars suggest that he likely sailed in a type of Greek cargo vessel known as the *holkas*. Unlike the oar-driven triremes often used in naval battles, the round-hulled *holkai* were popular for their sturdy build. With the ship's flat bottom, Pytheas was able to navigate shallow waters and haul large quantities of goods. The *holkas* was mainly propelled by sails. Despite not being particularly fast, this type of ship was reliable and a fitting choice for explorers like Pytheas who prioritized endurance and capacity rather than speed.

Pytheas likely began his voyage in Massilia. He would have then set sail westward, passing through the Pillars of Hercules (the modern-day Strait of Gibraltar) and into the Atlantic Ocean. This was where his voyage must have faced its first challenges. The Atlantic was an uncharted and treacherous frontier even for the most experienced Greek navigators. Nevertheless, Pytheas succeeded in overcoming all of the tests that the ocean had in store for him. He sailed northward along the coasts of Spain and France, observing the lands, and eventually made landfall in Brittany. Records claimed that Pytheas crossed the English Channel, reaching a place he referred to as "Belerion," which historians suspect to be Cornwall.

Ancient writers like Pliny the Elder and Timaeus also preserved Pytheas's record of an island he stumbled upon. Referred to as "Mictis," the island was said to be accessible by sailing inland from Britain for six days. This was where Pytheas observed the inhabitants mining tin. He also recorded his observation of the Britons traveling to the island using only lightweight wicker boats covered with animal hides. Tin was a crucial material for producing bronze, and the tin mined by the inhabitants was usually traded to Gaul. From there, it was transported to the Mediterranean markets. This was undoubtedly an important discovery for Pytheas, as it provided insights into the supply chain of one of antiquity's most valuable resources. While the exact location of Mictis remains unknown, some scholars speculate it could have been St. Michael's Mount in Cornwall, the Mount Batten peninsula in Devon, or even the Isle of Wight.

As a curious explorer, Pytheas's observations were not only limited to geography and trade. He was also said to have taken a keen interest in the people he encountered. He observed their way of life, culture, and customs. In one of his writings preserved by Diodorus Siculus, Pytheas noted that Britain was densely populated, which he thought was surprising given the region's cold climate. Its inhabitants lived in humble houses made of reed and timber, and the people were organized into tribal societies. Pytheas also wrote that they were governed by kings and aristocrats, which was pretty similar to other ancient societies. Agriculture was the Britons' main source of sustenance. Pytheas even described their unique method of harvesting grain. According to his observations, the people did not cut entire stalks; instead, they harvested only the heads of the grain. These heads were stored in roofed buildings until they ripened. Every day, the people would grind the ripened heads and use them as part of their diet.

Perhaps satisfied with his observations of Cornwall and southwestern Britain, Pytheas finally made the decision to continue his adventure. He sailed northward along the coast of Wales, where he explored rugged landscapes and possibly witnessed the lives of the remote tribes of the region. This was not his last stop; scholars suggest that he sailed farther north. Pytheas landed on the Isle of Man before continuing his exploration along the rugged western coast of Scotland. From here, he made his way between the Outer and Inner Hebrides. It is possible that the explorer made several landfalls in this area, where he studied the unfamiliar terrain and the people who inhabited it. The geographer Strabo noted that Pytheas explored as much of Britain as was accessible by foot, though Strabo also claimed that Pytheas might have exaggerated his adventures.

Pytheas did not venture into these unknown regions empty-handed. One of the tools he brought along on his journey was a gnomon, a vertical rod or stick used to measure the shadow cast by the sun. This ingenious device served as a precursor to modern navigational tools like sextants (used to measure the angular distance between two visible objects) and GPS. Many may agree that the gnomon was a relatively simple navigational tool, but it was highly effective at the time. Typically, a sailor would place the rod upright on a flat surface and record the shadow it cast when the sun finally reached its highest point in the sky. By calculating the length and angle of the shadow at noon, one could determine one's current latitude. Although the tool is considered crude by today's standards, back then, it was a groundbreaking innovation that allowed many explorers to venture farther into unknown regions.

A sundial with a gnomon (the triangular blade) on it.[51]

According to Pliny the Elder, Pytheas also explored another group of islands north of Britain that he referred to as the "Orcades." Scholars have suggested that the Orcades might be the Orkney Islands, yet this is nothing more than speculation. Pliny's count of the Orcades does not align with the actual number of islands in the Orkney archipelago. What we can be sure of, though, is that Pytheas moved on from Britain after exploring the Orcades. This time around, he sailed into the frigid waters of the North Sea.

This daunting journey took him six days before he finally reached a landmass he called Thule. This was where Pytheas finally got to answer his own question: was there really a part of the world where the sun refused to sink beyond the horizon? According to the ancient writers, Pytheas described the phenomenon in great detail. Although we will never uncover his exact words and description, it is safe to assume that Pytheas might have been in awe when he experienced continuous daylight during the summer months. After all, this concept where night ceased to exist—at least for several days or weeks—was almost mythical to the Greeks, who were well accustomed to the predictable cycles of day and night in the Mediterranean.

Pytheas documented what lay north of Thule. After sailing another day, the explorer was said to have come across what he called the "Congealed Sea." Scholars thought this was a term he used to refer to the icy waters of the Arctic Ocean. Pytheas wrote about the region being full of thick fog and floating ice floes, which were probably the main obstacles that stopped him from sailing further. Regardless, the extremely cold temperature, heavy mist, and dozens of ice floes were likely an alien sight for Pytheas and his crew, who all came from the temperate Mediterranean.

Perhaps one of the most intriguing parts of Pytheas's lost writings about his northern travels was something he referred to as "sea-lung." This term has long puzzled scholars and historians. Some believe that Pytheas was simply trying to describe something he had never seen before, and there was no existing word for it in Greek. What he saw was probably pancake ice, which is a type of sea ice that forms in circular patterns and floats on the water's surface.

Pancake ice.[52]

But why did he call it "sea-lung?" While we can never be entirely sure, some historians provided an explanation. Pytheas might have borrowed the term from jellyfish. According to Aristotle in his work *Parts of Animals*, jellyfish were known in Greek as *pleumōn thalattios*, or "sea lung." So, Pytheas, who had no word to refer to the pancake ice, might have thought of a jellyfish. These sea creatures are round and float near the surface of the water, just like pancake ice. Whether or not this is true, Pytheas's description of his northern travels really captured the bizarre and dynamic nature of the Arctic waters. It was indeed a place where the boundary between sea and land seemed to blur.

Of course, just like the Orcades, the exact location of Thule has been a topic of debate for many years. While some suggested Pytheas landed in Iceland, there are others who argued it was Norway or the Faroe Islands. The Canadian explorer Vilhjalmur Stefansson—best known for his Arctic expeditions—sided with the idea that Pytheas went to Iceland. Stefansson, in his book *Ultima Thule*, wrote that Pytheas's descriptions of Thule aligned with both Icelandic geography and astronomical details, especially the phenomenon of the midnight sun near the Arctic Circle. However, without definitive evidence, this is nothing more than just a theory. The exact identity of Thule and whether it was true that Pytheas succeeded in sailing as far as Iceland remains a debate.

Nevertheless, according to what remains of his records, the Congealed Sea and its "sea-lung" marked the northernmost point of Pytheas's journey. Since the environment was completely inhospitable, Pytheas began his return voyage home. Scholars suggest that he likely sailed down the eastern coast of Britain. He then rounded the Kentish peninsula, which he wrote down as "Kantion." This referred to the region of Kent, located at the southeastern tip of England, facing toward continental Europe (modern-day France).

This meant Pytheas had effectively achieved a circumnavigation of the island of Britain. Without modern navigational tools and the unpredictability of the fierce Atlantic water, this was a giant feat for his time. However, instead of turning westward and heading toward the Mediterranean, Pytheas made the decision to go on one last detour into uncharted territories.

He turned eastward and sailed along the northern coastline of Europe. Pliny the Elder recounted Pytheas's journey in his writing, narrating that the Greek explorer encountered various groups of people along the way. The Germanic tribe Gutones was one of them. They lived near the shores of an estuary (the tidal mouth of a large river) of the ocean he called "Mentonomon." This was possibly the mouth of the Elbe or another major river whose stream meets the North Sea. Always a keen observer, Pytheas likely recorded the people's customs, descriptions of their dwellings, and trade practices, all of which would have been invaluable to the Greeks who were unfamiliar with the northern Germanic tribes.

Pytheas also reached an island known for its amber. Some historians have proposed that the island he landed on was none other than Heligoland, a small yet historically significant archipelago off the coast of modern-day Germany. The Greeks considered amber to be extremely precious. Apart from its beauty, amber was revered for its mystical properties. The Greeks often associated it with sunlight and divine power. Referring to it as "electron," it was best known for its ability to attract lightweight objects when rubbed—a scientific phenomenon we now know as static electricity. Therefore, Pytheas's discovery of a land abundant with amber might have been a revelation.

Pytheas continued his journey, venturing into the Baltic Sea. Scholars suggested that he might have gone as far east as the Vistula River in present-day Poland. This theory is further supported by ancient accounts that recalled Pytheas's own descriptions of the amber trade and peoples living in the Baltic region. Moreover, given its proximity to rich amber deposits, it would have been a logical destination for someone keen on understanding the trade networks that brought this precious material to Mediterranean markets.

This region offered Pytheas a change of scenery. If he had indeed reached the Baltic, Pytheas might have encountered an environment that was vastly different from the rugged coasts of Britain or the biting cold of the north. The Baltic Sea was calmer compared to the harsh waters of the Atlantic and Arctic. The Baltic was also hugged by dense forests along its shores, providing Pytheas with rather green scenery.

It was only after he was done with exploring the Baltic that Pytheas continued the long journey back to the Mediterranean. It is unclear whether he decided to retrace his route along the northern European coast or took a different route southward. However, we can be sure that his return voyage was challenging.

Pytheas safely arrived at Massalia. With his memories fresh in his mind, the explorer dedicated himself to documenting the extraordinary voyage. Since his book *Things About the Ocean* was cited by Dicaearchus, a student of Aristotle, who lived between 350 BCE and 285 BCE, historians believe that Pytheas wrote his accounts sometime around 320 BCE, only a few years after he finished his expedition. This early acknowledgement of his work suggests that Pytheas's accounts were not only remarkable for their content but were also a significant contribution to the geographic and scientific understanding of the ancient world.

Things About the Ocean quickly gained traction and was widely circulated throughout Greece. It served as one of the primary sources of knowledge, especially about Britain and the mysterious lands far north, for over two centuries. His detailed descriptions of Britain, its inhabitants and trade, and stories of Thule and the Arctic were studied and dissected by a range of scholars and historians. It was not until the emergence of accounts by Tacitus and Julius Caesar that Pytheas's writings began to be overshadowed.

Unsurprisingly, despite his detailed writings, not everyone took his work in a favorable way. Strabo and Polybius, for example, were critical of Pytheas's work. As two of the most prominent ancient geographers, they often dismissed Pytheas's descriptions, claiming them to be exaggerated or fabricated. Strabo himself claimed Pytheas to be unreliable. He particularly mocked the explorer's claims about the midnight sun and the frozen sea, dismissing the descriptions as improbable and fantastical. Polybius also viewed Pytheas's accounts of the distant north with skepticism. Their criticisms, however, were less about Pytheas's methods and more about the incredible nature of his claims; to them, Pytheas's descriptions seemed to challenge the established understanding of the world at the time. The idea of a vast ocean filled with frozen sheets of ice and a land where the sun never set was so bizarre to the Greeks that many contemporaries found it easier to doubt his writings.

However, today, Pytheas's voyage has been acknowledged as one of the most incredible feats of the ancient world. His journey is often underappreciated in the history of exploration, often overshadowed by famous voyages of later explorers like Marco Polo and Christopher Columbus, but Pytheas's journey was no less daring. His curiosity led him to venture into uncharted territories with only his knowledge and the help of a primitive gnomon. Not only did he return to his homeland in one piece, but Pytheas also worked to compile his accounts, which ultimately expanded the geographic boundaries of his time.

Conclusion

Ancient Greece is a place that feels both familiar and endlessly fascinating. It was a world full of epic battles, intricate marble temples, and powerful gods who mirrored the mortals they ruled over with their flaws and passions. But beyond the famed story of the Trojan War or even the wisdom of the Olympian gods, one will discover a range of stories that reveal the Greeks as more than just legendary figures. They were also humans who were curious, contradictory, and delightfully peculiar.

Throughout this journey, we have encountered the unexpected. We have met Neaira, a woman whose trial provided us with a glimpse into the lives of those navigating a world where freedom was tenuous and societal expectations rigid. We followed Pytheas on his voyage to the frozen edges of the known world. There were narratives of ancient Greece's greatest minds and warriors who left us with ideas that shaped the world. We also learned about their odd deaths. Who would have thought that history could include a cryptic philosopher experimenting with manure to ease his sickness or a celebrated war general falling to his demise upon being hit by a roof tile?

Everyone knew the Greeks had a love for drama, but not everyone was aware that it was not confined only to their theaters. The Greeks wove drama through every aspect of their lives, from politics to war. Even their greatest city-states were not an exception. Athens, for one, had its history written with a dramatic flair. It reached incredible heights with its democracy, art, and naval power, yet the city was not invincible.

The city-state was eventually brought to its knees by an invisible enemy. The plague that wreaked havoc throughout Athens reshaped its destiny, giving the world a clear reminder of the fragility of human ambition.

What makes ancient Greece so captivating is not only its awe-inspiring achievements but also its many contradictions. True, this was the very civilization that built and championed democratic systems, yet it also marginalized much of its population. Ancient Greece was a melting pot of rational thought and groundbreaking philosophy, but the people were also deeply superstitious at the same time, often turning to the gods for even the smallest omens. For every gleaming temple or visionary thinker, there was also a tale of human error, rivalry, or unexpected tragedy.

It is clear that ancient Greece left us far more than myths and ruins. It provided us with stories and episodes that ask questions about life, ambition, and what it means to be human. These tales remind us that history is not just about polished monuments but also the rough edges that make it real, surprising, and relatable.

If you enjoyed this book, I'd greatly appreciate a review on Amazon because it helps me to create more books that people want. It would mean a lot to hear from you.

To leave a review:

1. Open your camera app.
2. Point your mobile device at the QR code.
3. The review page will appear in your web browser.

Thanks for your support!

Here's another book by Matt Clayton that you might like

Free Bonus from Captivating History (Available for a Limited time)

Hi History Lovers!

Now you have a chance to join our exclusive history list so you can get your first history ebook for free as well as discounts and a potential to get more history books for free!

Simply visit the link below to join.

Or, Scan the QR code!

captivatinghistory.com/ebook

Also, make sure to follow us on Facebook, X, and YouTube by searching for Captivating History.

Bibliography

Bogaard, Cecilia. "Empedocles of Acragas Commits Suicide by Jumping into a Volcano." *Ancient Origins,* August 28, 2022. https://www.ancient-origins.net/weird-facts/empedocles-acragas-0017197

Cartwright, Mark. "Battle of Marathon." *World History Encyclopedia,* May 19. 2013. www.worldhistory.org/marathon.

Cartwright, Mark. "Hetaira." *World History Encyclopedia,* January 22. 2021. www.worldhistory.org/Hetaira.

Chaliakopoulos, Antonis. "Heraclitus of Ephesus: The Philosopher of Change (Bio and Quotes)." *TheCollector,* March 5, 2023. www.thecollector.com/greek-philosopher-heraclitus-ephesus-quotes.

Copeland, Cody. "The Bizarre Death of Milo of Croton." *Grunge,* February 10, 2021. www.grunge.com/331467/the-bizarre-death-of-milo-of-croton.

Daley, Jason. "Was Alexander the Great Pronounced Dead Prematurely?" *Smithsonian Magazine,* February 5, 2019. www.smithsonianmag.com/smart-news/was-alexander-great-pronounced-dead-prematurely-180971419.

Davis, Lori. "4.2 Neaira: A Slave in Ancient Greece." *Her Half of History,* September 16, 2021. herhalfofhistory.com/2021/09/16/neaira-a-slave-in-ancient-greece.

Dilouambaka, Ethel. "This Greek Philosopher Died Laughing at His Own Joke." *Culture Trip,* October 29, 2024. theculturetrip.com/europe/greece/articles/this-greek-philosopher-died-laughing-at-his-own-joke.

Garlinghouse, Thomas S. "On The Ocean: The Famous Voyage of Pytheas." *World History Encyclopedia,* July 14, 2017. www.worldhistory.org/article/1078/on-the-ocean-the-famous-voyage-of-pytheas.

Hewitt, Nathan. "Alexander the Not-Feeling-Great: How Did Alexander the Great Die?" *TheCollector*, January 8, 2024, www.thecollector.com/how-did-alexander-the-great-die.

Marchant, Jo. "Decoding the Antikythera Mechanism, the First Computer." *Smithsonian Magazine*, February 2015. www.smithsonianmag.com/history/decoding-antikythera-mechanism-first-computer-180953979.

Mark, Joshua J. "Thucydides on the Plague of Athens: Text and Commentary." *World History Encyclopedia*, April 1, 2020. www.worldhistory.org/article/1535/thucydides-on-the-plague-of-athens-text--commentar.

Nel, Aiden. "Alcibiades: His Relationship With Socrates, Political Life, and Scandals." *TheCollector*, September 21, 2022. www.thecollector.com/alcibiades-general-and-lover.

Nel, Aiden. "Orpheus and the Mystery Cult of Orphism (Myths, Beliefs, Practices)." *TheCollector*, January 25, 2023, www.thecollector.com/orpheus-cult-orphism.

Nugent, Addison. "Why Heron's Aeolipile Is One of History's Greatest Forgotten Machines." *Popular Mechanics*, Nov 29, 2020. www.popularmechanics.com/science/energy/a34554479/heron-aeolipile.

Pruitt, Sarah. "Alexander the Great Died Mysteriously at 32. Now We May Know Why." *HISTORY*, February 5, 2024. www.history.com/news/alexander-the-great-death-cause-discovery.

Rees, Owen. "Did The Spartans Throw Babies Down Mountains?" *Bad Ancient*, Aug 31, 2020. www.badancient.com/claims/spartans-throw-babies-mountains.

Sahir. "Did Pythagoras' Bizarre Fear of Fava Beans Contribute to his Death?." *Ancient Origins,* July 24, 2022. https://www.ancient-origins.net/history-famous-people/pythagoras-beans-0017052

Scandelius, Carl. "The Sicilian Expedition." *The 1440 Review*, May 6, 2022. 1440review.com/2022/05/06/the-sicilian-expedition.

Silver, Carly. "The Ancient Spartans Had a Murderous Secret Police." *ThoughtCo*, Mar 7, 2017. www.thoughtco.com/ancient-spartans-murderous-secret-police-4031226.

Starkston, Judith. "Samothrace Mystery Cult." *Judith Starkston*, October 6, 2021. www.judithstarkston.com/2021/10/06/samothrace-mystery-cult.

"16 Dramatic and Bizarre Ways People Died in Ancient Greece and the Hellenistic World" *History Collection*, accessed December 10, 2024. historycollection.com/16-dramatic-and-bizarre-ways-people-died-in-ancient-greece-and-the-hellenistic-world.

"Battle of Marathon." *HISTORY,* July 13, 2023. www.history.com/topics/ancient-greece/battle-of-marathon.

"Battle of Tegyra (375 BC) – Breaking the Myth of Spartan Invincibility." *HistoryForce,* Nov 4, 2022. historyforce.com/battle-of-tegyra375-bc-breaking-the-myth-of-spartan-invincibility.

"Death of Alcibiades." *Heritage History,* Accessed December 12, 2024. www.heritage-history.com/index.php?c=read&author=guerber&book=greeks&story=alcibiades2.

"Odometer Was Invented in Ancient Greece." *Greek Boston,* accessed December 20, 2024. www.greekboston.com/culture/ancient-history/odometer.

"Secret Assassins of Ancient Sparta: The Krypteia and Their Murderous Missions." *History Skills,* Accessed December 8, 2024. www.historyskills.com/classroom/ancient-history/krypteia/?srsltid=AfmBOorPlAt3_m9Mk60TFMUvZRbwWL1-19POqA9NIqi5yIUo3Ot8Sj9g.

"The Battle of Marathon." *Heritage History,* Accessed December 9, 2024. www.heritage-history.com/index.php?c=read&author=macgregor&book=greece&story=marathon.

"The Diolkos, a Corinthian Curiosity. - AncientBlogger." *Ancient Blogger,* June 19, 2024. ancientblogger.com/the-diolkos-a-corinthian-curioisity.

"The Plague of Athens as Told by Thucydides: A Timeless Analysis of an Epidemic." *Greek News Agenda,* May 21, 2020. www.greeknewsagenda.gr/the-plague-of-athens-as-told-by-thucydides.

Image Sources

1 Map_athenian_empire_431_BC-fr.svg: Marsyasderivative work: Once in a Blue Moon, CC BY-SA 2.5 <https://creativecommons.org/licenses/by-sa/2.5>, via Wikimedia Commons: https://commons.wikimedia.org/wiki/File: Map_athenian_empire_431_BC-en.svg

2 https://commons.wikimedia.org/wiki/File:Pelopennesian_War,_Walls_ Protecting_the_City,_431_B.C.,JPG

3 https://commons.wikimedia.org/wiki/File:Plague_in_an_Ancient_City_ LACMA_AC1997.10.1_(1_of_2).jpg

4 George E. Koronaios, CC BY-SA 4.0 <https://creativecommons.org/licenses/by-sa/4.0>, via Wikimedia Commons: https://commons.wikimedia .org/wiki/File:Kerameikos_Cemetery_on_July_28,_2019.jpg

5 https://commons.wikimedia.org/wiki/File:Discurso_funebre_pericles.PNG

6 Generic Mapping Tools, CC BY-SA 3.0 <http://creativecommons.org/licenses/by-sa/3.0/>, via Wikimedia Commons: https://commons.wikimedia.org/wiki/File:MacedonEmpire.jpg

7 https://commons.wikimedia.org/wiki/File:Le_Brun,_Alexander_and_Porus.jpg

8 Peter Paul Rubens, CC0, via Wikimedia Commons: https://commons.wikimedia.org/wiki/File:Sir_Peter_Paul_Rubens,_Pan_Reclining,_ possibly_c._1610,_NGA_56608.jpg

9 https://commons.wikimedia.org/wiki/File:Greek_Phalanx.jpg

10 https://commons.wikimedia.org/wiki/File:Les_H%C3%A9ros_de_ Marathon_Georges_Rochegrosse_1859.jpg

11 https://commons.wikimedia.org/wiki/File:Phidippides.jpg

12 Sailko, CC BY-SA 4.0 <https://creativecommons.org/licenses/by-sa/4.0>, via Wikimedia Commons: https://commons.wikimedia.org/wiki/File: Volterra,_urna_cineraria_con_scena_di_combattimento_(guerriero_con_aratro)_01 .jpg

13 https://commons.wikimedia.org/wiki/File:Antique_Map_of_Classical_ City_of_Sparta.jpg

14 https://commons.wikimedia.org/wiki/File:Jean-Pierre_Saint-Ours_- _Gericht_%C3%BCber_die_Neugeborenen_Spartas_-_2358_- _Bavarian_State_Painting_Collections.jpg

15 AlMare, CC BY-SA 2.5 <https://creativecommons.org/licenses/by-sa/2.5>, via Wikimedia Commons: https://commons.wikimedia.org/wiki/File:Taygetos_From_Sparti.jpg

16 Metropolitan Museum of Art, CC BY 2.5 <https://creativecommons.org/licenses/by/2.5>, via Wikimedia Commons: https://commons.wikimedia.org/wiki/File:Banqueters_Met_1979.11.8.jpg

17 https://commons.wikimedia.org/wiki/File:Jean- L%C3%A9on_G%C3%A9r%C3%B4me,_Phryne_revealed_before_the_Areopagus _(1861)_-_01.jpg

18 https://commons.wikimedia.org/wiki/File:The_story_of_the_greatest_nations; _a_comprehensive_history,_extending_from_the_earliest_times_to_the_present,_f ounded_on_the_most_modern_authorities,_and_including_chronological_summar ies_and_(14783288925).jpg

19 https://commons.wikimedia.org/wiki/File:Do_Not_Eat_Beans.jpg

20 https://commons.wikimedia.org/wiki/File:Alcibades_being_taught_by_Socrates, _Fran%C3%A7ois-Andr%C3%A9_Vincent.jpg

21 https://commons.wikimedia.org/wiki/File:La_mort_d%27Alcibiade_Philippe _Ch%C3%A9ry_1791.jpg

22 https://commons.wikimedia.org/wiki/File:Greek_triremes_at_Salamis.jpg

23 https://commons.wikimedia.org/wiki/File:Illustrerad_Verldshistoria_band_I _Ill_116.png

24 https://commons.wikimedia.org/wiki/File:Canova_- _Urania,_the_Muse_of_Astronomy_Reveals_to_Thales_the_Secrets_of_the_Skies, _1798-1799_(crop).jpg

25 Jean Housen, CC BY-SA 3.0 <https://creativecommons.org/licenses/by-sa/3.0>, via Wikimedia Commons: https://commons.wikimedia.org/wiki/File:20140415_ioannina524.JPG

26 https://commons.wikimedia.org/wiki/File:The-Siege-Of-Sparta-By-Pyrrhus-319-272- Bc-1799-1800.jpg

27 https://commons.wikimedia.org/wiki/File:Franc_Kav%C4%8Di%C4%8D_- _Dekle_re%C5%A1i_Aristomena_iz_ujetni%C5%A1tva.jpg

28 Steve Swayne, CC BY 2.0 <https://creativecommons.org/licenses/by/2.0>, via Wikimedia Commons: https://commons.wikimedia.org/wiki/File:The_Parthenon_in_Athens.jpg

29 https://commons.wikimedia.org/wiki/File:1868_Lawrence_Alma-Tadema_-_Phidias_Showing_the_Frieze_of_the_Parthenon_to_his_Friends.jpg

30 InSapphoWeTrust from Los Angeles, California, USA, CC BY-SA 2.0 <https://creativecommons.org/licenses/by-sa/2.0>, via Wikimedia Commons: https://commons.wikimedia.org/wiki/File:Scale_model_of_Parthenon_Athena,_Ro yal_Ontario_Museum_(6222386828).jpg

31 Marsyas, CC BY-SA 2.5 <https://creativecommons.org/licenses/by-sa/2.5>, via Wikimedia Commons: https://commons.wikimedia.org/wiki/File:AGMA_Clepsydre.jpg

32 No machine-readable author provided. Marsyas assumed (based on copyright claims)., CC BY-SA 3.0 <http://creativecommons.org/licenses/by-sa/3.0/>, via Wikimedia Commons: https://commons.wikimedia.org/wiki/File: NAMA_Machine_d%27Anticyth%C3%A8re_1.jpg

33 https://commons.wikimedia.org/wiki/File:Aeolipile_(from_Pneumatica).jpg

34 Zdravko Pečar, CC BY-SA 4.0 <https://creativecommons.org/licenses/by-sa/4.0>, via Wikimedia Commons: https://commons.wikimedia.org/wiki/File:Irrigation_Pump_in_Egypt_-_1950s.tiff

35 Dan Diffendale, CC BY-SA 2.0 <https://creativecommons.org/licenses/by-sa/2.0>, via Wikimedia Commons: https://commons.wikimedia.org/wiki/File:Diolkos,_Western_End._Pic_04.jpg

36 Gts-tg, CC BY-SA 4.0 <https://creativecommons.org/licenses/by-sa/4.0>, via Wikimedia Commons: https://commons.wikimedia.org/wiki/File: Vitruve%27s_odometer,_1st_century_BC,_Roma_(reconstruction).jpg

37 https://commons.wikimedia.org/wiki/File:Plaque_Campana_-_Initiation_aux_myst%C3%A8res_d%27Eleusis_(Louvre,_Cp_4154).jpg

38 https://commons.wikimedia.org/wiki/File:%27Thesmophoria%27_by_ Francis_Davis_Millet,_1894-1897.jpg

39 https://commons.wikimedia.org/wiki/File:Regius_-_Orpheus_Beasts.jpg

40 https://commons.wikimedia.org/wiki/File:DSC00355_-_Orfeo_(epoca_romana)_-_Foto_G._Dall%27Orto.jpg

41 No machine-readable author provided. Marsyas assumed (based on copyright claims)., CC BY-SA 3.0 <http://creativecommons.org/licenses/by-sa/3.0/>, via Wikimedia Commons: https://commons.wikimedia.org/wiki/File: Samothraki_Arsinoe_rotunda.jpg

42 https://commons.wikimedia.org/wiki/File:The_Death_of_ Empedocles_by_Salvator_Rosa.jpg

43 https://en.wikipedia.org/wiki/File:Death_of_Aeschylus_in_Florentine_ Picture_Chronicle.jpg#Licensing

44 https://commons.wikimedia.org/wiki/File:Draco.webp

45 https://commons.wikimedia.org/wiki/File:Chrysippos_BM_1846.jpg

46 https://commons.wikimedia.org/wiki/File:Utrecht_Moreelse_Heraclite.JPG

47 Ishkabibble at the English Wikipedia, CC BY-SA 3.0
   <http://creativecommons.org/licenses/by-sa/3.0/>, via Wikimedia Commons:
   https://commons.wikimedia.org/wiki/File:Antikythera_philosopher.JPG

48 https://commons.wikimedia.org/wiki/File:Suv%C3%A9e,_Joseph-Benoit_-
   _Milo_of_Croton.jpg

49 Staatliche Antikensammlungen, CC BY-SA 3.0
   <http://creativecommons.org/licenses/by-sa/3.0/>, via Wikimedia Commons:
   https://commons.wikimedia.org/wiki/File:Pankratiasten_in_fight_copy_of_greek_sta
   tue_3_century_bC.jpg

50 Rvalette, CC BY-SA 3.0 <https://creativecommons.org/licenses/by-sa/3.0>, via
   Wikimedia Commons:
   https://commons.wikimedia.org/wiki/File:Pyth%C3%A9as.jpg

51 Photo taken by Alexandre Mirgorodski for http://www.taganrogcity.com Courtesy of
   Taganrog Local Government. © TaganrogCity.Com,
   https://commons.wikimedia.org/wiki/File:Sundial_Taganrog.jpg

52 Hans Kylberg from Stockholm Bagarmossen, Sweden, CC BY 2.0
   <https://creativecommons.org/licenses/by/2.0>, via Wikimedia Commons:
   https://commons.wikimedia.org/wiki/File:Islossning_(119329313).jpg

Printed in Dunstable, United Kingdom

76396937R00077